INTERMEDIATE WRITTEN
CHINESE

READ AND WRITE MANDARIN CHINESE AS THE CHINESE DO

CORNELIUS C. KUBLER

进阶中文: 读与写
進階中文：讀與寫

TUTTLE Publishing

Tokyo | Rutland, Vermont | Singapore

The Tuttle Story: "Books to Span the East and West"

Many people are surprised to learn that the world's leading publisher of books on Asia had humble beginnings in the tiny American state of Vermont. The company's founder, Charles E. Tuttle, belonged to a New England family steeped in publishing.

Immediately after WWII, Tuttle served in Tokyo under General Douglas MacArthur and was tasked with reviving the Japanese publishing industry. He later founded the Charles E. Tuttle Publishing Company, which thrives today as one of the world's leading independent publishers.

Though a westerner, Tuttle was hugely instrumental in bringing a knowledge of Japan and Asia to a world hungry for information about the East. By the time of his death in 1993, Tuttle had published over 6,000 books on Asian culture, history and art—a legacy honored by the Japanese emperor with the "Order of the Sacred Treasure," the highest tribute Japan can bestow upon a non-Japanese.

With a backlist of 1,500 titles, Tuttle Publishing is more active today than at any time in its past—still inspired by Charles Tuttle's core mission to publish fine books to span the East and West and provide a greater understanding of each.

Published by Tuttle Publishing, an imprint of Periplus Editions (HK) Ltd

www.tuttlepublishing.com

ISBN 978-0-8048-4020-0
Library of Congress Control Number: 2015940927

Distributed by:

North America, Latin America & Europe
Tuttle Publishing
364 Innovation Drive
North Clarendon, VT 05759-9436 U.S.A.
Tel: 1 (802) 773-8930 Fax: 1 (802) 773-6993
info@tuttlepublishing.com
www.tuttlepublishing.com

Japan
Tuttle Publishing
Yaekari Building, 3rd Floor
5-4-12 Osaki Shinagawa-ku Tokyo 141-0032
Tel: (81) 3 5437-0171 Fax: (81) 3 5437-0755
sales@tuttle.co.jp
www.tuttle.co.jp

Asia Pacific
Berkeley Books Pte. Ltd.
61 Tai Seng Avenue, #02-12, Singapore 534167
Tel: (65) 6280-1330 Fax: (65) 6280-6290
inquiries@periplus.com.sg
www.periplus.com

18 17 16 15   10 9 8 7 6 5 4 3 2 1
Printed in Singapore   1509CP

A Note to the Learner

Welcome to the second volume of an unusual and highly effective two-volume course in written Chinese!

As a native English speaker learning Chinese, working hard to learn Chinese is not enough; you have to work smart in order to learn this very different language efficiently. No matter why you've chosen to learn Chinese—for business, travel, cultural studies, or another goal—the Basic Chinese approach of two separate but integrated tracks in spoken and written Chinese will help you learn this language efficiently and successfully.

- *Intermediate Written Chinese* is a continuation of *Basic Written Chinese* (Tuttle Publishing, 2011).

- *Intermediate Written Chinese* systematically introduces **336 of the highest-frequency characters** (in both their simplified and traditional forms) and over **1,200 common words written with them**, showing their use in a variety of sentences and reading passages, to help you master Chinese reading and writing. Together with the 288 characters and some 700 words introduced in *Basic Written Chinese*, a total of 624 characters and more than 1,900 words are formally taught in this two-volume course. In addition, *Intermediate Written Chinese* introduces another supplementary 199 characters and over 700 words, meaning that students will have encountered a **grand total of 823 characters and over 2,600 words** by the end of this course.

- Each lesson introduces six new characters and a number of words written with them. By dividing the learning into small tasks, you maintain a sense of accomplishment rather than getting bogged down.

- The **structure and etymology** of each new character is explained in detail to make the learning of characters easier, and similar characters are compared and contrasted.

- Some lessons include **realia** such as photographs of street signs, name cards, e-mail messages, and handwritten notes.

- Lessons include both **printed and handwritten forms** of characters, as well as several **different printed fonts**.

- There are detailed, clear **English explanations** for the key points you need to understand to read and write Chinese correctly, plus information about Chinese usage, culture, and society, as well as recommended **study strategies** for learning written Chinese.

- *Intermediate Written Chinese* should be used in conjunction with the accompanying *Intermediate Written Chinese Practice Essentials*.

- Either before or at the same time that you study a lesson in *Intermediate Written Chinese*, you should study the companion lessons in *Intermediate Spoken Chinese* and *Intermediate Spoken Chinese Practice Essentials*, so

that you can learn of all the relevant information regarding Chinese culture and gain practice in Chinese pronunciation and grammar.

- The characters in *Intermediate Written Chinese* were chosen from those used in the Basic Conversation of the corresponding lesson in *Intermediate Spoken Chinese*, based on frequency of occurrence. Thus, when you begin a new lesson of *Intermediate Written Chinese*, you already know the pronunciation, meaning, and usage of the new words. You now need only to learn their written representations. This considerably **lightens your learning load!**

- Both **simplified and traditional characters** are taught in the same volume. This means students can learn either or both without having to purchase another book. Instructors have the flexibility to teach a combined class where some students read and write one type of character and other students the other type.

- *Intermediate Written Chinese* is designed to be used both in a class with an instructor and by independent learners working on their own.

- The course includes an **audio CD** of the new vocabulary and reading exercises, recorded by native speakers, to help with pronunciation, phrasing, and comprehension.

- The on-line **Instructor's Guide** (available gratis from the publisher) contains detailed suggestions for using these materials as well as a wealth of exercises for use by instructors in class or by tutors during practice sessions.

出版和使用说明

《进阶中文：读与写》专供读写课使用。这本教材通过各种练习有系统地介绍336个高频字（简体及繁体）和1,200多个高频词。这本教材另外还介绍199个补充生字及700多个补充生词，所以总共介绍823个生字和2,600多个生词。学习者宜与配套的《进阶中文：读与写》练习册、《进阶中文：听与说》及《进阶中文：听与说》练习册一起使用。

出版和使用說明

《進階中文：讀與寫》專供讀寫課使用。這本教材通過各種練習有系統地介紹336個高頻字（簡體及繁體）和1,200多個高頻詞。這本教材另外還介紹199個補充生字及700多個補充生詞，所以總共介紹823個生字和2,600多個生詞。學習者宜與配套的《進階中文：讀與寫》練習冊、《進階中文：聽與說》及《進階中文：聽與說》練習冊一起使用。

Contents

Acknowledgments

I am indebted to a number of people for their assistance in the preparation of this volume. It's not possible to mention everyone who participated, but special thanks are due the following for their contributions:

For assistance in drafting an earlier version of some of the reading exercises, parts of which survive in the present version, my good friend Qunhu Li, formerly my colleague in the Chinese Program at Williams College and now Director of New Century Language and Culture Center in Tianjin. Student research assistants Jenny Chen and Tron Wang also contributed to the reading exercises.

For corrections to the manuscript and helpful comments of all kinds, Jerling Guo Kubler, Eric Pelzl, and Shaopeng Zhang; and my colleagues in the Chinese Program at Williams College, present and past, Cecilia Chang, I-Ting Chao, Yu-yin Hsu, Nini Li, Christopher M. B. Nugent, Cathy Silber, Hsin-I Tseng, Weibing Ye, Zhang Mo, Wei Zhang and, especially, Hao-hsiang Liao and Li Yu. Yang Wang, my coauthor for *Basic Spoken Chinese Practice Essentials* and *Intermediate Spoken Chinese Practice Essentials*, went over the entire manuscript with a fine-toothed comb, for which I am deeply grateful. I would also like to thank my colleague and friend Professor Shengli Feng, formerly of Harvard University and now with the Chinese University of Hong Kong, for his valuable insights concerning register and prosody in written Chinese.

For making the accompanying audio recordings, Jerling Guo Kubler.

For advice and assistance with computer-related work, Adam Jianjun Wang, Senior Instructional Technology specialist at Williams College, and Peter Leimbigler of Asia Communications Québec Inc. All of the Chinese-language content in this volume was processed using the KEY 5.1 Chinese language software that Dr. Leimbigler and his colleagues developed.

For their careful editing and helpful suggestions during the production of this course, my editors June Chong and Sandra Korinchak. I also wish to express my appreciation for their enthusiastic support of the project and its development, and for their patience, to Tuttle's Publisher Eric Oey and Vice President Christina Ong; and to Nancy Goh, Ngo Su Yin, and the Tuttle Sales and Marketing Team for their expertise and assistance.

Last but not least, I wish to thank the students in the Basic Chinese classes at Williams College from 1993 through 2014 for their comments and suggestions. I should also state here that though many have helped me bring this volume to completion, I alone am responsible for the final form of the content and any mistakes or imperfections.

Cornelius C. Kubler
Department of Asian Studies
Williams College
Williamstown, Massachusetts, USA

About This Course

Intermediate Spoken Chinese and *Intermediate Written Chinese* constitute the second level of a comprehensive course in modern Chinese (Mandarin), the language with the largest number of native speakers in the world, the official language of mainland China and Taiwan and one of the official languages of Singapore. The focus of this course, which is designed for adult English-speaking learners, is on communicating in Chinese in practical, everyday situations. We have tried to keep in mind the needs of a wide range of users, from college and university students to business people and government personnel. With some adjustments in the rate of progress, high school students may also be able to use these materials to their advantage. By availing themselves of the detailed usage notes and making good use of the *Practice Essentials* books, the video, and the audio, it is even possible for motivated self-learners to work through these materials on their own, though it would be desirable for them to meet with a teacher or native speaker for an hour or two per week, if possible. Although users with specialized needs will, in the later stages of their study, require supplementary materials, we believe this course provides a solid general foundation or "base" (hence the title of the course) that all learners of Chinese need, on which they may build for future mastery.

The course is divided into spoken and written tracks, each with various types of ancillary materials. The following diagram will clarify the organization of the whole course:

Basic Spoken Chinese

Textbook   *Practice Essentials* Workbook

Video Software   CD-ROM
Audio Disc   (Audio + Printable resources)

Character Transcription

Basic Written Chinese

Textbook   *Practice Essentials* Workbook

Audio Disc   CD-ROM
(Audio + Printable resources)

**Instructor's Guide for
Basic Spoken Chinese and *Basic Written Chinese***

Intermediate Spoken Chinese

Textbook   *Practice Essentials* Workbook

Video Software   CD-ROM
Audio Disc   (Audio + Printable resources)

Character Transcription

Intermediate Written Chinese

Textbook   *Practice Essentials* Workbook

Audio Disc   CD-ROM
(Audio + Printable resources)

**Instructor's Guide for
Intermediate Spoken Chinese and *Intermediate Written Chinese***

Several modes of study are possible for these materials: (1) the spoken series only; (2) a lesson in the spoken series followed a few days, weeks, or months later by the corresponding lesson in the written series; and (3) a lesson in the spoken and written series studied simultaneously. What is not possible is to study the written series first or only, since the written series assumes knowledge of the pronunciation system and relevant grammatical and cultural information, which are introduced in the spoken series.

Students embarking upon the study of Chinese should be aware that, along with Japanese, Korean, and Arabic, Chinese is one of the most difficult languages for native English speakers. This course makes no pretensions of being an "easy" introduction to the language. However, students can be assured that if they make the effort to master thoroughly the material presented here, they will acquire a solid foundation in Chinese.

The proficiency goals in speaking and reading by completion of the *Intermediate Spoken Chinese* and *Intermediate Written Chinese* portions of the course are Intermediate-High on the American Council on the Teaching of Foreign Languages (ACTFL) Chinese Proficiency Guidelines, which correlates with S-1+/R-1+ on the U.S. government Interagency Language Roundtable (ILR) Language Skill Level Descriptions. By the time they attain this level, learners will be able to conduct simple, practical conversations with Chinese speakers on a variety of everyday topics. They will also be able to read simple, connected texts printed in simplified or traditional Chinese characters and recognize about 600 high-frequency characters and common words written with them. Of course, they will not yet be able to conduct conversations on professional topics or read newspapers or novels, skills that in the case of Chinese take a considerably longer time to develop.

Some of the special features of this course include:

Separate but integrated tracks in spoken and written Chinese. Most textbooks for teaching basic Chinese teach oral and written skills from the same materials, which are covered at a single rate of progress. Students typically study a dialog, learn how to use in their speech the words and grammar contained in the dialog, and also learn how to read and write every character used to write the dialog. But the fact is that, due to the inherent difficulty of Chinese characters, native English speakers can learn spoken Chinese words much faster than they can learn the characters used to write those words. As East Asian language pedagogues Eleanor H. Jorden and A. Ronald Walton have argued,* why must the rate of progress in spoken Chinese be slowed down to the maximum possible rate of progress in written Chinese? Moreover, in Chinese, more than in most languages, there are substantial differences between standard spoken style and standard written style, with many words and grammar patterns that are common in speech being rare in writing or vice versa. For all these reasons, this course uses separate but related materials for training in spoken and written Chinese. However, reflecting the fact that written Chinese is based on spoken Chinese, and so as to mutually reinforce the four skills (listening, speaking, reading, and writing), the written track is closely integrated with the spoken track. A day's spoken lesson is based on a conversation typically introducing one to three new grammar patterns and 15 to 20 new spoken words, while the corresponding written lesson introduces six new high-frequency characters and a number of words that are written using them, chosen from among (but not including all of) the characters used to write the basic conversation of the corresponding lesson. Experience shows that the learning of written skills in Chinese proceeds more efficiently if learners study for reading and writing the characters for words they have previously learned for speaking and comprehension. Under this approach, when students take up a new lesson in written Chinese, they already know the pronunciations, meanings, and usages of the new words, needing only to learn their written representations—which considerably lightens the learning load. Such an approach also allows students and instructors maximum flexibility concerning at which point, how, and even whether, to introduce reading and writing.

Graduated approach. There is so much to learn to become proficient in Chinese that Chinese language learning can easily become overwhelming. By dividing large tasks into a series of many smaller ones, the learning of Chinese becomes more manageable. Therefore, each spoken lesson consists of only one fairly short (five- to twelve-line) conversation, while each written lesson introduces only six new characters. An added bonus to this approach is the sense of accomplishment learners feel through frequent completion of small tasks, rather than getting bogged down in long lessons that seem never-ending.

Naturalness of the language. A special effort has been made to present natural, idiomatic, up-to-date Chinese as opposed to stilted "textbook style." This will be evident, for example, in the use of interjections, pause fillers,

---

* Cf. Eleanor H. Jorden and A. Ronald Walton, "Truly Foreign Languages: Instructional Challenges" in *The Annals of the American Academy of Political and Social Science*, March 1987.

and final particles, which occur more frequently in this text than in most other Chinese language textbooks. Occasionally, for comprehension practice, we have included recordings of slightly accented Mandarin speech, so as to familiarize learners with some of the more common variations in pronunciation they are likely to encounter.

Authenticity of the language. Chinese, like English, is a language spoken in a number of different societies, with multiple standards and varying usages. Although the emphasis of this course is on the core that is common to Mandarin Chinese wherever it is spoken, linguistic differences among the major Chinese speech communities as well as recent innovations are taken up where appropriate. Of the 96 basic conversations in *Basic Spoken Chinese* and *Intermediate Spoken Chinese*, the audio and video for 56 of them were recorded in Beijing, with another 31 recorded in Taipei, 3 in Hong Kong, one in Macao, 2 in Singapore, 2 in Malaysia, and one in the U.S. The relatively small number of terms that are restricted in use to a particular speech area are so indicated.

Emphasis on the practical and immediately useful. We have tried to present material that is high in frequency and has the most immediate "pay-off value" possible. An effort has been made to include the most useful words, characters, grammar patterns, situations, and functions, based on several published frequency studies as well as research by the author. The units of this course have been arranged in order of general usefulness and practical importance. Although the course is designed to be studied from beginning to end, learners with time for only, say, the first five or ten units will at least be exposed to many of the most useful characters, vocabulary items, and structural patterns.

Eclecticism of approach. We believe that language is so complex and the personalities of learners so different, that no single approach or method can possibly meet the needs of all learners at all times. For this reason, the pedagogical approach we have chosen is purposefully eclectic. This course is proficiency-oriented and situational in approach with a carefully ordered underlying grammatical foundation. We have borrowed freely from the audio-lingual, communicative, functional-notional, and grammar-translation approaches.

Maximum flexibility of use. Student and teacher needs and personalities vary widely, as do the types of programs in which Chinese is taught. We have tried to leave options open whenever possible. This is true, for example, in the question of how to teach pronunciation; whether to teach the spoken skills only or also the written skills; when to introduce reading and writing; whether to teach simplified or traditional characters or both; and which of the exercises to do and in which order to do them. There is detailed discussion of all these and other questions in the Instructor's Guide for *Basic Spoken Chinese* and *Basic Written Chinese*.

Attention to sociolinguistic and cultural features. Knowing how to say something with correct grammar and pronunciation is not sufficient for effective communication. Learners must know what to say and what not to say, when to say it, and how to adjust what they say for the occasion. How do the gender, age, and social position of the speaker and listener affect language? Finally, language does not exist apart from the culture of its speakers. What are the cultural assumptions of Chinese speakers? These are some of the matters to which we have tried to pay attention.

Extensive built-in review. In order to promote long-term retention of the material learned, a great effort has been made to recycle vocabulary and grammar periodically in later units in the textbook and *Practice Essentials* after they have been introduced.

Attention to the needs of learners with prior knowledge of Chinese. While the course is designed for beginners and assumes no prior knowledge of Chinese, it tries to take into account the special situation and needs of learners who possess some prior knowledge of the language acquired from home or residence overseas. Consequently, there are special notes on features of standard Mandarin pronunciation and usage that differ from the Cantonese or Taiwanese-influenced Mandarin to which some learners may have been exposed.

Organization and Use

Intermediate Written Chinese consists of fourteen units that parallel the fourteen units in *Intermediate Spoken Chinese*. Each of these units in turn consists of four parts, with each part presenting six characters, common words written with them, and reading exercises to help you master the new material.

The fourteen units of *Intermediate Written Chinese* systematically introduce 336 of the highest-frequency characters (in both their simplified and traditional forms) and over 1,200 common words and expressions written with them in context in sentences and a variety of reading passages, so as to help you master Chinese reading and writing. Together with the 288 characters and over 700 words introduced in *Basic Written Chinese*, this makes a total of 624 characters and about 1,900 words formally taught in the two-volume written Chinese course. In addition, *Intermediate Written Chinese* introduces another 199 new characters and over 700 new words for supplemental learning, making a grand total of 823 characters and over 2,600 words that students will have encountered by the end of the course.

The six characters in each lesson were chosen, based on frequency of occurrence, from the characters used to write the Basic Conversation of the corresponding lesson in *Intermediate Spoken Chinese**. Since each lesson of *Intermediate Written Chinese* was designed to be studied after the corresponding lesson of *Intermediate Spoken Chinese* and *Intermediate Spoken Chinese Practice Essentials*, when you begin a new lesson of *Intermediate Written Chinese*, you already know the pronunciations, meanings, and usages of the new words, so you need only learn their written representations. This considerably lightens your learning load!

NEW CHARACTERS AND WORDS

The first section of each part or lesson in *Intermediate Written Chinese* is called "New Characters and Words." It introduces the six new characters of the lesson as well as common words written with them. For each new character, the following information is provided:

1. **Number.** The blue-colored number at the beginning of the section for each new character is the number of the character in this course. Later in the course, characters are sometimes referred to by their number.

2. **Simplified form.** If only one large, blue-colored character is given, then the simplified form is the same as the traditional form.

3. **Traditional form.** If the traditional form of a character is different from the simplified form, it is given next, also in large, blue-colored font, but *enclosed in parentheses*. So that learners are always clear about which characters are simplified and which are traditional, whenever simplified and traditional characters occur together, simplified characters always come first, with traditional characters following, enclosed in parentheses.

4. **Pinyin.** The Pinyin transcription follows on the same line after the character.

5. **English.** The last item on the first line of each new character section is an English translation of the basic meaning of the character. The translation here is for reference only and does not need to be learned. The meaning of the individual character may be different from the meanings of words containing the character. Moreover, the English translation is not meant to be complete and includes only those meanings that are judged to be pedagogically useful for learners at this point in their study of Chinese.

---

* When there were no appropriate characters in the Basic Conversation of the corresponding lesson, characters from the Supplementary Vocabulary of the corresponding lesson were chosen, or characters from previous lessons where there had been an excess of appropriate characters were chosen.

6. **Radical.** Beginning on the second line of each new character section, the radical for the new character is given. If the character differs in its simplified and traditional forms, and if those two forms have different radicals, then both radicals are indicated. If the radical has a common colloquial name, that also is given.

7. **Phonetic.** If there is a pedagogically useful phonetic, it is indicated. If the character itself is a common phonetic, examples are given of characters in which the phonetic occurs.

8. **Other components.** Any other components of the character are mentioned and discussed.

9. **Structural explanation.** When something pedagogically useful can be said about the history and development of the character, it is included. Our primary consideration is helping students remember the character, so some explanations that have mnemonic value are mentioned even if they may not be historically accurate. On the other hand, explanations that are excessively complex and would not be helpful to the average learner have been omitted.

10. **Similar characters.** At the end of the new character section are listed any "look-alike" characters with which the new character should be contrasted.

11. **New words written with the character.** After each new character is a list of new words that can be written with that character. Sometimes related new words that have not previously occurred in the spoken materials are also listed here for supplemental learning; these are indicated with the symbol ⊙. All the new words are given in simplified characters, traditional characters (if different from simplified), Pinyin transcription, and English translation. The new words are also recorded on the accompanying audio disc.

12. **New words written with characters you already know.** This section presents new words from the corresponding lesson of *Intermediate Spoken Chinese* that are written with characters that have already been introduced in previous lessons of the course. These words are also recorded on the accompanying audio disc.

IMPORTANT NOTE TO LEARNERS: Before beginning the Reading Exercises and proceeding to the next lesson, you need only learn the *new words in sections (11) and (12) above that are followed by word class abbreviations in bolded brackets*. Everything else is for reference only.

READING EXERCISES

The next section of each lesson is the Reading Exercises. These should be the focus of study and practice, since they present the new characters, words, and other features of written Chinese in context. When doing the Reading Exercises, you should read the materials both orally and silently. Be sure to make frequent use of the accompanying audio disc to hear and practice correct pronunciation, phrasing, and intonation. The Reading Exercises are presented twice: first in simplified characters in horizontal format, and then again in traditional characters in vertical format. This is done to provide learners with practice in reading both types of characters and both formats. Of course, learners may choose to read only one version of the Reading Exercises, or they may read one version first and the other version later.

The Reading Exercises for Units 11 to 24 consist of the following components:

1. **Sentences.** These illustrate the use of the new characters and words in context. There are always ten sentences in this section, and they exemplify all the new characters and most of the new words of the lesson.

2. **Conversations.** The conversations are in spoken style. The first conversation is often similar to the Basic Conversation in the corresponding lesson of *Intermediate Spoken Chinese*. The name or role of each person speaking is included and should be studied along with the conversation itself. During class or practice sessions, you should find a partner or partners, and each of you should take a role. Then switch roles, so you can practice reading all of the lines.

3. **Narratives.** The purpose of the narratives is to give you practice in reading connected prose, which is different in a number of ways from a series of independent sentences. A few of the narratives include some elements of written-style Chinese. The first time you read a narrative, you should read it out loud; the second time, read silently and with gradually increased reading speed. Always think of the meaning of what you're reading.

4. **Notes.** These are miscellaneous comments to help you understand the meaning, structure, and cultural background of the material in the Reading Exercises. Be sure to study the notes carefully as you work your way through the Reading Exercises. No attempt is made to provide a systematic treatment of grammar, since that is provided in *Basic Spoken Chinese* and *Intermediate Spoken Chinese*. To allow the use of more interesting reading materials, some supplemental characters and words have been introduced in this volume, with the majority of these occurring in the later lessons. They are all fully explained in the notes, with the symbol ◆ indicating vocabulary written with new characters and the symbol ◉ indicating new vocabulary written with familiar characters.

Abbreviations

Word Classes*

[A]	Adverb
[AT]	Attributive
[AV]	Auxiliary Verb
[BF]	Bound Form
[CJ]	Conjunction
[CV]	Coverb
[EV]	Equative Verb
[EX]	Expression
[I]	Interjection
[IE]	Idiomatic Expression
[L]	Localizer
[M]	Measure
[MA]	Moveable Adverb
[N]	Noun
[NU]	Number
[P]	Particle
[PH]	Phrase
[PR]	Pronoun
[PT]	Pattern
[PV]	Postverb
[PW]	Place Word
[QW]	Question Word
[RC]	Resultative Compound
[RE]	Resultative Ending
[SN]	Surname
[SP]	Specifier
[SV]	Stative Verb
[TW]	Time Word
[V]	Verb
[VO]	Verb-Object Compound

Other Abbreviations and Symbols

(B)	Beijing
(T)	Taipei
lit.	literally
/	(separates alternate forms)
◆	(supplemental vocabulary written with new characters)
◉	(supplemental vocabulary written with familiar characters)

* For explanations of these word classes, see the section "Word Classes of Spoken Chinese" on pages 354–364 of *Basic Spoken Chinese* (Tuttle Publishing, 2011).

我做得到，你也可以的！

红酒的王国

一起來種樹

非買不可

您有房子要賣嗎？

第一个研究红山文化的中国人

五百元法國菜

第三週 11/3~11/9

你不知道的那些事儿

故事里的事

说再见

六百元

美国音乐

改变世界

3雙 2,000元

以前沒有，以後很難再有！

給A，還是給B？

欢迎

香港电影

百年
1909—2008

快去辦！

買1送1

Getting Around Taipei

COMMUNICATIVE OBJECTIVES

Once you've mastered this unit, you'll be able to use Chinese to read and write about:

1. Getting around the city of Taipei.

2. Hailing a taxi and telling the driver your destination.

3. Complaining that the driver is driving too fast and telling him or her to slow down.

4. Paying the driver and telling him or her to keep the change.

5. Inquiring about taking a bus.

6. Asking directions to a friend's home.

7. Filling up at a gas station.

8. A Chinese joke involving arithmetic.

By Taxi to the Bank of Taiwan

这个司机实在开得太快了！
(這個司機實在開得太快了！)

New Characters and Words

Study the six characters below and the common words written with them, paying careful attention to each character's pronunciation, meaning, and structure, as well as similar-looking characters. After you've studied a character, turn to the *Practice Essentials* volume and practice writing it on the practice sheet, making sure to follow the correct stroke order and direction as you pronounce it out loud and think of its meaning.

289 快   **kuài**   fast, quick; soon, quickly; happy

Radical is 心 **xīn** "heart" (262). When at the left side of a character, this radical is referred to colloquially as 心字旁 **xīnzìpáng** "side made up of the character 心" and is written as 忄. Phonetic is 夬 **kuài**. The "heart" 心 beats "fast" 快. Distinguish 快 from simplified 块 **kuài** (112).

     快   **kuài**   be fast, quick [SV]; soon, quickly [A]

290 慢   **màn**   slow; haughty, rude

Radical is 心 **xīn** "heart" (262). When at the left side of a character, this radical is referred to colloquially as 心字旁 **xīnzìpáng** "side made up of the character 心" and is written as 忄. Phonetic is 曼 **màn**, which is used in the city name 曼谷 **Màngǔ** "Bangkok."

     慢   **màn**   be slow [SV]
     慢走   **màn zǒu**   "take care" [IE]

291 题 (題)   **tí**   topic; problem

Radical is 页 (頁) **yè** "leaf," "page." The other component is 是 **shì** (76). Note how the bottom stroke in the 是 is elongated to make room for the 页 (頁). Distinguish 题 (題) from 是.

问题 (問題)	**wèntí**	question; problem [N]
没问题 (没問題)	**méi wèntí**	"no problem" [IE]

292 放   **fàng**   put; let go, set free

Radical is 攴 **pū** "rap," "tap." As a radical on the right-hand side of a character, it is usually written 攵. Phonetic is 方 **fāng** (158). Distinguish 放 from 方.

放心	**fàngxīn**	relax [VO]

293 解(解)   **jiě**   loosen

Radical is 角 **jiǎo** "horn." The whole character 解 itself serves as a phonetic in other characters, e.g., in the character 蟹 **xiè** which is used in the word 螃蟹 **pángxie** "crab." The character 解 has an alternate form 解.

◉ 解放 (解放)	**jiěfàng**	liberate, emancipate [V]¹
◉ 解放前 (解放前)	**jiěfàng qián**	before liberation, pre-liberation (i.e., before 1949 Chinese Communist revolution) [PH]
◉ 解放后 (解放後)	**jiěfàng hòu**	after liberation (i.e., after 1949) [PH]

Note that the difference between the official simplified form and the official traditional form of this character does not show up in all fonts; in some fonts, they both look the same.

294 决(決)   **jué**   decide

Radical of the simplified form is 冫 **bīng** "ice," which is referred to colloquially as 两点水 (兩點水) **liǎngdiǎn shuǐ** "two drops of water." Radical of the traditional form is 水 **shuǐ** "water," which is written 氵 and is referred to colloquially as 三点水 (三點水) **sāndiǎn shuǐ** "three drops of water" when it occurs at the left-hand side of a character. Phonetic is 夬 **kuài**, which you saw earlier in this lesson in 快 **kuài** (289). Distinguish 决 (決) from 快 and simplified 块 **kuài** (112).

解决 (解決)	**jiějué**	solve, resolve [V]
决定 (決定)	**juédìng**	decide, determine [V]; decision [N]

New Words in ISC 11-1 Written with Characters You Already Know

了	**le**	(indicates action continuing up to present) [P]
死	**-sǐ**	to the point of death [RE]
坐	**zuò**	sit in/on; take; by (car, boat, train, airplane, etc.) [CV]

Reading Exercises (Simplified Characters) 简体字²

Now practice reading the new characters and words for this lesson in context in sentences, conversations, and narratives. Be sure to refer to the Notes at the end of this lesson, and make use of the accompanying audio disc to hear and practice correct pronunciation, phrasing, and intonation.

---

1. Here and in the rest of this volume, the symbol ◉ indicates a new and useful word or expression that has not previously been introduced in the spoken course but that is written with characters you have already learned or are learning in the current lesson. You should learn this new word or expression at this time, since if it reoccurs later in this book, it will not be annotated again.

2. 简体字 (簡體字) **jiǎntǐzì** means "simplified character."

A. SENTENCES 句子[3]

Read out loud each of the following sentences, which include all the new characters of this lesson. The first time you read a sentence, focus special attention on the characters and words that are new to you, reminding yourself of their pronunciation and meaning. The second time, aim to comprehend the overall meaning of the sentence.

一、高老师，我能问您一个问题吗？

二、我觉得我们一定要快一点儿解决这个问题。

三、你的同屋没什么问题，你可以放心了。

四、解放前我表哥是一位小学老师，解放后他换了工作。

五、刚刚是谁开的门？请你快一点儿关上门，好不好？

六、校长，请您放心，这个问题很快就会解决的。

七、这么多的问题，你太慢了，快一点儿，我忙死了！

八、这家公司的东西贵死了，我们快去别家吧！

九、小何很喜欢中国，所以决定以后要到中国去住。

十、王大海气死了，他有很多问题，朋友也不给他解决。

B. CONVERSATIONS 对话[4]

Read out loud the following conversations, including the name or role of the person speaking. If possible, find a partner or partners and each of you play a role. Then switch roles, so you get practice reading all of the lines.

一、

美国学生：请您到天津街五十三号，谢谢。

中国司机：你的中国话说得不错！是在哪儿学的？

美国学生：我在美国跟香港都学过。

中国司机：你来了多长时间了？

美国学生：来了半年多了。司机先生，您开得太快了！可不可以开慢一点儿？

中国司机：没问题，你放心吧……前面就到了。

美国学生：多少钱？

中国司机：九十五块。

美国学生：好，给您钱。

中国司机：谢谢。

二、

金太太：李太太，我走了。今天真谢谢您了！

李太太：没事儿，没事儿，您慢走！

三、

小李：老张，你开得太快了！开慢一点儿，好吗？

---

3. 句子 **jùzi** means "sentence."
4. 对话 (對話) **duìhuà** means "dialog" or "conversation."

老张：好，没问题。

（过了一会儿）

小李：老张，对不起，现在你开得太慢了。请你开快一点儿，好吗？

四、

方先生：老林，你决定什么时候去成都了吗？

林先生：我还没决定，但是我大概下个月去。

方先生：你去四川一定得小心一点儿！

林先生：放心，不会有问题的。

五、

边美生：金金，你能给我解决一个问题吗？

王金金：那我得先知道是什么样儿的问题，对不对？

边美生：我表妹明天晚上要从上海来。她叫我去机场等她，但是我明
天有事。你能不能到机场去等她呢？

王金金：没问题，你放心好了，我一定去。她明天几点到？

边美生：六点三刻。

王金金：那么，我就六点半到机场等她吧。

边美生：金金，真谢谢你了！

王金金：没事儿。

C. NARRATIVE 短文[5]

Read the following narrative, paying special attention to punctuation and overall structure. The first time you read the narrative, read it out loud. The second time, read silently and try to gradually increase your reading speed. Always think of the meaning of what you're reading.

我姐姐快要三十岁了，我也已经二十五岁了。时间实在过得太快了！还
记得小的时候，我觉得三十岁一定很老，但是现在觉得三十岁不一定
那么老。其实，有很多事我还不太清楚，也有很多问题我还没解决。
不过我已经长大了，要决定的事，还是早一点决定吧。

Reading Exercises (Traditional Characters) 繁體字[6]

A. SENTENCES 句子

Read out loud each of the following sentences, which include all the new characters of this lesson. The first time you read a sentence, focus special attention on the characters and words that are new to you, reminding yourself of their pronunciation and meaning. The second time, aim to comprehend the overall meaning of the sentence.

---

5. 短文 **duǎnwén** means "short narrative."
6. 繁体字 (繁體字) **fántǐzì** means "complex character" or "traditional character."

一、高老師，我能問您一個問題嗎？

二、我覺得我們一定要快一點兒解決這個問題。

三、你的同屋沒什麼問題，你可以放心了。

四、解放前我表哥是一位小學老師，解放後他換了工作。

五、剛剛是誰開的門？請你快一點兒關上門，好不好？

六、校長，請您放心，這個問題很快就會解決的。

七、這麼多的問題，你太慢了，快一點兒，我忙死了！

八、這家公司的東西貴死了，我們快去別家吧！

九、小何很喜歡中國，所以決定以後要到中國去住。

十、王大海氣死了，他有很多問題，朋友也不給他解決。

B. CONVERSATIONS 對話

Read out loud the following conversations, including the name or role of the person speaking. If possible, find a partner or partners and each of you play a role. Then switch roles, so you get practice reading all of the lines.

一、

美國學生：請您到天津街五十三號，謝謝。

中國司機：你的中國話說得不錯！是在哪兒學的？

美國學生：我在美國跟香港都學過。

中國司機：你來了多長時間了？

美國學生：來了半年多了。司機先生，您開得太快了！可不可以開慢一點兒？

中國司機：沒問題，你放心吧……前面就到了。

美國學生：多少錢？

中國司機：九十五塊。

美國學生：好，給您錢。

中國司機：謝謝。

二、

金太太：李太太，我走了。今天真謝謝您了！

李太太：沒事兒，沒事兒，您慢走！

三、

小李：老張，你開得太快了！開慢一點兒，好嗎？

老張：好，沒問題。

（過了一會兒）

小李：老張，對不起，現在你開得太慢了。請你開快一點兒，好嗎？

四、

林先生：放心，不會有問題的。

方先生：你去四川一定得小心一點兒！

林先生：我還沒決定，但是我大概下個月去。

方先生：老林，你決定什麼時候去成都了嗎？

五、

王金金：沒事兒。

邊美生：金金，真謝謝你了！

王金金：那麼，我就六點半到機場等她吧。

邊美生：六點三刻。

王金金：沒問題，你放心好了，我一定去。她明天幾點到？

邊美生：我表妹明天晚上要從上海來。她叫我去機場等她，但是我明天有事。你能不能到機場去等她呢？

王金金：那我得先知道是什麼樣兒的問題，對不對？

邊美生：金金，你能給我解決一個問題嗎？

C. NARRATIVE 短文

Read the following narrative, paying special attention to punctuation and overall structure. The first time you read the narrative, read it out loud. The second time, read silently and try to gradually increase your reading speed. Always think of the meaning of what you're reading.

我姐姐快要三十歲了，我也已經二十五歲了。時間實在過得太快了！還記得小時候，我覺得三十歲一定那麼老。是現在覺得三十歲不一定那麼老。其實，有很多事我還不太清楚，我也還有很多問題。不過我還沒很多解決。已經長大了，要決定的事，還是早一點決定吧。

Notes 注解[7]

A5. 关上门 (關上門) "close the door"

A6. 这个问题很快就会解决的 (這個問題很快就會解決的) "This problem will be solved soon." The pattern 会…的 (會…的) means "be likely to" or "will" and expresses the writer's conviction that something will most likely be a certain way (BSC 10-1: 2B, ISC 13-2: 7C).

A8. 别家 (別家) here stands for 别家公司 (別家公司) "another company."

A10. ⊙ 气死 (氣死) **qìsǐ** "become extremely angry" [RC]

B1. 司机先生 (司機先生) "Mr. Chauffeur" is a polite way to refer to a male chauffeur or driver. Referring to him simply as 先生 would also be acceptable.

B4. 不会有问题的 (不會有問題的) "There won't be (any) problems." See note A6 above on 会…的 (會…的).

C1. You learned 过 (過) "pass," "go by" in BWC 8-3. The sentence 时间实在过得太快了 (時間實在過得太快了) means "Time really passes too quickly."

C2. 要决定的事，还是早一点决定吧 (要決定的事，還是早一點決定吧) lit. "The matters that should be decided, on reflection it would be better to decide them a little earlier." A more idiomatic translation might be "I'd better decide the things that need to be decided as soon as possible." Note that 要 here means "need to," "should" (BWC 8-3).

Store Sign in Taipei

"Which Bus Do I Take to Muzha?"

 New Characters and Words

Study the six characters below and the common words written with them, paying careful attention to each character's pronunciation, meaning, and structure, as well as similar-looking characters. After you've studied a character, turn to the *Practice Essentials* volume and practice writing it on the practice sheet, making sure to follow the correct stroke order and direction as you pronounce it out loud and think of its meaning.

295 久 **jiǔ** for a long time

Radical is 丿 **piě** left curving stroke. The character 久 depicts a "person" 人 trying to walk but being impeded by an obstacle 丿, so it takes the person "a long time" 久 to get anywhere. 久 can itself serve as a phonetic, e.g., in 玖 **jiǔ**, the more complex form of the number 九 **jiǔ** (10). The character 玖 is used on checks instead of 九 to avoid mistakes and alterations. Distinguish 久 from 人 **rén** (30) and 次 **cì** (134).

久	jiǔ	be long (of time) [SV]
好久	hǎo jiǔ	for a very long time [PH]
多久	duō jiǔ	for how long? [PH]

296 完 **wán** finish, complete

Radical is 宀 **mián** "roof." This radical is referred to colloquially as 宝盖头 (寶蓋頭) **bǎogàitóu** "top made up of a canopy." Phonetic is 元 **yuán** "dollar" (377). Distinguish 完 from 定 **dìng** (270) and simplified 园 **yuán** (252).

完	wán	finish, complete [V/RE]
卖完 (賣完)	màiwán	finish selling, be sold out
吃完	chīwán	finish eating
说完话 (說完話)	shuōwán huà	finish talking

三、

中国同学：你来这个学校多久了？
老外：　　　已经很久了，快一年了。
中国同学：你吃过饭了吗？
老外：　　　我刚刚吃完。
中国同学：我还没吃呢，现在就去吃。再见！
老外：　　　再见！

四、

张老师：老李，好久不见了！
李老师：是，好久不见！
张老师：你准备什么时候去香港？
李老师：我下个星期六或者星期天就要走了。
张老师：你要去多久呢？
李老师：还不知道，因为去了香港以后，还要去广州。
张老师：是吗？时间不早了，我得先走了。明天见！
李老师：再见！

C. NARRATIVES 短文

Read the following narratives, paying special attention to punctuation and overall structure. The first time you read a narrative, read it out loud. The second time, read silently and try to gradually increase your reading speed. Always think of the meaning of what you're reading.

一、　小学五年级的时候，我有一个同学住在我们家对面。他是美国人，
　　　但是中国话说得比中国人还好！小学六年级的时候，他和他家人
　　　回美国去了，听说他们现在住在美国的西岸。我已经好久没见到
　　　他了。不知道他最近怎么样，也不知道什么时候会再见到他。

二、　老温
　　　我有一个朋友姓温，名字叫温安然。他现在是记者，住在我们家
　　　对面，不过我很久没见到他了。老温是我以前上大学时候的同
　　　屋，很喜欢买东西。有一次，他买了一个大钟。我问他："你为什
　　　么要买那个钟？你家里不是已经有好几个钟了吗？"老温说他很
　　　需要那个钟，别人家里都没有，买了以后只有他一个人有，所以
　　　一定要买。还有一次，老温买了一个很贵的汽车。我问他："你为
　　　什么要买那么贵的汽车？你真的需要吗？"老温说因为别人都有
　　　这样的车，所以他不能不买。我真不知道说什么好。

Reading Exercises (Traditional Characters) 繁體字

A. SENTENCES 句子

Read out loud each of the following sentences, which include all the new characters of this lesson. The first time you read a sentence, focus special attention on the characters and words that are new to you, reminding yourself of their pronunciation and meaning. The second time, aim to comprehend the overall meaning of the sentence.

一、我弟弟很久沒說日本話了，大概已經忘了很多了。

二、老張那個人說一是一，說二是二，你別再問了。

三、我和我的小學六年級同學說了再見以後，就很久沒再見到他們了。

四、原來你說還有很多公車票，怎麼現在都賣完了？

五、你大概已經忘了我了吧？我們已經好久沒見了。

六、你從公司給我打電話或者找一個公共電話給我打都可以。

七、飯也吃完了，東西也買完了，我們可以回家了。

八、你要是需要換錢的話，可以去機場或者比較大的飯店換。

九、這個地方天天下大雨或是毛毛雨，我們已經好久沒見到太陽了。

十、我們等王大海已經等了好久了，但是他還沒吃完晚飯，叫我們再等他一會兒。

B. CONVERSATIONS 對話

Read out loud the following conversations, including the name or role of the person speaking. If possible, find a partner or partners and each of you play a role. Then switch roles, so you get practice reading all of the lines.

一、（在台北）

老外：請問，到台北動物園去要坐幾號？

第一個台北人：我好久沒坐公車了，不太清楚。你到對面的7-ELEVEN去問問看。要不然，你也可以坐MRT去動物園。

老外：謝謝。我買一張車票。

第二個台北人：236或是237都可以到。

老外：大概多久一班？

第二個台北人：237比較久。236好像五分鐘一班，很快的。

第二個台北人：對不起，車票已經賣完了。你上了車再買吧。

二、

老師：我叫你寫的字你都寫完了嗎？

學生：都寫完了。

老師：這個字寫錯了，請你再寫一次。

三、

中國同學：你來這個學校多久了？

老外：已經很久了，快一年了。

中國同學：你吃過飯了嗎？

老外：我剛剛吃完。

中國同學：我還沒吃呢，現在就去吃。再見！

老外：再見！

四、

張老師：老李，好久不見了！

李老師：是，好久不見！

張老師：你準備什麼時候去香港？

李老師：我下個星期六或者星期天就要走了。

張老師：你要去多久呢？

李老師：還不知道，因為去了香港以後，還要去廣州。

張老師：是嗎？時間不早了，我得先走了。明天見！

李老師：再見！

C. NARRATIVES 短文

Read the following narratives, paying special attention to punctuation and overall structure. The first time you read a narrative, read it out loud. The second time, read silently and try to gradually increase your reading speed. Always think of the meaning of what you're reading.

一、

小學五年級的時候，我有一個同學住在我們家對面。他是美國人，但是中國話說得比中國人還好！小學六年級的時候，他和他家人回美國去了，聽說他們現在住在美國的西岸。我已經好久沒見到他了。不知道他最近怎麼樣，也不知道什麼時候會再見到他。

二、

老溫

我有一個朋友姓溫，名字叫溫安然。他現在是記者，住在我家對面，不過我很久沒見到他了。老溫是我以前上大學時候的同屋，很喜歡買東西。有一次，他買了一個大鐘。我問他：「你為什麼要買那個鐘？你家裡不是已經有好幾個鐘了嗎？」老溫說他很需要那個鐘，別人家裡都沒有，買了以後只有他一個人有，所以一定要買。還有一次，老溫買了一個很貴的汽車。我問他：「你為什麼要買那麼貴的汽車？你真的需要這樣的車嗎？」老溫說因為別人都有這樣的車，所以他不能不買。我這樣真不知道說甚麼好。

Notes 注解

A2.   说一是一，说二是二 (說一是一，說二是二) lit. "Say one and it's one, say two and it's two" or, in idiomatic English, "Mean what you say" or "Stand by your word."

A3.   In this sentence, notice that the two 再见 (再見) have very different meanings. The first occurs in 说再见 (說再見), and means "Say goodbye." The second occurs in 很久没再见到他们 (很久沒再見到他們), and means "(I) didn't see them again for a long time."

B1.   In Taiwan, 公车 (公車) is the word for "bus." In mainland China, 公交车 (公交車) is usually used instead.

B2.   You've learned 叫 in the sense of "be called" or "call." 叫 can also mean "tell" (someone to do something). Therefore, 我叫你写的字 (我叫你寫的字) means "the characters that I told you to write."

C1.   比中国人还好 (比中國人還好) means "even better than Chinese people."

C2.   你家里不是已经有好几个钟了吗？(你家裏不是已經有好幾個鐘了嗎？) "Don't you already have quite a few clocks at your home?" This is a rhetorical question, in other words, the speaker believes that the person he or she is speaking to does have a lot of clocks at their home. 好几个 (好幾個) means "quite a few," "several," or "a lot of."

Street Sign in Hong Kong

Asking Directions to a Friend's House

公用電話

我跟你讲，我转来转去
怎么找也找不到你说的那条路。
(我跟你講，我轉來轉去怎麼找
也找不到你說的那條路。)

New Characters and Words

Study the six characters below and the common words written with them, paying careful attention to each character's pronunciation, meaning, and structure, as well as similar-looking characters. After you've studied a character, turn to the *Practice Essentials* volume and practice writing it on the practice sheet, making sure to follow the correct stroke order and direction as you pronounce it out loud and think of its meaning.

301 转（轉）   **zhuǎn/zhuàn**   turn, revolve

Radical is 车（車）**chē** "cart" (224). Phonetic is 专（專）**zhuān** "special." The wheels of a "cart" 车（車) are there for a "special" 专（專）purpose, i.e., to "turn" 转（轉）. Distinguish 转（轉）from 专（專）.

转 （轉）	**zhuǎn/zhuàn**	turn; go around; revolve [V]
左转 （左轉）	**zuǒ zhuǎn**	turn left
往右转 （往右轉）	**wàng yòu zhuǎn**	turn toward the right
转进来 （轉進來）	**zhuǎnjìnlai**	turn in [RC]
转来转去 （轉來轉去）	**zhuànlái zhuànqù**	turn back and forth

302 跟   **gēn**   with, and; heel

Radical is 足 **zú** "foot" (546), which at the left side of a character is referred to colloquially as 足字旁 **zúzìpáng** "side made up of the character 足." When this character is written as a radical, its last two strokes are different, with the last stroke angling up to make room for the component on the right. Phonetic is 艮 **gèn**, which is one of the Eight Trigrams in the *Book of Changes*. Distinguish 跟 from 很 **hěn** (58).

跟	**gēn**	and [CV]; with [CJ]
我跟你	**wǒ gēn nǐ**	you and I

我跟你走	**wǒ gēn nǐ zǒu**	I'll go with you
跟…说 (跟…說)	**gēn...shuō**	say to, tell (someone something); repeat after someone [PT]
我跟你说 (我跟你說)	**wǒ gēn nǐ shuō**	I say to you; let me tell you
你跟我说 (你跟我說)	**nǐ gēn wǒ shuō**	repeat after me

---

303 讲 (講)   **jiǎng**   speak, say, explain

Radical is 讠(言) **yán** "speech" (336). The colloquial name for this radical is 言字旁 **yánzìpáng** "side made up of the character 言." Phonetic of the simplified form is 井 **jǐng** "a well." Distinguish 讲 (講) from 清 **qīng** (245) and 请 (請) **qǐng** (67), and distinguish simplified 讲 from simplified 进 **jìn** (278).

讲 (講)	**jiǎng**	speak, say, talk about, explain [V]
讲话 (講話)	**jiǎnghuà**	speak [VO]
跟…讲 (跟…講)	**gēn...jiǎng**	say to, tell (someone something) [PT]
我跟你讲 (我跟你講)	**wǒ gēn nǐ jiǎng**	I say to you; let me tell you
讲中国话 (講中國話)	**jiǎng Zhōngguo huà**	speak Chinese

---

304 具   **jù**   implement, tool

Radical is 八 **bā** "eight" (9). Distinguish 具 from 真 **zhēn** (173) and simplified 县 **xiàn** (194).

| 家具 | **jiājù** | furniture [N] |
| 家具店 | **jiājù diàn** | furniture store [PH] |

---

305 手   **shǒu**   hand

This character is itself a common radical. When 手 is at the left side of a character, it is written as 扌 and is referred to colloquially as 提手 **tíshǒu** "raised hand." 手 is a pictograph, being a side view of a person's hand with the fingers stretched out. Be sure to distinguish 手 from 毛 **máo** (258).

手	**shǒu**	hand [N]
左手	**zuǒshǒu**	left hand [N/PW]
右手	**yòushǒu**	right hand [N/PW]
左手边 (左手邊)	**zuǒshǒubiān**	left-hand side [PW]
右手边 (右手邊)	**yòushǒubiān**	right-hand side [PW]

---

306 房   **fáng**   house; room

Radical is 戶 **hù** "door." Phonetic is 方 **fāng** "square" (158), which you already encountered in 放 **fàng** (292). "Houses" 房 have "doors" 戶 and are often "square" 方 in shape. Distinguish 房 from 方.

房	**Fáng**	Fang [SN]
房子	**fángzi**	house [N]
房间 (房間)	**fángjiān**	room [N]

New Words in ISC 11-3 Written with Characters You Already Know

错过 (錯過)	**cuòguo**	miss (a bus, an opportunity, etc.) [V]
店	**diàn**	shop, store [PW]
过 (過)	**-guò**	(indicates motion past or by) [RE]
看到	**kàndào**	see [RC]
一会儿见 (一會兒見)	**yìhuǐr jiàn**	"see you in a while" [IE]
来…去 (來…去)	**VERB lái VERB qù**	VERB all over [PT]
找来找去 (找來找去)	**zhǎolái zhǎoqù**	look all over
怎么…也不 (怎麼…也不)	**zěnme...yě bù**	no matter how hard...don't [PT]
怎么…也没 (怎麼…也沒)	**zěnme...yě méi**	no matter how hard...didn't [PT]

Reading Exercises (Simplified Characters) 简体字

Now practice reading the new characters and words for this lesson in context in sentences, conversations, and narratives. Be sure to refer to the Notes at the end of this lesson, and make use of the accompanying audio disc to hear and practice correct pronunciation, phrasing, and intonation.

A. SENTENCES 句子

Read out loud each of the following sentences, which include all the new characters of this lesson. The first time you read a sentence, focus special attention on the characters and words that are new to you, reminding yourself of their pronunciation and meaning. The second time, aim to comprehend the overall meaning of the sentence.

一、这个事儿我已经跟你讲过很多次了，你怎么不听？

二、在那个中文中心里面一定得讲中国话，不可以讲外国话。

三、林先生在房间里走来走去，好像有很多问题还没解决的样子。

四、那个地方离这儿不远，你先往左转，再往右转，很快就到了。

五、我们这儿十月的天气最好，你来得正是时候，别错过！

六、我今天得去家具店买几件家具，你要不要跟我一起去？

七、我不小心，错过了三点钟的那班公共汽车，只好等三点半的了。

八、弟弟，别那样动你的手，实在太难看了，我跟你讲过很多次了！

九、你的房间是几号？在左手边，在右手边？我找来找去，怎么找也找不着！

十、王大海说他有一个问题，就是："没有家具的房子怎么能住呢？"

B. CONVERSATIONS 对话

Read out loud the following conversations, including the name or role of the person speaking. If possible, find a partner or partners and each of you play a role. Then switch roles, so you get practice reading all of the lines.

一、

何大安：小谢，我是小何。我跟你讲，我转来转去怎么找也找不到你说
的那条路。

谢百里：你现在在哪里？

何大安：我在你说的那个小学门口打电话给你。

谢百里：好，你听我讲。你往"中美公司"那边走，就会看到一家家具
店。店不太大，不要错过。从那条路转进来左手边就是我们
住的房子。

何大安：好，知道了。一会儿见！

二、

房先生：钱小姐，你家里的家具都很好看。是在哪儿买的？

钱小姐：我们是在和平家具店买的。

房先生：和平家具店在哪儿？离这儿远吗？

钱小姐：不太远，很近。要是从这里走的话，一直往前走，到了公共汽
车站往左转，然后一直往前走就到了。

房先生：那好。有时间我一定去看看。谢谢你了，再见！

钱小姐：不谢。明天见！

"**Xǐshǒujiān**" (sign in Beijing)

C. NARRATIVE 短文

Read the following narrative, paying special attention to punctuation and overall structure. The first time you read the narrative, read it out loud. The second time, read silently and try to gradually increase your reading speed. Always think of the meaning of what you're reading.

我要跟你们讲一讲我小时候的房子。这已经是很久以前的事了，但是我到现在还记得很清楚。那时候我跟我家里人住在北京城外头一个叫房山的地方。我们住的房子不大，只有两个小房间，不过我那时候还很小，所以对我来说那个房子好像很大！房子里家具也不多，但是我们也不需要那么多东西。房子的左手边有一个中学，右手边有一家小店。我们后来在对面买了一个大一点的房子，可是我觉得那个房子住起来没有以前的房子那么好。我真喜欢我小时候的房子！

 ## Reading Exercises (Traditional Characters) 繁體字

A. SENTENCES 句子

Read out loud each of the following sentences, which include all the new characters of this lesson. The first time you read a sentence, focus special attention on the characters and words that are new to you, reminding yourself of their pronunciation and meaning. The second time, aim to comprehend the overall meaning of the sentence.

一、這個事兒我已經跟你講過很多次了，你怎麼不聽？

二、在那個中文中心裡面一定得講中國話，不可以講外國話。

三、林先生在房間裡走來走去，好像有很多問題還沒解決的樣子。

四、那個地方離這兒不遠，你先往左轉，再往右轉，很快就到了。

五、我們這兒十月的天氣最好，你來得正是時候，別錯過！

六、我今天得去家具店買幾件家具，你要不要跟我一起去？

七、我不小心，錯過了三點鐘的那班公共汽車，只好等三點半的了。

八、弟弟，別那樣動你的手，我跟你講過很多次了！

九、你的房間是幾號？在左手邊，在右手邊？我找來找去，怎麼找也找不著！

十、王大海說他有一個問題，就是：「沒有家具的房子怎麼能住呢？」

B. CONVERSATIONS 對話

Read out loud the following conversations, including the name or role of the person speaking. If possible, find a partner or partners and each of you play a role. Then switch roles, so you get practice reading all of the lines.

一、

何大安：小謝，我是小何。我跟你講，我轉來轉去怎麼找也找不到你說的那條路。

謝百里：你現在在哪裡？

何大安：我在你說的那個小學門口打電話給你。

謝百里：好，你聽我講。你往「中美公司」那邊走，就會看到一家家具店。店不太大，不要錯過。從那條路轉進來左手邊就是我們住的房子。

何大安：好，知道了。一會兒見！

二、

房先生：錢小姐，你家裡的家具都很好看。是在哪兒買的？

錢小姐：我們是在和平家具店買的。

房先生：和平家具店在哪兒？離這兒遠嗎？

錢小姐：不太遠，很近。要是從這裡走的話，一直往前走，到了公共汽車站往左轉，然後一直往前走就到了。

房先生：那好。有時間我一定去看看。謝謝你了，再見！

錢小姐：不謝。明天見！

C. NARRATIVE 短文

Read the following narrative, paying special attention to punctuation and overall structure. The first time you read the narrative, read it out loud. The second time, read silently and try to gradually increase your reading speed. Always think of the meaning of what you're reading.

我要跟你們講一講我小時候的房子。這已經是很久以前的事了，但是我到現在還記得很清楚。那時候我跟我家裡人住在一個叫京城外頭的山北的地方，只有兩個小房間，不大，不過那時候我還小，所以對我來說那個房子好像很大！那房子裡家具也不需要那麼多，東西也不多，房子的左右手邊有一個小房子。後來在對面一家店買了一個大一點的房子，可是我覺得那個房子，住起來沒有以前那個房子真好。我那麼喜歡我小時候的房子！

Notes 注解

A3. 好像有很多问题还没解决的样子 (好像有很多問題還沒解決的樣子) "It appeared that he had a lot of problems that he hadn't yet solved." Review the pattern 好像…的样子 (好像…的樣子) "it appears that, it seems that" (BSC 10-3: 1C, BWC 10-3).

A8. ⊙难看 (難看) **nánkàn** "be ugly," "unattractive" [SV]

A9. ⊙找不着 (找不著) **zhǎobuzháo** "can't find" [RC]. This is a synonym of 找不到 (BWC 9-4).

B2. ⊙不谢 (不謝) **búxiè** "don't thank me" or "you're welcome" [IE]

B3. 讲一会儿话 (講一會兒話) **jiǎng yìhuǐr huà** means "talk for a little while." Some in the younger generation now pronounce 一会儿 (一會兒) as **yíhuìr**.

C1. 很久以前的事 means "a matter from a long time ago."

Filling Up at a Gas Station

请问，你加什么油？
（請問，你加什麼油？）

95. 我看还是加满好了。
（95. 我看還是加滿好了。）

New Characters and Words

Study the six characters below and the common words written with them, paying careful attention to each character's pronunciation, meaning, and structure, as well as similar-looking characters. After you've studied a character, turn to the *Practice Essentials* volume and practice writing it on the practice sheet, making sure to follow the correct stroke order and direction as you pronounce it out loud and think of its meaning.

307 加 **jiā** add

Radical is 力 **lì** "strength" (478). The other element is 口 **kǒu** "mouth" (140). "Strength" 力 is "added" to the "mouth" 口 to make 加. Distinguish 加 from 叫 **jiào** (78).

加	**jiā**	add [V]
加州	**Jiāzhōu**	California [PW]

308 油 **yóu** oil; gasoline

Radical is 水 **shuǐ** "water" (333), since oil is a liquid like water. This radical is written 氵 and is referred to colloquially as 三点水 (三點水) **sāndiǎn shuǐ** "three drops of water" when occurring at the left-hand side of a character. Phonetic is 由 **yóu** "from."

油	**yóu**	oil; gasoline [N]
加油	**jiāyóu**	add gasoline, refuel, tank up [VO]; "All power to you!", "Hang in there!" (said when rooting for someone or to encourage them) [IE]
加油站	**jiāyóuzhàn**	gas station [PW]
◉汽油	**qìyóu**	gasoline [N]

四、

小李：小王，你去過加州嗎？

小王：我就是加州人。我是在加州出生的，也是在那兒長大的。

小李：加州怎麼樣？聽說西岸的天氣不錯。

小王：對，那兒的氣候特別好，不冷也不熱，但是加州買東西比較貴。

小李：聽說最近加州的油價特貴，是真的嗎？

小王：是的。以前還好，可是從今年起，汽油和其他東西的價錢都越來越貴了，所以現在不少人需要加油的時候就到別的州去加，不在加州加油。

C. NARRATIVES 短文

Read the following narratives, paying special attention to punctuation and overall structure. The first time you read a narrative, read it out loud. The second time, read silently and try to gradually increase your reading speed. Always think of the meaning of what you're reading.

一、

我們家住在美國西岸的加州。這是一個汽車特別多的州，所以很多路口都有加油站。前天我的車子快沒有油了，所以我就停在一個加油站準備要加油，但是那裡的油價實在太貴了，還好，對面就有一個加油站，但是那裡的油價比第一家還要貴。然後我轉來轉去，去了十幾家加油站，價錢都很貴，最後我的車子沒有油了！最近油價越來越貴，我看以後車子就停在家裡，坐公車或者走路去上班比較好。

二、

東山大學很小，有汽車的人也不太多，但是這個大學有一個特別大的停車場。離那兒不遠還有一個大學叫西山大學。西山大學很大，開車的人也特別多，但是西山大學的停車場特別小，天天都會停滿，還有很多人怎麼找也找不到停車的位子。聽說西山大學的林校長今天要去見東山大學的高校長。不知道這兩位大學校長能不能解決停車的問題？

Notes 注解

A4.   全票 (全票) means "full-price ticket" while 半价票 (半價票) means "half-price ticket."

A5.   成 here means "become" (BWC 10-1).

A6.   油价要贵很多 (油價要貴很多) "The price of oil is going to become much more expensive."

A10.   到现在 (到現在) here means "by now."

C1a.   ⊙ 州 **zhōu** "district," "prefecture," "state," or "canton" **[N]**. You first encountered this word in BWC B-1 in the city name 广州 (廣州) "Guangzhou". When the context is the United States, 州 means "state," for example, one could say 美国有五十个州 (美國有五十個州) "The U.S. has 50 states." In the word 加州 "California," the syllable 加 **jiā** represents the "Ca-" sound in "California" and 州 means "state," so 加州 literally means "the state of California."

C1b.   还好 (還好) lit. means "still good." When followed by a statement, as here, it means "luckily" or "fortunately" and implies the situation could have been worse (i.e., there might not have been another gas station nearby).

C1c.   对面就有一个加油站 (對面就有一個加油站) "Right on the other side there was a gas station" or "There was a gas station right across from where I was." The 就 here implies "as close as that; that close," so in this context 就 could be translated as "right."

C1d.   十几家加油站 (十幾家加油站) lit. means "ten plus a few gas stations," which in good English we could render as "over a dozen gas stations." The actual number is at least 11 and at most 19. 几 (幾) is used here to mean "few," "several," or "some" (BSC 7-2: 7B, BWC 7-2).

C2a.   停满 (停滿) lit. "park to the point where it (the parking lot) is full."

C2b.   停车的位子 (停車的位子) means "a place for parking" or "a parking spot" (BSC 5-2, BWC 5-2).

C2c.   不知道 here means 我不知道. In contexts like this, the pronoun 我 is frequently omitted. It would be acceptable to translate this 不知道 as "I don't know," but an even better translation would be "I wonder if…"

Street Sign in Taipei

UNIT 12

Shopping (I)

COMMUNICATIVE OBJECTIVES

Once you've mastered this unit, you'll be able to use Chinese to read and write about:

1. Purchasing various items in a department store.

2. Buying different kinds of vegetables and fruit.

3. Alternatives: This one or that one? Big ones or small ones? etc.

4. The names of common academic fields and majors.

5. Reading books and newspapers and visiting bookstores.

6. A simple discussion of Chinese languages and dialects.

Buying Ice Pops

 New Characters and Words

Study the six characters below and the common words written with them, paying careful attention to each character's pronunciation, meaning, and structure, as well as similar-looking characters. After you've studied a character, turn to the *Practice Essentials* volume and practice writing it on the practice sheet, making sure to follow the correct stroke order and direction as you pronounce it out loud and think of its meaning.

313 根 **gēn** root; (measure for long, thin things)

Radical is the pictograph 木 **mù** "tree." This radical is referred to colloquially as 木字旁 **mùzìpáng** "side made up of the character 木." When 木 is written at the left of a character as a radical, its last stroke is shortened so that it doesn't touch the component to its right. Phonetic is 艮 **gèn** (one of the Eight Trigrams in the *Book of Changes*). Distinguish 根 from 很 **hěn** (58) and 跟 **gēn** (302).

根	**gēn**	(measure for long, thin things) [M]
一根毛	**yìgēn máo**	a hair (on the body)
根本	**gēnběn**	basically, fundamentally [A]
根本 + NEGATIVE	**gēnběn**	not at all, completely not [PT]

314 拿 **ná** take; hold

Radical is 手 **shǒu** "hand" (305), which is usually at the left side of a character and written as 扌 and referred to colloquially as 提手 **tíshǒu** "raised hand" but is here at the bottom of the character. Phonetic is 合 **hé** "merge" or "combine." In order to "take" 拿 something, one's "hand" 手 must "merge" 合 with the object. Distinguish 拿 from 手.

拿	ná	take, hold [V]
拿好	náhǎo	hold on to well, hold firmly [RC]
加拿大	Jiā'nádà	Canada [PW]
加拿大人	Jiā'nádà rén	Canadian person [PH]

315 专 (專) zhuān   special; expert

Radical is 寸 **cùn** "inch." 专 (專) can serve as a phonetic in other characters, e.g., 转 (轉) **zhuǎn** (301). Distinguish 专 (專) from 转 (轉).

| 专家 (專家) | zhuānjiā | specialist, expert [N] |
| 外国专家 (外國專家) | wàiguo zhuānjiā | foreign expert [PH] |

316 业 (業) yè   business, industry; course of study; undertaking

Radical of the simplified form is 一 **yī** "one" (1). Radical of the traditional form is 木 **mù** "tree." Distinguish simplified 业 from simplified 个 **ge** (87), simplified 开 **kāi** (122), and 小 **xiǎo** (24).

| 专业 (專業) | zhuānyè | major (in college) [N] |
| ⊙作业 (作業) | zuòyè | homework [N] |

317 办 (辦) bàn   do; handle, take care of

Radical of the simplified form is 力 **lì** "strength" (478). Radical of the traditional form is 辛 **xīn** "arduous." In the traditional form, note the character 力 **lì** "strength" (478) in between the two 辛. Distinguish simplified 办 from 九 **jiǔ** (10) and simplified 为 **wèi** (182).

办 (辦)	bàn	do, handle, take care of [V]
办事 (辦事)	bànshì	take care of matters [VO]
怎么办？(怎麼辦？)	Zěnme bàn?	"What should be done?" [IE]

318 法 fǎ/fá   way, method

Radical is 水 **shuǐ** "water" (333), which is written 氵 and is referred to colloquially as 三点水 (三點水) **sāndiǎn shuǐ** "three drops of water" when it occurs at the left-hand side of a character. The other component is 去 **qù** (53). Distinguish 法 from 去.

法子	fázi	way, method [N] (Note that 法 is here pronounced **fá**, not **fǎ**.)
办法 (辦法)	bànfǎ	way of managing or handling something [N]
⊙想法	xiǎngfǎ	way of thinking, idea, opinion [N]
⊙做法	zuòfǎ	way of doing something [N]
法国 (法國)	Fǎguo	France [PW]
法国人 (法國人)	Fǎguo rén	French person [PH]
法文	Fǎwén	written French [N]

New Words in ISC 12-1 Written with Characters You Already Know

还是 (還是)	**háishi**	or [CJ]
好	**-hǎo**	so that something is good [RE]
生物	**shēngwù**	biology [N]
天文	**tiānwén**	astronomy [N]
文学 (文學)	**wénxué**	literature [N]
比较文学 (比較文學)	**bǐjiào wénxué**	comparative literature [PH]
样 (樣)	**yàng(r)**	kind, variety [M][1]

Reading Exercises (Simplified Characters) 简体字

Now practice reading the new characters and words for this lesson in context in sentences, conversations, and narratives. Be sure to refer to the Notes at the end of this lesson, and make use of the accompanying audio disc to hear and practice correct pronunciation, phrasing, and intonation.

A. SENTENCES 句子

Read out loud each of the following sentences, which include all the new characters of this lesson. The first time you read a sentence, focus special attention on the characters and words that are new to you, reminding yourself of their pronunciation and meaning. The second time, aim to comprehend the overall meaning of the sentence.

一、你说得不对，我根本没有说过这样儿的话！

二、在中国，大一的学生就已经决定了要学什么专业。

三、我的表哥姓高，是一位天文专家，你可能听说过他。

四、你不可以拿我的东西，以后请你不要拿我这里的东西！

五、这个大学有生物和比较文学专业，但是没有天文。

六、对不起，我还得去办点儿事，先走了，明天见！

七、你没有钱买车票我也没有办法，因为我也没带钱。

八、我上个星期到加拿大去了，但是天气不好，根本没办法出门。

九、中国有很多"美国专家"，美国也有很多"中国专家"，但是有的问题专家也没法子解决。

十、王大海好高兴，他今天早上在他家外头的地上找到了一百块钱。

---

1. In this volume, to simplify the presentation and save space, if a word can occur with an optional (r) suffix, this is indicated in the Pinyin column by (r) at the end of the word, but the (r) suffix is not indicated in the Chinese character column. This actually corresponds to Chinese writing practice, since the (r) suffix is seldom indicated in standard Chinese writing. For more information on the (r) suffix, see pp. 40–42 in *Basic Spoken Chinese*.

B. CONVERSATIONS 对话

Read out loud the following conversations, including the name or role of the person speaking. If possible, find a partner or partners and each of you play a role. Then switch roles, so you get practice reading all of the lines.

一、

加拿大人：多少钱？

中国人　：五毛钱一根儿。

加拿大人：买两根。

中国人　：你要这样儿的还是要那样儿的？

加拿大人：一样一根吧。

中国人　：一共一块。

加拿大人：给您五块。

中国人　：找您四块。您拿好！

二、

男生：要学法文的话，去法国好还是去加拿大好？

女生：我们的老师是法国人，她说法国的法文听起来比较好听。

男生：听说小何下个月要去法国。

女生：小何最近太忙了，我看他根本还没决定去还是不去。

三、

小文：小李，我有个大问题，真不知道怎么办。

小李：你有什么问题？

小文：这个月我们不是要决定专业了吗？家里要我学生物专业，可是我
　　　要学的是比较文学专业。

小李：那，你能不能学两个专业？也学生物，也学比较文学。这样你家
　　　里人高兴，你也能学你喜欢的专业。

小文：对，这是一个好办法。

C. NARRATIVES 短文

Read the following narratives, paying special attention to punctuation and overall structure. The first time you read a narrative, read it out loud. The second time, read silently and try to gradually increase your reading speed. Always think of the meaning of what you're reading.

一、刚刚走的那个人是我一个大学同学。他是一个比较文学专家。他刚
　　刚来我家拿一点儿东西。因为他还有一点儿事得办，所以先走了。他
　　可能明天还要再来我家找我。

二、我在高中的时候很喜欢生物，后来也喜欢天文。可是到了大学，我
　　越来越喜欢文学，特别是法国文学。现在我的专业是法文，明年我
　　要到法国或是加拿大去多学一点法文。我真的很喜欢法文，不过以
　　后要找什么样儿的工作，我现在根本不知道。

Reading Exercises (Traditional Characters) 繁體字

A. SENTENCES 句子

Read out loud each of the following sentences, which include all the new characters of this lesson. The first time you read a sentence, focus special attention on the characters and words that are new to you, reminding yourself of their pronunciation and meaning. The second time, aim to comprehend the overall meaning of the sentence.

一、你說得不對，我根本沒有說過這樣兒的話！

二、在中國，大一的學生就已經決定了要學甚麼專業。

三、我的表哥姓高，是一位天文專家，你可能聽說過他。

四、你不可以拿我的東西，以後請你不要拿我這裡的東西！

五、這個大學有生物和比較文學專業，但是沒有天文。

六、對不起，我還得去辦點兒事，先走了，明天見！

七、你沒有錢買車票我也沒有辦法，因為我也沒帶錢。

八、我上個星期到加拿大去了，但是天氣不好，根本沒辦法出門。

九、中國有很多「美國專家」，美國也有很多「中國專家」，但是有的問題專家也沒法子解決。

十、王大海好高興，他今天早上在他家外頭的地上找到了一百塊錢。

B. CONVERSATIONS 對話

Read out loud the following conversations, including the name or role of the person speaking. If possible, find a partner or partners and each of you play a role. Then switch roles, so you get practice reading all of the lines.

一、

加拿大人：多少錢？
中國人：五毛錢一根兒。
加拿大人：買兩根。
中國人：你要這樣兒的還是要那樣兒的？
加拿大人：一樣一根吧。
中國人：一共一塊。
加拿大人：給您五塊。
中國人：找您四塊。您拿好！

二、

男生：要學法文的話，去法國好還是去加拿大好？
女生：我們的老師是法國人，她說法國的法文聽起來比較好聽。
男生：聽說小何下個月要去法國。
女生：小何最近太忙了，我看他根本還沒決定去還是不去。

三、

小文：小李，我有個大問題，真不知道怎麼辦。

小李：你有甚麼問題？

小文：這個月我們不是要決定專業了嗎？家裡要我學的是比較文學專業。

小李：那，你能不能學兩個專業？也學生物，也學比較文學。這樣你也能讓家里人高興，你也能學你喜歡的專業。

小文：對，這是一個好辦法。

C. NARRATIVES 短文

Read the following narratives, paying special attention to punctuation and overall structure. The first time you read a narrative, read it out loud. The second time, read silently and try to gradually increase your reading speed. Always think of the meaning of what you're reading.

一、

剛剛走的那個人是我一個大學同學。他是一個比較文學專家。他剛剛來我家拿一點兒東西。因為他還有一點兒事得辦，所以先走了。他可能明天還要再來我家找我。

二、

我在高中的時候很喜歡生物，後來也喜歡天文學，可是到了大學，我特別喜歡文學，我現在越來越喜歡文學了。我喜歡的專業是法國文學或法文。現在明年我要到法國去多學一點兒法文。不過以後我真的很喜歡法文，我要找什麼樣兒的工作，我現在根本不知道。

Notes 注解

A2. The adverb 就 here implies "as early as then" or "that early."

A7. 你没有钱买车票我也没有办法 (你沒有錢買車票我也沒有辦法) "If you don't have money to buy a bus ticket, there's nothing I can do about it" or "There's nothing I can do about your not having money to buy a bus ticket."

A9. 有的问题专家也没法子解决 (有的問題專家也沒法子解決) "Some problems even specialists have no way to solve." The 也 here implies "even."

A10. 地上, composed of the noun 地 and the localizer 上, means "on the ground."

B3. 也学生物,也学比较文学 (也學生物,也學比較文學) "Study both biology and comparative literature." 也…也 is a pattern meaning "both...and."

Purchasing Pens

 New Characters and Words

Study the six characters below and the common words written with them, paying careful attention to each character's pronunciation, meaning, and structure, as well as similar-looking characters. After you've studied a character, turn to the *Practice Essentials* volume and practice writing it on the practice sheet, making sure to follow the correct stroke order and direction as you pronounce it out loud and think of its meaning.

319 想 **xiǎng** think; want

Radical is 心 **xīn** "heart" (262). This radical is referred to colloquially as 心字底 **xīnzìdǐ** "bottom made up of the character 心." Phonetic is 相 **xiāng** "mutually" (459).

想	**xiǎng**	think [V]; want to, would like to [AV]
想想看	**xiángxiang kàn**	try and think
◉想要	**xiǎngyào**	want to, would like to [AV]

320 种 (種) **zhǒng** seed; kind

Radical is 禾 **hé** "growing grain." Phonetic of the simplified form is 中 **zhōng** "middle" (23). Phonetic of the traditional form is 重 **zhòng** "heavy" (462). The "heavy" 重 end of the "growing grain" 禾 is laden with "seeds" (種). Distinguish simplified 种 from simplified 钟 **zhōng** "clock" (119) and distinguish traditional 種 from traditional 動 **dòng** "move" (250).

种 (種)	**zhǒng**	kind [M]
这种 (這種)	**zhèizhǒng**	this kind
那种 (那種)	**nèizhǒng**	that kind

哪种 (哪種)	**něizhǒng**	which kind?
一种 (一種)	**yìzhǒng**	a kind of

---

321 书 (書)   **shū**   book

Radical of the simplified form is 丨 **gǔn**, called 一竖 (一豎) **yíshù** "vertical line." Radical of the traditional form is 曰 **yuē** "speak." The rest of the traditional form consists of 聿 **yù**, an archaic word for "pen." A "book" (書) is the product of a "pen" 聿 that "speaks" 曰. Distinguish simplified 书 from 中 **zhōng** (23), simplified 为 **wèi** (182), and simplified 东 **dōng** (29).

书 (書)	**shū**	book [N]
一本书 (一本書)	**yìběn shū**	one book
书店 (書店)	**shūdiàn**	bookstore [PW]
书房 (書房)	**shūfáng**	study [PW]
看书 (看書)	**kànshū**	read a book [VO]

---

322 些   **xiē**   some

Radical is 二 **èr** "two" (2). The other component is 此 **cǐ** "this," or "here" (605). If there are "two" 二 of some item "here" 此, then it can be said that there are "some" 些. Distinguish 些 from 比 **bǐ** (143) and 北 **běi** (16).

些	**xiē**	some [M]
有些人	**yǒu xiē rén**	(there are) some people (who...)
这些 (這些)	**zhèixiē**	these
那些	**nèixiē**	those
哪些	**něixiē**	which ones?
一些	**yìxiē**	some

---

323 报 (報)   **bào**   newspaper

Radical of the simplified form is 手 **shǒu** "hand" (305), which at the left side of a character is written as 扌 and is referred to colloquially as 提手 **tíshǒu** "raised hand." Radical of the traditional form is 土 **tǔ** "earth."

报 (報)	**bào**	newspaper [N]
报上 (報上)	**bàoshang**	in the newspaper
看报 (看報)	**kànbào**	read a newspaper [VO]

---

324 纸 (紙)   **zhǐ**   paper

Radical is 丝 (絲) **sī** "silk." When at the left side of a character, this radical is referred to colloquially as 绞丝旁 (絞絲旁) **jiǎosīpáng** "side made up of twisted silk" and is written as 纟 (糹). Phonetic is 氏 **shì** "family name." Distinguish 纸 (紙) from 级 (級) **jí** (174).

纸 (紙)	**zhǐ**	paper [N]
一张纸 (一張紙)	**yìzhāng zhǐ**	a piece of paper
报纸 (報紙)	**bàozhǐ**	newspaper [N]

New Words in ISC 12-2 Written with Characters You Already Know

本	**běn(r)**	(measure for books, dictionaries)	[M]
本子	**běnzi**	notebook	[N]
市	**shì**	city, municipality	[BF]

Reading Exercises (Simplified Characters) 简体字

Now practice reading the new characters and words for this lesson in context in sentences, conversations, and narratives. Be sure to refer to the Notes at the end of this lesson, and make use of the accompanying audio disc to hear and practice correct pronunciation, phrasing, and intonation.

A. SENTENCES 句子

Read out loud each of the following sentences, which include all the new characters of this lesson. The first time you read a sentence, focus special attention on the characters and words that are new to you, reminding yourself of their pronunciation and meaning. The second time, aim to comprehend the overall meaning of the sentence.

一、你想买什么样的钟？这种还是那种？

二、我天天早上第一件事就是看报，你呢？

三、这些东西是谁的？请你快一点从地上拿走。

四、那张纸上是不是有我的名字？

五、我想加个油，你说哪种汽油比较好？

六、我记得那家书店的左手边好像有一个家具店。

七、我在报上看到，你们有一些家具想卖，是不是？

八、《百家姓》是一本书的名字，这本书里头都是中国人的姓。

九、这种本子好像有两百张纸，那种好像只有一百五十张。

十、王大海去书店买了书和报纸，所以现在没有钱买饭了。

B. CONVERSATIONS 对话

Read out loud the following conversations, including the name or role of the person speaking. If possible, find a partner or partners and each of you play a role. Then switch roles, so you get practice reading all of the lines.

一、

老外　　：我想买书和报纸。

卖东西的：对不起，我们这儿不卖这些东西，您可以到对面的书店去买。

老外　　：好，谢谢您。

卖东西的：不谢。

二、

房国书：你在想什么呢？

李国林：我正在想我上个星期看过的一本书。

房国书：你还记得那本书叫什么名字吗？

李国林：我想想看……书好像叫……对不起，我忘了！

三、

李明　：今天的报纸你拿到了吗？

林文子：没有。你呢？

李明　：我也没拿到。是不是今天没有报纸呢？

林文子：不可能的！天天都有报纸，今天怎么会没有呢？

四、

边小姐：你去过和平街上的书店吗？

万先生：还没有时间去。你呢？

边小姐：我已经去过几次了。我觉得那家书店还不错。

万先生：我很想去看看。那儿都卖一些什么样儿的东西？

边小姐：书、报、本子、纸都有，价钱也不贵。

C. NARRATIVES 短文

Read the following narratives, paying special attention to punctuation and overall structure. The first time you read a narrative, read it out loud. The second time, read silently and try to gradually increase your reading speed. Always think of the meaning of what you're reading.

一、我因为小的时候没有朋友，所以特别喜欢看书跟报纸。我最喜欢去的地方就是书店。我去一回书店，就一定会买几本书，所以我的书房里书特别多！那个时候，我已经决定长大以后要在书店里工作。我觉得我一定会很喜欢这种工作的。

二、我早上看了报纸，报上说今天台北市又要下雨。没错，真的下了很大的雨。我现在很想到书店去给女儿买些本子，但是外面还在下雨。我只好坐在这儿看看书、写写东西。现在已经四点半了，我看今天大概出不去了。最近天天都下雨，这种天气根本没办法出门！

三、我们学校一共有两个书店，一个在东门，一个在西门。这两个书店一个比较大，里边卖的东西很多，可是离我家很远；还有一个比较小，里边卖的东西比较少，可是离我家很近。上个星期日我去这个小书店买一本书，书名是《为什么中国人会这样，外国人会那样？》，作者是王定和先生。可是小书店没有我要的这本书，所以我只好明天到大书店去找找看。

Store Sign in Harbin

Reading Exercises (Traditional Characters) 繁體字

A. SENTENCES 句子

Read out loud each of the following sentences, which include all the new characters of this lesson. The first time you read a sentence, focus special attention on the characters and words that are new to you, reminding yourself of their pronunciation and meaning. The second time, aim to comprehend the overall meaning of the sentence.

一、你想買什麼樣的鐘？這種還是那種？

二、我天天早上第一件事就是看報，你呢？

三、這些東西是誰的？請你快一點從地上拿走。

四、那張紙上是不是有我的名字？

五、我想加個油，你說哪種汽油比較好？

六、我記得那家書店的左手邊好像有一個家具店。

七、我在報上看到，你們有一些家具賣，是不是？

八、《百家姓》是一本書的名字，這本書裡頭都是中國人的姓。

九、這種本子好像有兩百張紙，那種好像只有一百五十張。

十、王大海去書店買了書和報紙，所以現在沒有錢買飯了。

B. CONVERSATIONS 對話

Read out loud the following conversations, including the name or role of the person speaking. If possible, find a partner or partners and each of you play a role. Then switch roles, so you get practice reading all of the lines.

一、

老外　：我想買書和報紙。

賣東西的：對不起，我們這兒不賣這些東西，您可以到對面的書店去買。

老外　：好，謝謝您。

賣東西的：不謝。

二、

房國書：你在想甚麼呢？

李國林：我正在想我上個星期看過的一本書。

房國書：你還記得那本書叫甚麼名字嗎？

李國林：我想看……書好像叫……對不起，我忘了！

三、

李明　：今天的報紙你拿到了嗎？

林文子：沒有。你呢？

李明　：我也沒拿到。是不是今天沒有報紙呢？

林文子：不可能的！天天都有報紙，今天怎麼會沒有呢？

四、

邊小姐：你去過和平街上的書店嗎？

萬先生：還沒有時間去。你呢？

邊小姐：我已經去過幾次了。我覺得那家書店還不錯。

萬先生：我很想去看看。那兒都賣一些什麼樣兒的東西？

邊小姐：書、報、本子、紙都有，價錢也不貴。

Sign in Singapore

C. NARRATIVES 短文

Read the following narratives, paying special attention to punctuation and overall structure. The first time you read a narrative, read it out loud. The second time, read silently and try to gradually increase your reading speed. Always think of the meaning of what you're reading.

一、

我因為小的時候沒有朋友，所以特別喜歡看書跟報紙。我最喜歡去的地方就是書店。我去一回書店，就一定會買幾本書！那個時候，我已經決定我以後要在書店裡工作。我覺得我一定會很喜歡這種工作的。

二、

我早上看了報紙，報上說今天台北市又要下雨。沒錯，真的下了很大的雨。我現在很想到書店去給女兒買些本子，但是外面還在下雨。我只好坐在這兒看看書、寫寫東西。現在已經四點半了，我看今天大概出不去了。最近天天都下雨，這種天氣根本沒辦法出門！

三、

我們學校一共有兩個書店，一個在東門，一個在西門。這兩個書店一個比較大，裡邊賣的東西很多，可是離我家很遠；還有一個比較小，裡邊賣的東西比較少，可是離我家很近。上個星期日我去這個小書店買一本書，書名是《為什麼中國人會那樣？》，作者是王定和先生。可是小書店沒有我要的這本書，所以我只好明天到大書店去找找看。

"Xiǎoxīn Pèng Tóu" (Be Careful About Hitting Your Head; sign in Harbin)

Notes 注解

A3. 请你快一点从地上拿走 (請你快一點從地上拿走) lit. "Please you more quickly take them away from the ground" or, in idiomatic English, "Please pick them up off the ground as fast as you can." The resultative verb compound 拿走 means "take away."

A5. 加个油 (加個油) lit. "add a gasoline" is a more relaxed and casual way to say 加油 "add gas," "fill up," or "tank up." If you're talking about having a meal, instead of saying 吃饭 (吃飯) you could also say 吃个饭 (吃個飯), with essentially the same meaning.

A7a. Note that in English one says "*in* the newspaper," but in Chinese one says 报上 (報上) lit. "*on* the newspaper."

A7b. 你们有一些家具想卖 (你們有一些家具想賣) "You have some furniture that you want to sell."

A8. ◉ 《百家姓》 **Bǎi Jiā Xìng** *The Book of One Hundred Family Names* [N]. This book, which would more accurately be translated as "Surnames of the General Population," is a well-known Classical Chinese text composed during the Song Dynasty. It lists all the Chinese surnames that existed at the time, most of which are still in use today. The work is a long poem in lines of eight characters with a rhyme at the end of each line. Children used to have to memorize this poem as part of their basic education. The brackets 《 》 are called 书名号 (書名號) and indicate book and article titles (BWC 7-2: E1).

B2. 你在想什么呢？(你在想什麼呢？) "What are you thinking about?" Note the use of 在 as an auxiliary verb to indicate progressive aspect (BSC 10-3: 2A). Similarly, in the next line, 我正在想我上个星期看过的一本书 (我正在想我上個星期看過的一本書) "I'm just thinking about a book that I read last week." The addition of the adverb 正 "just" strengthens the progressive sense (ISC 17-2: 7A).

B3a. 拿到 is a resultative compound verb that means "get," so 你拿到了吗？(你拿到了嗎？) means "Did you get it?"

B3b. 不可能的！ is an exclamation meaning "Impossible!" The final 的 is optional; one could also say just 不可能！

C2. 出不去 is a negative potential resultative compound meaning "can't go out."

C3. ◉ 书名 (書名) **shūmíng** "book title" [N]

"Yíngyè Zhōng"
(lit. "in the midst of doing business"; sign in Taipei)

Shopping for Vegetables

 New Characters and Words

Study the six characters below and the common words written with them, paying careful attention to each character's pronunciation, meaning, and structure, as well as similar-looking characters. After you've studied a character, turn to the *Practice Essentials* volume and practice writing it on the practice sheet, making sure to follow the correct stroke order and direction as you pronounce it out loud and think of its meaning.

325 才   **cái**   not until, then and only then, just

Radical is 一 **yī** "one" (1). The character 才 is a common phonetic within other characters, e.g., in 材 as in 材料 **cáiliào** "material." Distinguish 才 from 方 **fāng** (158) and simplified 万 **wàn** (142).

才	**cái**	not until, then and only then, just [A]

....

326 斤   **jīn**   catty (unit of weight, about 1⅓ lbs.)

This character is itself both a radical and a phonetic. For example, it serves as a phonetic in 近 **jìn** "be close" (221). Distinguish 斤 from 近 and simplified 听 **tīng** (215).

斤	**jīn**	catty (unit of weight, about 1⅓ lbs.) [M]
半斤	**bànjīn**	half a catty
公斤	**gōngjīn**	kilogram [M]

....

327 菜   **cài**   vegetable; dish of food

Radical is 艹 **cǎo** "grass," which is written as 草 when it occurs as an independent word (456). When it occurs as a radical at the top of a character, the "grass" radical is written as ⁺⁺, and is then known as 草字头 (草字頭) **cǎozìtóu** "top made up of the character 草." The phonetic within 菜 is 采 **cǎi** "gather." As a mnemonic, remember this: "gather" 采 "grass" ⁺⁺ and end up with "vegetables" 菜.

菜	**cài**	vegetable; dish of food [N]
中国菜 (中國菜)	**Zhōngguo cài**	Chinese food
生菜	**shēngcài**	lettuce [N]
菜场 (菜場)	**càichǎng**	food market, greenmarket, marketplace [N]
◉菜市场 (菜市場)	**càishìchǎng**	food market, greenmarket, marketplace [N]

328 白   **bái**   white

This character is itself both a radical and a phonetic, e.g., it is used in 百 **bǎi** "hundred" (113). Distinguish 白 from 百 and 日 **rì** (132).

白	**Bái**	Bai [SN]
白	**bái**	be white [SV]
白菜	**báicài**	cabbage [N]
白天	**báitiān**	during the day, daytime [TW]
◉白人	**Báirén**	White (person), Caucasian [N]
◉长白山 (長白山)	**Chángbái Shān**	Changbai Mountains (on the border between China and North Korea) [PW]

329 保   **bǎo**   protect; guarantee

Radical is 人 **rén** "person" (30), which is written 亻 when occurring at the left side of a character so as not to get in the way of the component at the right. The colloquial name for this radical is 人字旁 **rénzìpáng** "side made up of the character 人." The rest of the character is composed of a 口 **kǒu** "mouth" (140) and a 木 **mù** "tree." The whole character can serve as a phonetic, e.g., in 堡 **bǎo** "fort." As a mnemonic, you might remember that a "person" 人, a "mouth" 口, and a "tree" 木 equals "protection" 保.

330 证 (證)   **zhèng**   evidence; prove

Radical is 讠 (言) **yán** "speech" (336). The colloquial name for this radical is 言字旁 **yánzìpáng** "side made up of the character 言." Phonetic of the simplified form is 正 **zhèng** "just" (276). Phonetic of the traditional form is 登 **dēng** "ascend." The idea is to "climb" 登 to a high place and "speak" 言 to give "evidence" 证 (證). Distinguish simplified 证 from 正.

保证 (保證)	**bǎozhèng**	guarantee [V/N]

New Words in ISC 12-3 Written with Characters You Already Know

进口 (進口)	jìnkǒu	import [V/N]
出口	chūkǒu	export [V/N]
多谢 (多謝)	duō xiè	"thanks" [IE]
怎么这么… (怎麼這麼 …)	zěnme zhème...	how come so...? [PT]
怎么那么… (怎麼那麼 …)	zěnme nàme...	how come so...? [PT]

Reading Exercises (Simplified Characters) 简体字

Now practice reading the new characters and words for this lesson in context in sentences, conversations, and narratives. Be sure to refer to the Notes at the end of this lesson, and make use of the accompanying audio disc to hear and practice correct pronunciation, phrasing, and intonation.

A. SENTENCES 句子

Read out loud each of the following sentences, which include all the new characters of this lesson. The first time you read a sentence, focus special attention on the characters and words that are new to you, reminding yourself of their pronunciation and meaning. The second time, aim to comprehend the overall meaning of the sentence.

一、我同屋保证这次一定会早到，但是他最后还是很晚才到。

二、我今天白天在外面特别忙，晚上只想在家里看报，不想再出门了。

三、我们在机场等了快两个钟头，小白才到。

四、从前中国人不太喜欢吃生菜，可是最近几年他们好像越来越喜欢吃了。

五、到了加拿大我才知道这个比中国还大的地方人口比北京还少。

六、这本书写得特别好，我保证你会喜欢！

七、这种车子是从外国进口的，又好看又好开。

八、日本往外国出口很多汽车，从外国进口很多吃的东西。

九、有些美国人觉得美国汽车没有从外国进口的汽车那么好。

十、王大海到菜场给他的动物买了十公斤的白菜，但是动物不吃。

B. CONVERSATIONS 对话

Read out loud the following conversations, including the name or role of the person speaking. If possible, find a partner or partners and each of you play a role. Then switch roles, so you get practice reading all of the lines.

一、

张太太：白菜怎么卖？

卖菜的：白菜……半斤二十五块。

张太太：半斤二十五块？怎么这么贵？

卖菜的：太太，这种白菜是从日本进口的，今天才到的。比台湾的好，
　　　　保证好吃。

张太太：好，给我一斤好了。这是五十块。

卖菜的：好，多谢。你拿好！再来！

二、

李安：小白，你怎么这么晚才来？

白喜：我都忘了今天我是要来找你的。

李安：下次你得记得，别再忘了！

白喜：放心吧。我下次一定很早就来。

李安：好吧，你可不能忘了你今天说的话。

白喜：没有问题，我可以保证！

C. NARRATIVES 短文

Read the following narratives, paying special attention to punctuation and overall structure. The first time you read a narrative, read it out loud. The second time, read silently and try to gradually increase your reading speed. Always think of the meaning of what you're reading.

一、我跟你讲，我以前是什么菜都吃，只有白菜不吃。后来因为听朋友说从日本进口的白菜特别好吃，所以就决定买一些吃吃看。今天早上我就买了差不多三斤。很贵，但是真好吃！我先生也喜欢，他问我："这种白菜特别好吃，你在哪里买的？"朋友，你也去买一点儿从日本进口的白菜吧。我保证你一定会喜欢吃！

二、我们家住在湖北省老河口市。离我们家不远有两个菜市场。一个在路的左手边，叫"四号路菜市场"，一个在路的右手边，叫"王家台菜市场"。"四号路菜市场"的菜很多都是从外国进口的，又贵又不好吃。"王家台菜市场"卖的差不多都是本地菜，比进口的菜好吃，也没有进口的菜那么贵。要是我们家的人去买菜的话，我保证他们会去"王家台菜市场"，不会去"四号路菜市场"。

"**Zhuānmén Diàn**" (Specialty Store; sign in Taipei)

Reading Exercises (Traditional Characters) 繁體字

A. SENTENCES 句子

Read out loud each of the following sentences, which include all the new characters of this lesson. The first time you read a sentence, focus special attention on the characters and words that are new to you, reminding yourself of their pronunciation and meaning. The second time, aim to comprehend the overall meaning of the sentence.

一、我同屋保證這次一定會早到，但是他最後還是很晚才到。

二、我今天白天在外面特別忙，晚上只想在家裡看報，不想再出門了。

三、我們在機場等了快兩個鐘頭，小白才到。

四、從前中國人不太喜歡吃生菜，可是最近幾年他們好像越來越喜歡吃了。

五、到了加拿大我才知道這個比中國還大的地方人口比北京還少。

六、這本書寫得特別好，我保證你會喜歡！

七、這種車子是從外國進口的，又好看又好開。

八、日本往外國出口很多汽車，從外國進口很多的東西。

九、有些美國人覺得美國汽車沒有從外國進口的汽車那麼好。

十、王大海到菜場給他的動物買了十公斤的白菜，但是動物不吃。

B. CONVERSATIONS 對話

Read out loud the following conversations, including the name or role of the person speaking. If possible, find a partner or partners and each of you play a role. Then switch roles, so you get practice reading all of the lines.

一、

張太太：白菜怎麼賣？

賣菜的：白菜⋯⋯半斤二十五塊。

張太太：半斤二十五塊？怎麼這麼貴？

賣菜的：太太，這種白菜是從日本進口的，今天才到的，比台灣的好，保證好吃。

張太太：好，給我一斤好了。這是五十塊。

賣菜的：好，多謝。你拿好！再來！

二、

李安：小白，你怎麼這麼晚才來？

白喜：我都忘了今天我是要來找你的。

李安：下次你得記得，別再忘了！

白喜：放心吧。我下次一定很早就來。

李安：好吧，你可不能忘了你今天說的話。

白喜：沒有問題，我可以保證！

C. NARRATIVES 短文

Read the following narratives, paying special attention to punctuation and overall structure. The first time you read a narrative, read it out loud. The second time, read silently and try to gradually increase your reading speed. Always think of the meaning of what you're reading.

一、
我跟你講，我以前是甚麼菜都吃，只有白菜不吃。後來因為聽朋友說從日本進口的白菜特別好吃，所以就決定買一些吃吃看。今天早上我就買了差不多三斤。很貴，但是真好吃！我先生也喜歡，他問我：「這種白菜特別好吃，你在哪兒買的？」朋友，你也去買一點兒從日本進口的白菜吧。我保證你一定會喜歡吃！

二、
我們家住在湖北省老河口市。離我們家不遠有兩個菜市場。一個在路的左手邊，叫「四號路菜市場」，一個在路的右手邊，叫「王家臺菜市場」。「四號路菜市場」的菜很多都是從外國進口的，又貴又不好吃。「王家臺菜市場」賣的差不多都是本地菜，比進口的菜好吃，也沒有進口的菜那麼貴。要是我們家的人去買菜的話，我保證他們會去「王家臺菜市場」，不會去「四號路菜市場」。

Notes 注解

A5a. 这个比中国还大的地方人口比北京还少(這個比中國還人的地方人口比北京還少) "This place that is even bigger than China has a population even smaller than Beijing." This is a topic-comment structure. A literal translation would be "This compared to China even bigger place, population compared to Beijing even fewer."

A7. ⊙ 从⋯进口 (從⋯進口) **cóng... jìnkǒu** "import from" [PT]

A8. ⊙ 往⋯出口 **wǎng...chūkǒu** "export to" [PT]

B2a. 我都忘了今天我是要来找你的 (我都忘了今天我是要來找你的) "I completely forgot that I was going to come looking for you today." The 都 here functions as an intensifier.

B2b. 你可不能忘了 "You really can't forget." The adverb 可 here is also an intensifier and could be translated as "really" or "indeed."

C1. 我以前是什么菜都吃 (我以前是甚麼菜都吃) lit. "I used to be a situation of eating any vegetable" or, in idiomatic English, "It used to be that I would eat any vegetable."

At a Fruit Stand

New Characters and Words

Study the six characters below and the common words written with them, paying careful attention to each character's pronunciation, meaning, and structure, as well as similar-looking characters. After you've studied a character, turn to the *Practice Essentials* volume and practice writing it on the practice sheet, making sure to follow the correct stroke order and direction as you pronounce it out loud and think of its meaning.

331 总 (總)　　**zǒng**　　collect; unite; sum up; always

Radical of the simplified form is 心 **xīn** "heart" (262). This radical when occurring at the bottom of a character, as here, is referred to colloquially as 心字底 **xīnzìdǐ** "bottom made up of the character 心." Radical of the traditional form is 丝 (絲) **sī** "silk." When at the left side of a character, this radical is referred to colloquially as 绞丝旁 (絞絲旁) **jiǎosīpáng** "side made up of twisted silk" and is written as 纟 (糹). Phonetic of the traditional character is 悤 **cōng**. One can "collect" various things and "unite" (總) them with a strand of "silk" (絲). Distinguish simplified 总 from 只 **zhǐ** (238).

　　　　总共 (總共)　　　**zǒnggòng**　　　altogether, in all [A]

332 包　　**bāo**　　wrap

Radical is 勹 **bāo**. The whole character is itself a common phonetic, e.g., in 饱 (飽) **bǎo** "full, satiated," 抱 **bào** "embrace," and 跑 **pǎo** "run" (484). Distinguish 包 from 呢 **ne** (54).

包	**Bāo**	Bao [SN]
包	**bāo**	wrap [V]
包起来 (包起來)	**bāoqilai**	wrap up [RC]
公事包	**gōngshìbāo**	briefcase, attaché case [N]

333 水 shuǐ water

This character is itself a radical. At the left-hand side of a character, it is written 氵 and is then referred to colloquially as 三点水 (三點水) **sāndiǎn shuǐ** "three drops of water." Distinguish 水 from 小 **xiǎo** (24) and 家 **jiā** (191).

水	**shuǐ**	water [N]
冷水	**lěng shuǐ**	cold water
热水 (熱水)	**rè shuǐ**	hot water
◉香水	**xiāngshuǐ(r)**	perfume (lit. "fragrant water") [N]
◉口水	**kǒushuǐ**	saliva (lit. "mouth water") [N]

334 果 guǒ fruit

Radical is the pictograph 木 **mù** "tree." The other component is 田 **tián** "field." "Fruit" 果 often grows on "trees" 木 and in "fields" 田. The character 果 occurs as a phonetic in a number of other characters, e.g., in the character 裹 which is used in 包裹 **bāoguǒ** "package", and in the character 课 (課) **kè** "class" (428). Distinguish 果 from 早 **zǎo** "early" (259).

水果	**shuǐguǒ**	fruit [N]

335 语 (語) yǔ language

Radical is 讠 (言) **yán** "speech" (336). The colloquial name for this radical is 言字旁 **yánzipáng** "side made up of the character 言." Phonetic is 吾 **wú** "I," which is in turn composed of 五 **wǔ** "five" (5) and 口 **kǒu** "mouth" (140). The structure of this character would suggest that "five" 五 "mouths" 口 produce "language" 语 (語), an idea that is further reinforced by the radical 言 "speech." Distinguish 语 (語) from 话 (話) **huà** (201).

国语 (國語)	**Guóyǔ**	Mandarin (language) [N]
日语 (日語)	**Rìyǔ**	Japanese (language) [N]
法语 (法語)	**Fǎyǔ**	French (language) [N]
越南语 (越南語)	**Yuènányǔ**	Vietnamese (language) [N]
◉美语 (美語)	**Měiyǔ**	American English [N]
外国语 (外國語)	**wàiguoyǔ**	foreign language [N]
北京外国语大学 (北京外國語大學)	**Běijīng Wàiguóyǔ Dàxué**	Beijing Foreign Studies University [PW]

336 言 yán speech, word

This character is itself a radical. It frequently occurs at the left side of a character and is then referred to as 言字旁 **yánzipáng** "side made up of the character 言." 言 is a picture of a 口 **kǒu** "mouth" (140) with "words" issuing forth above it. Distinguish 言 from traditional 這 **zhè** (96) and 高 **gāo** (62).

语言 (語言)	**yǔyán**	language [N]
语言学 (語言學)	**yǔyánxué**	linguistics [N]
方言	**fāngyán**	dialect [N]
北京语言大学 (北京語言大學)	**Běijīng Yǔyán Dàxué**	Beijing Language & Culture University [PW]

C. NARRATIVES 短文

Read the following narratives, paying special attention to punctuation and overall structure. The first time you read a narrative, read it out loud. The second time, read silently and try to gradually increase your reading speed. Always think of the meaning of what you're reading.

一、我以后要是有钱，一定天天开进口的车子去公司上班，晚上吃进口的菜和进口的水果。我以后总共要七个房子，这样我可以一天住一个。星期六的房子得比其他的房子大得多，因为那一天我可能要请朋友来我家住。有钱多好！

二、中国的方言
中国总共有几百种方言，但是大方言只有七、八种。北京话、上海话、广东话、台湾话和湖南话都是这些大方言的一种。大方言还分成很多小方言，要是你学过语言学你就知道这些小方言也叫"次方言"。有几位西方的语言学专家说，其实中国的大方言就是语言，不是方言，因为要是你只会北京话，没学过其他方言的话，你根本不可能知道一个说那种方言的人在讲什么。不过因为中国是一个大国，不是好几个小国，所以中国人很少这么说，他们还是觉得说这都是"方言"比较好。

 ## Reading Exercises (Traditional Characters) 繁體字

A. SENTENCES 句子

Read out loud each of the following sentences, which include all the new characters of this lesson. The first time you read a sentence, focus special attention on the characters and words that are new to you, reminding yourself of their pronunciation and meaning. The second time, aim to comprehend the overall meaning of the sentence.

一、我總共只去過中國兩回。你去過幾回了？

二、他會講國語、日語和越南語，不知道他會不會講其他的語言？

三、手裡拿著公事包的那位老師叫包美生，是學語言學的。

四、李校長總共會說三種外國語：日語、法語跟美語。

五、我前天好像在菜場看見李老師在買水果。

六、為什麼有錢的人越來越有錢，沒錢的人越來越沒錢？

七、我大哥說因為很久沒下雨，所以現在很多種水果跟菜都比以前貴得多。

八、北京語言大學叫「北語」，北京外國語大學叫「北外」，現在清楚了吧？

九、老毛剛剛生氣了，要是我是你的話，會離他遠一點兒！

十、王大海很難過，他給他的女朋友買了從法國進口的香水，可是她不喜歡。

B. CONVERSATIONS 對話

Read out loud the following conversations, including the name or role of the person speaking. If possible, find a partner or partners and each of you play a role. Then switch roles, so you get practice reading all of the lines.

一、

法國女生：這種水果，您給我來兩斤吧。

賣水果的：您要一塊一斤的還是要一塊五一斤的？

法國女生：我要一塊五的。

賣水果的：一塊五的比一塊的大得多！還要別的嗎？

法國女生：不要了，就這些了吧。一共多少錢？

賣水果的：總共是七塊四。

法國女生：給您十塊。請您給我包起來。

賣水果的：沒問題。找您兩塊六，請您點一下兒。

法國女生：謝謝，再見！

賣水果的：您拿好。再見！

二、

老師：明天要聽寫，同學們都聽到了嗎？

學生：知道了！

三、

張老師：校長的話，你聽得見嗎？

白老師：太遠了，聽不見。

四、

小何：今天我們家沒有熱水，只有冷水。

老班：有冷水就不錯了。我們家停水了，根本沒有水！

五、

哥哥：我買的車比你的車好看得多！

弟弟：可是我的車比你的車快得多！

哥哥：我的車比你的車大得多！

弟弟：對，可是你的車比我的車貴得多！

哥哥：對，那是因為我的錢比你的錢多得多！

"Tèjià" (Special Price; sign in Singapore)

C. NARRATIVES 短文

Read the following narratives, paying special attention to punctuation and overall structure. The first time you read a narrative, read it out loud. The second time, read silently and try to gradually increase your reading speed. Always think of the meaning of what you're reading.

一、

我以後要是有錢，一定天天開進口的車子去公司上班，晚上吃進口的菜和進口的水果。我以後總共要七個房子，這樣我可以一天住一個。星期六的房子得比其他的房子大得多，因為那一天我可能要請朋友來我家住。有錢多好！

二、中國的方言

中國總共有幾百種方言，但是大方言只有七、八種。北京話、上海話、廣東話、台灣話和湖南話都是這些大方言的一種。大方言還分成很多小方言，要是你學過語言學你就知道這些小方言也叫「次方言」。有幾位西方的語言學專家說，其實中國的大方言就是語言，不是方言，因為要是你只會北京話，沒學過其他方言的話，你根本不可能知道那一個說那種方言的人在講甚麼。不過因為中國是一個大國，不是好幾個小國，所以中國人很少這麼說，他們還是覺得說這都是「方言」比較好。

Notes 注解

A3. 手里拿着公事包的那位老師 (手裏拿著公事包的那位老師) "That teacher who is holding a briefcase in his/her hand."

B2a. 听写 (聽寫) means "take a dictation quiz" (cf. BWC p. 26, Classroom Expression 1).

B2b. 同学们都听到了吗？(同學們都聽到了嗎？) "Did you all hear?" 同学 (同學) literally means "classmate," but when a teacher or school principal addresses students as 同学们 (同學們), he or she means "students". 同学 (同學) is one of a fairly small group of nouns referring to humans that can add an optional plural suffix 们 (們). Another common example is 朋友们 (朋友們) "friends."

B4. ⊙停水 **tíngshuǐ** "stop the water; suffer a disruption of the water supply" [VO]

C1. 有钱多好！(有錢多好！) lit. "To have money how good it is!" or, in more idiomatic English, "How wonderful it is to be rich!" The character 多 is used in exclamations to mean "How…!"

C2a. 都是这些大方言的一种 (都是這些大方言的一種) "Are all a variety of these major dialects."

C2b. ⊙次方言 **cìfāngyán** "subdialect" [N]

C2c. 中国是一个大国不是好几个小国 (中國是一個大國不是好幾個小國) "China is one large country, not a whole bunch of little countries."

C2d. In this passage, the discussion of Chinese languages and dialects—a fascinating but complex topic—has had to be greatly simplified so as to remain within the limitations of the vocabulary, grammar, and characters we have studied so far.

Shopping (II)

COMMUNICATIVE OBJECTIVES

Once you've mastered this unit, you'll be able to use Chinese to read and write about:

1. Buying meat at a traditional market.

2. Buying groceries at a supermarket.

3. Purchasing shoes in a shoe store.

4. Buying pants in a clothing store.

5. Inquiring whether you can exchange something.

6. Requesting a better price.

7. Expressing similarity and dissimilarity.

8. Emphasizing your main point while conceding minor points.

9. A well-known Chinese joke.

Buying Meat at a Traditional Market

其实都差不多。
(其實都差不多。)

您给我切那边儿的吧。
(您給我切那邊兒的吧。)

New Characters and Words

Study the six characters below and the common words written with them, paying careful attention to each character's pronunciation, meaning, and structure, as well as similar-looking characters. After you've studied a character, turn to the *Practice Essentials* volume and practice writing it on the practice sheet, making sure to follow the correct stroke order and direction as you pronounce it out loud and think of its meaning.

337 切　　**qiē**　　cut, slice

The radical, on the right side, is 刀 **dāo** "knife." The phonetic, on the left side, is 七 **qī** "seven." Distinguish 切 from 地 **dì** (157) and 加 **jiā** (307).

切　　**qiē**　　cut, slice [V]

338 肉　　**ròu**　　meat

This character is itself a common radical. It is a picture of two strips of "meat" 人人 hanging on a drying rack 冂. As a radical, 肉 is usually written 月. For example, this character appears as a radical in 能 **néng** (186). Distinguish 肉 from simplified 从 **cóng** (211).

肉　　**ròu**　　meat [N]

339 牛　　**niú**　　ox, cow

This character is itself a common radical. At the left side of a character it is written as 牛 and is referred to colloquially as 牛字旁 **niúzìpáng** "side made up of the character 牛." It appears as a radical in 物 **wù** (251) and in 特 **tè** (310). Distinguish 牛 from 干 **gān** (275), 半 **bàn** (117), 平 **píng** (241), and 年 **nián** (104).

牛　　**Niú**　　Niu [SN]

牛	**niú**	OX, COW [N]
牛肉	**niúròu**	beef [N]
⊙牛油	**niúyóu**	butter [N]

---

340 极（極） **jí**   utmost, very, extremely

Radical is the pictograph 木 **mù** "tree." This radical is referred to colloquially as 木字旁 **mùzìpáng** "side made up of the character 木." When 木 is written at the left of a character as a radical, its last stroke is shortened so that it doesn't collide with the component to its right. Phonetic of the simplified form is 及 **jí** "reach" or "come up to," while the phonetic of the traditional version is 亟 **jí**. "Trees" 木 can "reach" 及 an "extreme" 极（極）height.

…极了（…極了）	**-jíle**	extremely [PT]
近极了（近極了）	**jìnjíle**	extremely close
好极了（好極了）	**hǎojíle**	"Great!" "Fantastic!" [IE]

---

341 食 **shí**   eat

This character is itself a very common radical meaning "eat," which is written as 饣（飠）when occurring at the left-hand side of a character. The colloquial name for this radical is 食字旁 **shízìpáng** "side made up of the character 食." The radical 食 often indicates food, e.g., 饭（飯）**fàn** (152). Distinguish 食 from traditional 會 **huì** (199).

---

342 品 **pǐn**   goods, product

Radical is the pictograph 口 **kǒu** "mouth" (140). The character 口 is here written three times as 品, representing the idea of "a multitude of goods or products." Distinguish 品 from 口.

食品	**shípǐn**	food product, groceries [N]
食品店	**shípǐn diàn**	grocery store [PH]

New Words in ISC 13-1 Written with Characters You Already Know

差不多（差不多）	**chàbuduō**	be about the same [PH]
面包（麵包）	**miànbāo**	bread [N]
面包店（麵包店）	**miànbāo diàn**	bakery [PH]
一点…也不 （一點…也不）	**yìdiǎn(r) yě bù…**	not at all, not the least bit [PT]

慢慢来 (慢慢來)	**mànmàn lái**	"take your time" [IE]
…什么的 (…什麼的)	**…shénmede**	…and so on [PT]
为了 (爲了)	**wèile**	in order to, for [PT]
像	**xiàng**	resemble, be like [V]
一…比一…	**yī…bǐ yī…**	one…more…than the next [PT]
一年比一年贵 (一年比一年貴)	**yìnián bǐ yìnián guì**	more expensive year by year

Reading Exercises (Simplified Characters) 简体字

Now practice reading the new characters and words for this lesson in context in sentences, conversations, and narratives. Be sure to refer to the Notes at the end of this lesson, and make use of the accompanying audio disc to hear and practice correct pronunciation, phrasing, and intonation.

A. SENTENCES 句子

Read out loud each of the following sentences, which include all the new characters of this lesson. The first time you read a sentence, focus special attention on the characters and words that are new to you, reminding yourself of their pronunciation and meaning. The second time, aim to comprehend the overall meaning of the sentence.

一、中文难极了，可是我觉得学起来很有意思。

二、中文跟日文比起来，你觉得哪种比较难学？

三、小姐，你走错了，这儿是出口，入口在那边。

四、牛先生看起来像一头牛，可是高先生不高，白先生也不白。

五、我弟弟、妹妹都主张卖我们家的那块土地，可是我哥哥不想卖。

六、你节省一点儿，先别买汽车。你还年轻，慢慢来，以后还有机会买。

七、我们的中文老师好极了，所以我们班上的同学，中文一天比一天好。

八、不好意思，我的中文不好，请问，"禁止携犬进入"这六个字是什么意思？

九、他们家土地不少但是没钱，所以那次他们需要钱的时候，没有别的办法，只好卖了一些土地，这样才解决了问题。

十、有一天早上，王大海跟他的同屋说："我有一个好主意，星期六早上我们都去动物园，你们觉得怎么样？"

"Niúròu Miàn" (Beef Noodles)

B. CONVERSATIONS 对话

Read out loud the following conversations, including the name or role of the person speaking. If possible, find a partner or partners and each of you play a role. Then switch roles, so you get practice reading all of the lines.

一、

台湾同学：我要去食品店买点东西。你要不要和我一起去？
美国同学：好。我也正想买点水果、土司什么的。
台湾同学：这样好了，为了节省时间，你买你的，我买我的。我们五分钟
　　　　　以后在出口见，怎么样？
美国同学：好主意。
台湾同学：你觉得台湾的食品店跟美国的食品店比起来怎么样？
美国同学：都差不多。大概比美国的小一点，也不像在美国那么多。
台湾同学：可能要慢慢来吧。我想以后会一年比一年多吧。

二、

小牛：八点一刻了，我们吃早饭吧！
小白：好主意。你准备吃什么？
小牛：我早饭喜欢吃土司。
小白：你吃干土司？
小牛：不，土司加一点牛油就很好吃了。你呢？你准备吃什么？
小白：我吃一点水果就行了。

三、

太太：为了节省时间，你进市场买你的牛肉、白菜什么的，我开车去加油
　　　站加油。我们差不多半个小时以后在市场的入口见，怎么样？
先生：好主意。市场看起来好像人很多，所以你慢慢加你的油吧。如果
　　　半个小时以后我还没出来的话，你等我一会儿，好吗？
太太：好，没问题。

C. NARRATIVES 短文

Read the following narratives, paying special attention to punctuation and overall structure. The first time you read a narrative, read it out loud. The second time, read silently and try to gradually increase your reading speed. Always think of the meaning of what you're reading.

一、上大学真是没意思。我天天为了上学很早就得起来。我和我的同学
　　都忙得要死，得准备第二天的中文听写，还有很多很多其他的作业，
　　根本没时间出去。大学跟高中比起来，我觉得还是高中有意思。

二、我有两个哥哥、一个弟弟。我长得比较像大哥，弟弟长得比较像二
　　哥。大哥比我大四岁，可是看起来我的年纪比他大，所以有的人不太
　　清楚谁是哥哥，谁是弟弟。你看得出来吗？

C. NARRATIVES 短文

Read the following narratives, paying special attention to punctuation and overall structure. The first time you read a narrative, read it out loud. The second time, read silently and try to gradually increase your reading speed. Always think of the meaning of what you're reading.

一、

上大學真是沒意思。我天天為了上學很早就得起來。我和我的同學都忙得要死，得準備第二天的中文聽寫，還有很多很多其他的作業，根本沒時間出去。大學跟高中比起來，我覺得還是高中有意思。

二、

我有兩個哥哥、一個弟弟。我長得比較像大哥，弟弟長得比較像二哥。大哥比我大四歲，可是看起來我的年紀比他大，所以有的人不太清楚誰是哥哥，誰是弟弟。你看得出來嗎？

三、

星期天我出去買報紙，在書店看見了我的老朋友張國林。他說正想去我家裡找我呢。我們兩個人好久沒見了，我覺得他好像一年比一年老了。從書店出來，他就和我一起回家了。我太太看到我的老朋友來了，也很高興。她一定要張國林在我們家吃中飯。為了買到最好的牛肉和白菜，她去了離我們家比較遠的市場，然後給我們準備了很好吃的中飯。

Notes 注解

A8a. ◆ 禁止 **jìnzhǐ** "forbid," "prohibit," or "ban" [V][1]

A8b. ◆ 犬 **quǎn** "canine, dog" [BF]. 犬, to be differentiated carefully from the character 太, is a formal, written-style Chinese word for colloquial 狗 **gǒu** "dog". The street sign 禁止携犬进入 (禁止攜犬進入) **Jìnzhǐ xié quǎn jìnrù** means lit. "Forbid bring dogs enter", or in more idiomatic English, "It is not permitted to enter if you are bringing a dog." Many Chinese street signs begin with the word 禁止. Like most street signs, this sign is in 书面语 (書面語), or formal, written-style Chinese (BWC 4-2: note A1). The verb 携 (攜) **xié** is a more formal, written-style equivalent of 带 (帶)(93). In fact, these two syllables can be used together to create the word 携带 (攜帶), which still means "carry" or "bring."

(cf. Note A8b. to left)

Purchasing New Shoes

 New Characters and Words

Study the six characters below and the common words written with them, paying careful attention to each character's pronunciation, meaning, and structure, as well as similar-looking characters. After you've studied a character, turn to the *Practice Essentials* volume and practice writing it on the practice sheet, making sure to follow the correct stroke order and direction as you pronounce it out loud and think of its meaning.

349 双（雙） shuāng pair

Radical of the simplified form is 又 **yòu** (210). The simplified form 双 represents the idea of "pair" with two 又. Radical of the traditional form is 隹 **zhuī** "short-tailed bird." The explanation of the traditional form is that two "birds" 隹隹 held in one "hand" 又 make a "pair" 雙. Note that 又 is an ancient form of 手 **shǒu** (305). Distinguish simplified 双 from 又.

双（雙）	**shuāng**	pair [M]
一双（一雙）	**yìshuāng**	a pair
◉ 双号（雙號）	**shuānghào**	even number [N] (cf. 388 for "odd number")
◉ 双人房（雙人房）	**shuāngrénfáng**	double room (as in a hotel) [N]

350 鞋 xié shoe

Radical is 革 **gé** "animal skin." Phonetic is 圭 **guī**, which refers to a musical instrument used on ceremonial occasions.

鞋	**xié**	shoe [N]
一双鞋（一雙鞋）	**yìshuāng xié**	a pair of shoes
雨鞋	**yǔxié**	rain shoes [N]

Buying Pants

 New Characters and Words

Study the six characters below and the common words written with them, paying careful attention to each character's pronunciation, meaning, and structure, as well as similar-looking characters. After you've studied a character, turn to the *Practice Essentials* volume and practice writing it on the practice sheet, making sure to follow the correct stroke order and direction as you pronounce it out loud and think of its meaning.

355 应 (應)　　**yīng**　　should

Radical of the simplified form is 广 **yǎn** "eaves." This radical is referred to colloquially as 广字头 (廣字 頭) **guǎngzìtóu** "top made up of the character 广." Radical of the traditional form is 心 **xīn** "heart." This radical, when at the bottom of a character, is referred to colloquially as 心字底 **xīnzìdǐ** "bottom made up of the character 心." The feeling of obligation that one "should" (應) do something comes from the "heart" 心. Distinguish simplified 应 from simplified 厂 **chǎng** (197) and simplified 广 **guǎng** (270).

356 该 (該)　　**gāi**　　should, ought

Radical is 讠 (言) **yán** "speech" (336). The colloquial name for this radical is 言字旁 **yánzìpáng** "side made up of the character 言." Phonetic is 亥 **hài**, which is the last of the twelve earthly branches. Distinguish 该 (該) from 刻 **kè** (116).

该 (該)	**gāi**	should, ought [AV]
应该 (應該)	**yīnggāi**	should [AV]
◉该你了 (該你了)	**gāi nǐ le**	"it's your turn" [IE]

357 衣   yī   clothing

This character is itself both a radical and a phonetic. When at the side of a character as a radical, it is written 衤. As a phonetic, it occurs in 依 **yī** "rely on." Distinguish 衣 from 表 **biǎo** (193).

衣	**Yī**	Yi [SN]
毛衣	**máoyī**	sweater [N]
大衣	**dàyī**	overcoat [N]
雨衣	**yǔyī**	raincoat [N]

358 服   fú   clothing

Radical is 月 **yuè** "moon" (130). The colloquial name for this radical is 月字旁 **yuèzìpáng** "side made up of the character 月." Distinguish 服 from 报（報）**bào** (323).

衣服	**yīfu**	clothes [N]

359 如   rú   if; be like, equal

Radical is 女 **nǚ** "woman" (101). This radical is referred to colloquially as 女字旁 **nǚzìpáng** "side made up of the character 女." Note that when 女 is written at the left of a character as a radical, its last stroke is shortened so that it doesn't collide with the component to its right. Phonetic is 口 **kǒu** "mouth" (140). The traditional explanation of this character is to speak with one's "mouth" 口 "like" 如 a "woman" 女. Distinguish 如 from 加 **jiā** (307) and 始 **shǐ** (208).

如果	**rúguǒ**	if [A]
如果…的话（如果…的話）	**rúguǒ...de huà**	if [PT]

360 内（內）   nèi   inside, within

Radical is 冂 **jiōng** "space." The simplified character has a 人 **rén** "person" (30) "inside" 内 the "space" 冂, while the traditional character has the character 入 **rù** "enter" (345) "inside" 內 the "space" 冂. Distinguish 内（內）from 因 **yīn** (181) and 肉 **ròu** (338).

…以内（…以內）	**...yǐnèi**	within... [PT]
…之内（…之內）	**...zhīnèi**	within... [PT]
三天之内（三天之內）	**sāntiān zhīnèi**	within three days
内衣（內衣）	**nèiyī**	underwear [N]

New Words in ISC 13-4 Written with Characters You Already Know

本来（本來）	**běnlái**	originally [MA]
表（錶）	**biǎo**	watch (for telling time) [N]
手表（手錶）	**shǒubiǎo**	wristwatch [N]
刚好（剛好）	**gānghǎo**	it just happens that [MA]

过来 (過來)	guòlai	come over [RC]
过来 (過來)	-guòlai	(indicates movement from there to here) [RE]
过去 (過去)	guòqu	go over, pass by [RC]
过去 (過去)	-guòqu	(indicates movement from here to there) [RE]
拿来 (拿來)	nálai	bring over [RC]
拿去	náqu	take over [RC]
拿过去 (拿過去)	náguoqu	take over [RC]
现金 (現金)	xiànjīn	cash [N]
小男生	xiǎo nánshēng	little boy [PH]
小女生	xiǎo nǔshēng	little girl [PH]

Reading Exercises (Simplified Characters) 简体字

Now practice reading the new characters and words for this lesson in context in sentences, conversations, and narratives. Be sure to refer to the Notes at the end of this lesson, and make use of the accompanying audio disc to hear and practice correct pronunciation, phrasing, and intonation.

A. SENTENCES 句子

Read out loud each of the following sentences, which include all the new characters of this lesson. The first time you read a sentence, focus special attention on the characters and words that are new to you, reminding yourself of their pronunciation and meaning. The second time, aim to comprehend the overall meaning of the sentence.

一、如果下雨的话，应该穿雨衣跟雨鞋。

二、下一站就是动物园儿了，您该准备下车了！

三、那个女的好像在叫我，你看我应该不应该过去？

四、我下星期六刚好有时间，到你家去应该没有问题。

五、地上本来没有路，走的人多了，也就有了路了。

六、这双鞋，您如果不喜欢的话，只要是五天之内都可以拿来换。

七、小何，这些牛肉和白菜你拿过去给对面的王老太太，好不好？

八、今天是老高的生日，朋友准备送他大衣、毛衣、内衣什么的。

九、我知道我应该节省一点，所以我决定从明年起不买贵的衣服了。

十、王大海因为没有钱买手表，所以到哪儿去都带着一个小钟。

B. CONVERSATIONS 对话

Read out loud the following conversations, including the name or role of the person speaking. If possible, find a partner or partners and each of you play a role. Then switch roles, so you get practice reading all of the lines.

一、

美国太太：小姐，你们有没有小朋友穿的毛衣？

卖衣服的：有，请过来看看。小朋友几岁了？

美国太太：六岁多，快七岁了。

卖衣服的：穿九号应该没有问题。看看这件。

美国太太：看起来不错，但是不知道会不会太大或太小？

卖衣服的：你放心。如果有问题的话，七天以内可以拿来换。

美国太太：这件多少钱？

卖衣服的：这种毛衣本来是一千二一件，这个星期刚好半价，只要六百块。

美国太太：好，那我就买这件吧。我给你现金，这是一千块。

卖衣服的：好的，请等一下。……找您四百块。谢谢，下次再来！

二、

小张：你知道现在外头差不多多少度吗？

老万：好像今天最高温度二十五度，最低温度二十度。

小张：你看我出去要不要穿大衣？

老万：如果我是你的话，不会穿大衣，可是一定会穿一件毛衣。

小张：好，那我就穿毛衣吧。

三、

美国人：房应国老先生死了，你觉得我应不应该到房家去看看房太太？

中国人：我觉得你应该去。

美国人：听说在中国，人死了要穿白色的衣服，是真的吗？

中国人：对，有时候是这样子，可是也不一定。你是外国人，你穿黑衣服、黑鞋就可以了。

四、

年家平：李老师，不好意思，今天的作业我忘了。

李老师：你忘了？那你什么时候能给我呢？

年家平：我两天之内一定给老师，真对不起。

李老师：两天之内？不行！你最晚明天早上八点给我，要不然太晚了。

C. NARRATIVES 短文

Read the following narratives, paying special attention to punctuation and overall structure. The first time you read a narrative, read it out loud. The second time, read silently and try to gradually increase your reading speed. Always think of the meaning of what you're reading.

一、广州在中国的南方。以前有不少朋友跟我讲过，那个地方热得要死，所以去年一月我去那儿看我表哥的时候，我想天气一定很热吧。但是我错了，刚好我去的那个星期广州的天气冷极了，还天天下大雨。我应该带的很多衣服，像大衣、毛衣、雨衣、雨鞋什么的，都没有带。所以我在那儿的那几天就觉得很冷。我保证下次如果还去广州的话，一定会多带一点儿衣服，特别是一月去的话。

二、很久没看到白老师的儿子了。三年前他跟白老师一起来学校的时候
　　还很小。今天看到他，好像不是以前的那个小男孩儿了。三年时间他
　　就长这么大了！我想他应该上学了，可是白老师说他明年才可以上学。
　　他长得那么高，看起来好像有六、七岁的样子，其实他还不到五岁。

D. SUPPLEMENT: A CHINESE JOKE

Read the following Chinese joke, which makes repeated use of the verb 该 that is introduced in this lesson.

以前有一个姓王的，人人都叫他老王。老王特别不会说话。有一天，他请
了四个朋友到家里来吃饭，可是只来了三个人。他说："该来的没来！"
第一个人听到了，对老王说："你说该来的没来，你的意思是不该来的
来了！"第一个人很不高兴，走了。老王说："不该走的走了！"第二个人
说："不该走的走了，你的意思是我该走！"所以他也走了。第三个人对
老王说："以后说话小心一点。"老王说："我又没说他们！"第三个人
说："你没说他们，那你说的就是我了！"第三个人生气了，也走了。最后
老王的朋友都走了，所以他只好一个人吃饭。

Reading Exercises (Traditional Characters) 繁體字

A. SENTENCES 句子

Read out loud each of the following sentences, which include all the new characters of this lesson. The first time
you read a sentence, focus special attention on the characters and words that are new to you, reminding yourself
of their pronunciation and meaning. The second time, aim to comprehend the overall meaning of the sentence.

一、如果下雨的話，應該穿雨衣跟雨鞋。

二、下一站就是動物園兒了，您該準備下車了！

三、那個女的好像在叫我，你看我應該不應該過去？

四、我下星期六剛好有時間，到你家去應該沒有問題。

五、地上本來沒有路，走的人多了，也就有了路了。

六、這雙鞋，您如果不喜歡的話，只要是五天之內都可以拿來換。

七、小何，這些牛肉和白菜你拿過去給對面的王老太太，好不好？

八、今天是老高的生日，朋友準備送他大衣、毛衣、內衣什麼的。

九、我知道我應該節省一點，所以我決定從明年起不買貴的衣服了。

十、王大海因為沒有錢買手錶，所以到哪兒去都帶著一個小鐘。

B. CONVERSATIONS 對話

Read out loud the following conversations, including the name or role of the person speaking. If possible, find a partner or partners and each of you play a role. Then switch roles, so you get practice reading all of the lines.

一、

美國太太：小姐，你們有沒有小朋友穿的毛衣？

賣衣服的：有，請過來看看。小朋友幾歲了？

美國太太：六歲多，快七歲了。

賣衣服的：穿九號應該沒有問題。看看這件。

美國太太：看起來不錯，但是不知道會不會太大或太小？

賣衣服的：你放心。如果有問題的話，七天以內可以拿來換。

美國太太：這件多少錢？

賣衣服的：這種毛衣本來是一千二一件，這個星期剛好半價，只要六百塊。

美國太太：好，那我就買這件吧。我給你現金，這是一千塊。

賣衣服的：好的，請等一下。……找您四百塊。謝謝，下次再來！

二、

小張：你知道現在外頭差不多多少度嗎？

老萬：好像今天最高溫度二十五度，最低溫度二十度。

小張：你看我出去要不要穿大衣？

老萬：如果我是你的話，不會穿大衣，可是一定會穿一件毛衣。

小張：好，那我就穿毛衣吧。

"Mother Zhang's Beef Noodles" (restaurant in Taipei)

三、

美國人：房應國老先生死了，你覺得我應該不應該到房家去看看房太太？

中國人：我覺得你應該去。

美國人：聽說在中國，人死了要穿白色的衣服，是真的嗎？

中國人：對，有時候是這樣子，可是也不一定。你是外國人，你穿黑衣服、黑鞋就可以了。

四、

年家平：李老師，不好意思，今天的作業我忘了。

李老師：你忘了？那你什麼時候能給我呢？

年家平：我兩天之內一定給老師，真對不起。

李老師：兩天之內？不行！你最晚明天早上八點給我，要不然太晚了。

C. NARRATIVES 短文

Read the following narratives, paying special attention to punctuation and overall structure. The first time you read a narrative, read it out loud. The second time, read silently and try to gradually increase your reading speed. Always think of the meaning of what you're reading.

一、

廣州在中國的南方。以前有不少朋友跟我講過，那個地方熱得要死，所以去年一月我去那兒看我表哥的時候，我想天氣一定很熱吧。但是我錯了，剛好我去的那個星期廣州的天氣冷極了，還天天下大雨。我應該帶的很多衣服，像大衣、毛衣、雨衣、雨鞋什麼的，都沒有帶。所以我在那兒的那幾天就覺得很冷。我保證下次如果還去廣州的話，一定會多帶一點兒衣服，特別是一月去的話。

二、

很久沒看到白老師的兒子了。三年前他跟白老師一起來學校的時候還很小。今天看到他，好像不是以前的那個小男孩兒了。三年時間他就長這麼大了！我想他應該上學了，可是白老師說他明年才可以上學。他長得那麼高，看起來好像有六、七歲的樣子，其實他還不到五歲。

D. SUPPLEMENT: A CHINESE JOKE

Read the following Chinese joke, which makes repeated use of the verb 該 that is introduced in this lesson.

以前有一個姓王的，人人都叫他老王。老王特別不會說話。有一天，他請了四個朋友到家裡來吃飯，可是只來了三個人。他說：「該來的沒來！」第一個人聽到了，對老王說：「你說該來的沒來，不該來的來了！」第一個人很不高興，走了。老王說：「不該走的走了！」第二個人說：「你的意思是我該走的走了！」所以他也走了。第三個人對老王說：「小心一點。」老王說：「我又沒說他們！」第三個人說：「你沒說他們，那你說的就是我了！」第三個人生氣了，也走了。最後老王的朋友都走了，所以他只好一個人吃飯。

Notes 注解

A3. 好像在叫我 "It seems she's calling me."

B3. 人死了要穿白色的衣服 "When a person dies, you should wear white clothing."

C2. 三年时间他就长这么大了！(三年時間他就長這麼大了！) "In three years' time he has grown to be so big!" or "In the space of three years he's gotten so big!" Be sure to pronounce 长（長）here as **zhǎng** "grow."

D1. 只来了三个人 (只來了三個人) lit. "There only came three people." In Chinese, indefinite subjects sometimes follow rather than precede the verb (ISC 19-3: 2).

D2. 该来的没来 （該來的沒來）lit. "(The) one who should have come didn't come."

D3. 不该来的来了(不該來的來了) lit. "(The) one who shouldn't have come did come."

D4. 我又没说他们！(我又沒說他們！) "I wasn't talking about them at all!" The verb 说（說）here means "talk about" and the adverb 又 makes the negative 没说（沒說）even more emphatic.

(bottom four characters are **shǒugōng shuǐjiǎo** "hand-made dumplings")

Eating and Drinking (I)

龙凤酒店

COMMUNICATIVE OBJECTIVES

Once you've mastered this unit, you'll be able to use Chinese to read and write about:

1. A discussion with a friend about where to go for a meal.

2. Eating various foods and drinking different kinds of beverages.

3. Reserving a formal banquet in a restaurant.

4. Some of the different cuisines of China.

5. The issue of increasing exports and decreasing imports.

6. Rice prices in Guangzhou.

7. Several Chinese jokes.

Ordering a Meal in a Restaurant

你想吃什么？
(你想吃什麼？)

随便，什么都可以。
(隨便，什麼都可以。)

New Characters and Words

Study the six characters below and the common words written with them, paying careful attention to each character's pronunciation, meaning, and structure, as well as similar-looking characters. After you've studied a character, turn to the *Practice Essentials* volume and practice writing it on the practice sheet, making sure to follow the correct stroke order and direction as you pronounce it out loud and think of its meaning.

361 随 (隨)　　**suí**　　follow

Radical is 阜 **fù** "mound," which is written ⻖ when occurring at the left-hand side of a character. This radical is referred to colloquially as 左耳旁 **zuǒ'ěrpáng** "side made up of a left ear." Phonetic of the traditional form is 遀 **suí**.

随 (隨)	**Suí**	Sui [SN]

362 便　　**biàn**　　convenient

Radical is 人 **rén** "person" (30), which is written 亻 when occurring at the left side of a character so as not to get in the way of the component at the right. The colloquial name for this radical is 人字旁 **rénzìpáng** "side made up of the character 人." The other constituent of this character is 更 **gēng** "to change." The idea is that "people" 人 "change" 更 matters so as to make them more "convenient" 便 for themselves.

随便 (隨便)	**suíbiàn**	"as you wish" [IE]; be casual, informal [SV]
便鞋	**biànxié**	slipper [N]
◉大便	**dàbiàn**	defecate (lit. "big convenience") [V]; feces [N]
◉小便	**xiǎobiàn**	urinate (lit. "small convenience") [V]; urine [N]

二、美国进口的东西太多，出口的东西太少，这已经成了一个很大的问题。今年美国的国会有人主张美国应该多出口一些东西到外国去，我觉得这个想法很对。不过今天我在报上看到，国会也有人主张少从外国进口东西，或者一、两年之后可能根本不进口外国的东西，特别是从中国来的东西，这个想法我觉得是不对的，不是解决问题的好办法。

三、"你们好！我姓张，叫张子文。很高兴今天有机会跟你们说说话。我们先来看看最近几个星期广州的米价是多少。你们都知道，不同的米，价钱也不一样。那么，如果到米店去买米的话，最近白米一公斤要十二块钱左右，黑米一公斤大概要十三块五，香米一公斤差不多十四块钱。不过如果你到米厂去买就不会那么贵了，白米一公斤只要十块钱，黑米只要十一块，香米只要十二块。我这样讲你们都清楚了吧？有没有人有什么问题？"

Reading Exercises (Traditional Characters) 繁體字

A. SENTENCES 句子

Read out loud each of the following sentences, which include all the new characters of this lesson. The first time you read a sentence, focus special attention on the characters and words that are new to you, reminding yourself of their pronunciation and meaning. The second time, aim to comprehend the overall meaning of the sentence.

一、喝一點兒酒沒關係，但是不能多喝。

二、你現在吃不完沒有關係，等一會兒再吃吧。

三、她們是不是有甚麼急事？怎麼這麼早就要走了？

四、小牛，你看起來比我高。我一米七八。你有多高？

五、喝酒以後不可以開車！你長這麼大，怎麼還不知道呢？

六、米飯是中國南方人的主食，沒有米飯他們會吃得很不高興。

七、我真受不了生物專業，所以決定明年從生物系轉到比較文學系。

八、不好意思，可是我還是想問你：金小姐跟李先生是甚麼關係？

九、在美國年滿二十一歲才可以喝酒，在中國年滿十八歲就可以喝了。

十、王大海不喜歡喝酒，白酒、米酒什麼的，他都不喝。

B. CONVERSATIONS 對話

Read out loud the following conversations, including the name or role of the person speaking. If possible, find a partner or partners and each of you play a role. Then switch roles, so you get practice reading all of the lines.

一、

王先生：小姐，這些菜，請你們少放點兒油，我這位美國朋友可能受不了。

何小姐：沒問題，您放心好了。主食要甚麼？

王先生：我看……四兩米飯好了。

何小姐：行。兩位喝點兒甚麼？喝不喝酒？

王先生：我們不喝酒。就這些了吧。我們有急事，請您快點兒上菜。

二、

小文：小李，你先吃了飯再走吧。

小李：不行，我有一些急事得現在去辦。

小文：那沒關係，你先去辦你的事吧。

小李：好。再見，明天見！

小文：再見，慢走。

三、

金老師：小車，你喜歡你們學校的飯嗎？

車大山：我一點兒都不喜歡。我吃了快一年了，已經受不了了。

金老師：真的嗎？為什麼這麼不喜歡呢？

車大山：我也不太清楚。可能吃來吃去都是差不多一樣的，所以就不喜歡了。

金老師：那，你最想吃甚麼？

車大山：我就想吃我媽媽做的菜。我們家裡的米飯也特別香。

Eating and Drinking (II)

开饭时间

早 7:00 - 8:00

午 11:00 - 1:00

晚 5:00 - 6:30

周末 早 7:30 - 9:00

COMMUNICATIVE OBJECTIVES

Once you've mastered this unit, you'll be able to use Chinese to read and write about:

1. Eating food and drinking beverages as part of breakfast, lunch, or dinner.

2. Hosting or participating as a guest in a formal banquet.

3. Inviting someone to your home for dinner, or accepting or declining an invitation if you are invited to dinner.

4. Making various kinds of foods.

5. Several Chinese jokes.

6. Various other situations that require use of the new characters and vocabulary introduced in this unit.

The Peking Duck Banquet

 New Characters and Words

Study the six characters below and the common words written with them, paying careful attention to each character's pronunciation, meaning, and structure, as well as similar-looking characters. After you've studied a character, turn to the *Practice Essentials* volume and practice writing it on the practice sheet, making sure to follow the correct stroke order and direction as you pronounce it out loud and think of its meaning.

385 非 **fēi** not; Africa

This character is itself both a radical and a phonetic. For example, it serves as a phonetic in 匪 **fěi** "bandit." Distinguish 非 from 三 **sān** (3).

⊙南非 **Nánfēi** South Africa [PW]

386 常 **cháng** often; common

Radical is 巾 **jīn** "towel." Phonetic is 尚 **shàng** "still." Distinguish 常 from 带 (帶) **dài** (93) and 度 **dù** (269).

常	**Cháng**	Chang [SN]
常	**cháng**	often [A]
常常	**chángcháng**	often [A]
平常	**píngcháng**	usually, ordinarily [A]
非常	**fēicháng**	extremely [A]
⊙常用字	**chángyòngzì**	frequently used character [N]

387 简（簡） **jiǎn**   simple

Radical is 竹 **zhú** "bamboo." The colloquial name for this radical is 竹字头 (竹字頭) **zhúzìtóu** "top made up of the character 竹." When it is a radical, the third and sixth strokes of 竹 are shortened. Phonetic is 间 (間) **jiān** "between" (232). Distinguish 简 (簡) from 间 (間).

简（簡）	**Jiǎn**	Jian [SN]

388 单（單） **dān**   single, alone; odd-numbered; list

Radical is 口 **kǒu** "mouth" (140). This radical is referred to colloquially as 口字旁 **kǒuzìpáng** "side made up of the character 口." The whole character is itself a phonetic, e.g., in 弹 (彈) as in 子弹 (子彈) **zǐdàn** "bullet." Distinguish 单 (單) from 早 **zǎo** (259) and 果 **guǒ** (334).

简单（簡單）	**jiǎndān**	be simple [SV]
菜单（菜單）	**càidān**	menu [N]
单位（單位）	**dānwèi**	work unit; organization [PW]
◉ 名单（名單）	**míngdān**	name list, list of names [N]
◉ 单子（單子）	**dānzi**	list [N]
◉ 单号（單號）	**dānhào**	odd number [N] (cf. 349 for "even number")
◉ 单人房（單人房）	**dānrénfáng**	single room (as in a hotel) [N]

389 句 **jù**   phrase; sentence

Radical is 口 **kǒu** "mouth" (140). The other component is 勹 **bāo**. Distinguish 句 from 司 **sī** (95), 同 **tóng** (80), and 够 (夠) **gòu** (364).

句	**jù**	phrase; sentence [M]
一句话（一句話）	**yíjù huà**	a phrase; a sentence
句子	**jùzi**	sentence [N]

390 活 **huó**   live

Radical is 水 **shuǐ** "water" (333). This radical is written 氵 and is referred to colloquially as 三点水 (三點水) **sāndiǎn shuǐ** "three drops of water" when it occurs at the left-hand side of a character. The other element is 舌 **shé** "tongue." Carefully distinguish 活 from 话 (話) **huà** (201).

生活	**shēnghuó**	life [N]; live [V]
◉ 活	**huó**	live [V]

New Words in ISC 15-1 Written with Characters You Already Know

大家	**dàjiā**	everybody, everyone [PR]
地	**-de**	(adverbial marker) [P] (e.g., 简单地 [簡單地] **jiǎndānde** "simply"; note that 地 is here usually pronounced -**de**)
来（來）	**lái**	(indicates one is about to do something) [AV]
同时（同時）	**tóngshí**	at the same time [MA]

Reading Exercises (Simplified Characters) 简体字

Now practice reading the new characters and words for this lesson in context in sentences, conversations, and narratives. Be sure to refer to the Notes at the end of this lesson, and make use of the accompanying audio disc to hear and practice correct pronunciation, phrasing, and intonation.

A. SENTENCES 句子

Read out loud each of the following sentences, which include all the new characters of this lesson. The first time you read a sentence, focus special attention on the characters and words that are new to you, reminding yourself of their pronunciation and meaning. The second time, aim to comprehend the overall meaning of the sentence.

一、老师, 请问, 这个句子是什么意思?

二、这几年以来, 中国人的生活越来越好了。

三、那位同学一句中文都不会, 可是他的日语讲得非常好。

四、大家好! 谢谢你们来参加今天晚上的酒席, 我先来简单地说几句……

五、先生, 我们可以看看菜单吗? 你们今天有没有什么比较特别的菜?

六、大家好! 我姓简。我非常高兴今年能有机会到中国来跟你们一起工作!

七、因为美国的大学非常好, 还有工作的机会比较多, 所以美国的外国留学生特别多。

八、最简单的中国字是 "一"; 最难写的中国字可能是 "齉" nàng, 真的非常难写!

九、我觉得法语很难, 比西语难得多, 你为什么说法语很简单呢?

十、王大海同时有两个女朋友, 他的两个女朋友知道了这件事, 都非常生气。

B. CONVERSATIONS 对话

Read out loud the following conversations, including the name or role of the person speaking. If possible, find a partner or partners and each of you play a role. Then switch roles, so you get practice reading all of the lines.

一、

姐姐: 妹妹, 在北京开车要特别小心。

妹妹: 姐姐, 我知道, 你放心! 我会非常小心的。

二、

老何: 我还有几句话想跟大家说……

小李: 老何, 你刚才已经说了很多, 我们吃饭吧!

三、

老师: 同学们, 你们听老师讲。"。" 叫句号, 也叫句点; "?" 叫问号; "; " 叫分号; "《》" 叫书名号。现在同学们都清楚了吧? 有没有问题?

学生: 老师, 知道了。

四、

小林：小王，你平常几点上班，几点下班？

小王：我应该八点上班，但是我常常会晚一点儿到。

小林：是吗？那你几点才到呢？

小王：我有的时候晚十分钟，有的时候晚半个钟头。

小林：你的上司不会不高兴吗？

小王：我的上司？他一句话也没说！

C. NARRATIVES 短文

Read the following narratives, paying special attention to punctuation and overall structure. The first time you read a narrative, read it out loud. The second time, read silently and try to gradually increase your reading speed. Always think of the meaning of what you're reading.

一、我常常同时做很多不一样的事。我喜欢吃饭的时候看报，或是做饭的时候讲电话，或是走路的时候想我第二天应该做的事。我妈妈常常说我这个人都是"一半在这儿，一半在那儿"。

二、我们家喜欢过简单的生活。我们不需要住大房子，小房子就够我们住了。因为房子小，所以我们不需要买很多很贵的家具。因为我们平常都走路，所以我们也不需要买很大的汽车，小车就行了。我们也很少去那些很高级的饭店或者买很多从外国进口的衣服什么的。我们不做这些事，还是可以过得非常高兴。我们家的人都觉得过简单的生活真的比较好！

三、我已经上完大学了，现在自己一个人住在台北市。在台北市住没有我想得那么简单。我平常下午五点半、六点才下班，下班以后得先买菜，然后回家自己做饭，忙死了。自己一个人生活非常没有意思。我现在知道为什么大家都说我应该找个男朋友了。

"Dàjiā Gòuwù Zhōngxīn" (Everybody Shopping Center; in Kuala Lumpur)

Reading Exercises (Traditional Characters) 繁體字

A. SENTENCES 句子

Read out loud each of the following sentences, which include all the new characters of this lesson. The first time you read a sentence, focus special attention on the characters and words that are new to you, reminding yourself of their pronunciation and meaning. The second time, aim to comprehend the overall meaning of the sentence.

一、老師，請問，這個句子是甚麼意思？

二、這幾年以來，中國人的生活越來越好了。

三、那位同學一句中文都不會，可是他的日語講得非常好。

四、大家好！謝謝你們來參加今天晚上的酒席，我先來簡單地說幾句……

五、先生，我們可以看看菜單嗎？你們今天有沒有甚麼比較特別的菜？

六、大家好！我姓簡。我非常高興今年能有機會到中國來跟你們一起工作！

七、因為美國的大學非常好，還有工作的機會比較多，所以美國的外國留學生特別多。

八、最簡單的中國字是「一」；最難寫的中國字可能是「鸞」nǎng，真的非常難寫！

九、我覺得法語很難，比西語難得多，你為什麼說法語很簡單呢？

十、王大海同時有兩個女朋友，他的兩個女朋友知道了這件事，都非常生氣。

B. CONVERSATIONS 對話

Read out loud the following conversations, including the name or role of the person speaking. If possible, find a partner or partners and each of you play a role. Then switch roles, so you get practice reading all of the lines.

一、

姐姐：妹妹，在北京開車要特別小心。

妹妹：姐姐，我知道，你放心！我會非常小心的。

二、

老何：我還有幾句話想跟大家說……

小李：老何，你剛才已經說了很多，我們吃飯吧！

三、

老師：同學們，你們聽老師講。「。」叫句點，也叫句號；「？」叫問號；「；」叫分號；「《》」叫書名號。現在同學們都清楚了吧？有沒有問題？

學生：老師，知道了。

四、

小林：小王，你平常幾點上班，幾點下班？

小王：我應該八點上班，但是我常常會晚一點兒到。

小林：是嗎？那你幾點才到呢？

小王：我有的時候晚十分鐘，有的時候晚半個鐘頭。

小林：你的上司不會不高興嗎？

小王：我的上司？他一句話也沒說！

C. NARRATIVES 短文

Read the following narratives, paying special attention to punctuation and overall structure. The first time you read a narrative, read it out loud. The second time, read silently and try to gradually increase your reading speed. Always think of the meaning of what you're reading.

一、

我常常同時做很多不一樣的事。我喜歡吃飯的時候看報，或是做飯的時候講電話，或是走路的時候想我第二天應該做的事。我媽媽常常說我這個人都是「一半在這兒，一半在那兒」。

二、

我們家喜歡過簡單的生活。我們不需要住大房子，小房子就夠我們住了。因為房子小，所以我們不需要買很多很貴的家具。因為我們平常都走路，所以我們也不需要買很大的汽車，小車就行了。我們也很少去那些很高級的飯店或者買很多從外國進口的衣服什麼的。我們不做這些事，還是可以過得非常高興。我們家的人都覺得過簡單的生活真的比較好！

三、

我已經上完大學了，現在自己一個人住在台北市。在台北市住沒有我想得那麼簡單。我平常下午五點半、六點才下班，下班以後得先買菜，然後回家自己一個人生活非常沒有意思。我現在知道為什麼大家都說我應該找個男朋友了。

Notes 注解

A8. The word 齉 **nàng**, which means "have a nasal twang," contains a total of 36 strokes, and is thus the character with the largest number of strokes that can be found in modern Chinese dictionaries.

A9. ⊙西语 (西語) **Xīyǔ** "Spanish" [N]. This is an abbreviation of 西班牙语 (西班牙語) **Xībānyáyǔ**.

B4. ⊙上司 **shàngsi** "boss" or "one's superior" [N]

The Peking Duck Banquet (cont.)

各位请看！
(各位請看！)

 New Characters and Words

Study the six characters below and the common words written with them, paying careful attention to each character's pronunciation, meaning, and structure, as well as similar-looking characters. After you've studied a character, turn to the *Practice Essentials* volume and practice writing it on the practice sheet, making sure to follow the correct stroke order and direction as you pronounce it out loud and think of its meaning.

391 各   **gè**   each, every

Radical is 口 **kǒu** "mouth" (140). This radical, when occurring at the bottom of a character, is referred to colloquially as 口字底 **kǒuzìdǐ** "bottom made up of the character 口." The other component is 夊 **zhǐ**. Distinguish 各 from 名 **míng** (83), 路 **lù** (36), and simplified 备 **bèi** (264).

各	**gè**	each, every [SP]
各位	**gèwèi**	each person (polite)
各国 (各國)	**gèguó**	each country; the various countries

392 客   **kè**   visitor, guest

Radical is 宀 **mián** "roof." This radical is referred to colloquially as 宝盖头 (寶蓋頭) **bǎogàitóu** "top made up of a canopy." Phonetic is the previous new character, 各 **gè** "each" (391). "Each" 各 person is welcome to stay under the "roof" 宀 as a "guest" 客. Distinguish 客 from 各 **gè** (391), 名 **míng** (83), 完 **wán** (296), 定 **dìng** (270), and 路 **lù** (36).

客人	**kèrén**	guest [N]
主客	**zhǔkè**	main guest [N]
不客气 (不客氣)	**bú kèqi**	"you're welcome" [IE]

| 客家话 (客家話) | **Kèjiā huà** | Hakka language [PH] |
| ◉客家人 | **Kèjiā rén** | Hakka person, Hakka people [PH] |

393 习 (習)   **xí**   practice

Radical of the simplified form is 冫 **bīng** "ice," the colloquial term for which is 两点水 (兩點水) **liǎngdiǎn shuǐ** "two drops of water." Radical of the traditional form is 羽 **yǔ** "feather." The other element in the traditional form is 白 **bái** (328).

习 (習)	**Xí**	Xi [SN]
习近平 (習近平)	**Xí Jìnpíng**	Xi Jinping (President of the People's Republic of China, 2013–)
习主席 (習主席)	**Xí Zhǔxí**	Chairman Xi
学习 (學習)	**xuéxí**	learn, study [V]; study, studies [N]

394 惯 (慣)   **guàn**   be accustomed to

Radical is 心 **xīn** "heart" (262). When at the left side of a character, this radical is referred to colloquially as 心字旁 **xīnzìpáng** "side made up of the character 心" and is written as 忄. Phonetic is 贯 (貫) **guàn** "pass through." Distinguish 惯 (慣) from 慢 **màn** (290).

惯 (慣)	**-guàn**	be used to, be accustomed to [RE]
吃惯 (吃慣)	**chīguàn**	be used to eating something [RC]
吃得惯 (吃得慣)	**chīdeguàn**	can get used to eating something [RC]
吃不惯 (吃不慣)	**chībuguàn**	can't get used to eating something [RC]
习惯 (習慣)	**xíguàn**	be accustomed to [V]; custom, habit [N]

395 认 (認)   **rèn**   recognize; know; admit

Radical is 讠 (言) **yán** "speech" (336). The colloquial name for this radical is 言字旁 **yánzìpáng** "side made up of the character 言." Phonetic of the simplified form is 人 **rén** "person" (30). Phonetic of the traditional form is 忍 **rěn** "endure." Distinguish simplified 认 from 人 and 以 **yǐ** (146).

396 识 (識)   **shí**   know; recognize

Radical is 讠 (言) **yán** "speech" (336). The colloquial name for this radical is 言字旁 **yánzìpáng** "side made up of the character 言." Phonetic of the simplified form is 只 **zhǐ** (238). Phonetic of the traditional form is 戠 **zhí** "sword." Distinguish simplified 识 from 只 and simplified 总 **zǒng** (331).

| 认识 (認識) | **rènshi** | become acquainted with; recognize; know [V] |

New Words in ISC 15-2 Written with Characters You Already Know

吃得来 (吃得來)	chīdelái	can eat or like to eat something [RC]
但	dàn	but [CJ]
来(來)	lái	(verb substitute) [V] (e.g., 我自己来 (我自己來) "I'll help myself")
味道	wèidao	taste, flavor [N]
一直	yìzhí	always, all along [A]
越 A 越 B	yuè A yuè B	the more A the more B [PT]
早就	zǎo jiù	long ago, long since [PH]
主人	zhǔrén	host [N]

Reading Exercises (Simplified Characters) 简体字

Now practice reading the new characters and words for this lesson in context in sentences, conversations, and narratives. Be sure to refer to the Notes at the end of this lesson, and make use of the accompanying audio disc to hear and practice correct pronunciation, phrasing, and intonation.

A. SENTENCES 句子

Read out loud each of the following sentences, which include all the new characters of this lesson. The first time you read a sentence, focus special attention on the characters and words that are new to you, reminding yourself of their pronunciation and meaning. The second time, aim to comprehend the overall meaning of the sentence.

一、各国的语言和生活习惯都不一样。

二、我认识的中国字, 有的会写, 有的还不会。

三、客家人讲客家话, 他们的生活习惯跟别的中国人也不完全一样。

四、你们在哪儿学习中文? 学了多长时间了? 中文是不是越学越有意思?

五、有的人习惯用左手拿东西, 有的人习惯用右手拿东西, 我觉得都
　　一样。

六、习近平主席是在北京出生的, 也是在北京长大的, 所以他说一口北
　　京话。

七、各位同学, 你们如果已经学到这个地方了, 就已经认识三百九十
　　六个中国字了!

八、在法国, 喝酒已经成了一种生活习惯, 如果家里有客人也常请客
　　人喝酒。

九、要是你认识差不多一千五百个中国常用字, 你就可以开始看一点
　　中文的书和报纸了。

十、你们都认识王大海吧? 他正在写一本书, 越写越长。

Reading Exercises (Simplified Characters) 简体字

Now practice reading the new characters and words for this lesson in context in sentences, conversations, and narratives. Be sure to refer to the Notes at the end of this lesson, and make use of the accompanying audio disc to hear and practice correct pronunciation, phrasing, and intonation.

A. SENTENCES 句子

Read out loud each of the following sentences, which include all the new characters of this lesson. The first time you read a sentence, focus special attention on the characters and words that are new to you, reminding yourself of their pronunciation and meaning. The second time, aim to comprehend the overall meaning of the sentence.

一、你能不能把桌子上的报纸拿给我看看？谢谢。

二、中国北方人习惯吃面，南方人更喜欢吃米饭。

三、非常感谢各位今天晚上找时间来参加这次的酒席！

四、我们现在生活过得这么好，得感谢我的表姐及表姐夫。

五、你为什么觉得美国西岸的生活比东岸的生活更有意思呢？

六、有的美国人习惯把鞋子放在桌子上，在中国这是不可以的！

七、我住的房子在一所黑色的房子跟一所白色的房子的中间，不难找。

八、何夫人，对不起，您的车子不能停在这儿，请您把车子停在停车场，好吗？

九、火车六点十分开，现在已经五点四十了，你还要找个地方吃晚饭，我想大概来不及。

十、因为王大海的同学常常笑话他，所以他心里很难过。

B. CONVERSATIONS 对话

Read out loud the following conversations, including the name or role of the person speaking. If possible, find a partner or partners and each of you play a role. Then switch roles, so you get practice reading all of the lines.

一、

主人　：司先生，这个中国话叫"薄饼"。您得先拿一张薄饼，把肉放在中间，再放上一点儿这个东西，然后就可以吃了。

主客　：好。这样对不对？（他吃了之后）好吃极了！

主人　：司夫人，您吃得太少了，再来一点儿这个菜吧！

司夫人：我已经吃了很多了。别一直给我拿菜，您自己也要吃！

主人　：司先生，您怎么不吃了？多吃点儿吧！

主客　：我吃得太多了，实在是吃不下了。（等大家都吃完了）今天的菜太好吃了！非常感谢主人以及在这儿的各位！

二、

男：请问，和平食品店怎么走？

女：你走着去或者坐公车去都可以。

男：哪个更方便呢？

女：两个都行。走路去可能更快一点儿。

男：那，我应该怎么走呢？

女：这条街你先一直往前走，走差不多五分钟。到了第一个路口往左转。再走差不多两、三分钟，然后在路的右手边你会看到一个加油站跟一家大饭店。和平食品店很小，就在加油站和饭店的中间。

男：行，那我知道了。谢谢你了！

女：不用谢。

三、

包先生：高先生，听说您的夫人是外语专家，会讲好多种语言！她总共会讲几种语言呢？

高先生：她好像一共会说七、八种吧，还会说一些中国的方言，像客家话、广东话、台湾话什么的。

包先生：七、八种语言？还会几种方言？真不简单！您的夫人上大学学的是不是语言学专业？

高先生：其实不是，她是法文专业，后来也在加拿大留了一、两年学。

包先生：会那么多语言一定很方便。如果她需要到外国去办什么事的话，跟老外讲话根本就不成问题。

高先生：是的，是很方便。我们这几年以来到各国各地，认识了不知道多少外国朋友，我太太还常常用外语跟他们讲笑话呢！

C. NARRATIVE 短文

Read the following narrative, paying special attention to punctuation and overall structure. The first time you read the narrative, read it out loud. The second time, read silently and try to gradually increase your reading speed. Always think of the meaning of what you're reading.

我小时候很喜欢笑。有时候我家里人或是我同学随便说什么或是做什么，我都会一直笑。有时候我自己给自己讲笑话，然后就一直笑。有一次我跟爸妈和姐姐到火车站坐火车，可是火车已经走了，我那时不知道为什么，觉得非常好笑，就笑个不停，我的家人很不高兴。还有一次爸妈请了很多客人，都是他们最好的朋友，爸爸说"这是我们的小女儿美美，"我听了就开始笑，一直笑个不停。那天晚上回家以后，爸爸很生气，打了我几下，我一直到现在还记得。他说以后不可以再这样笑了，要不然大家会不喜欢我，以后我也会没有朋友，长大了也会找不到工作。从那天起，我就不笑了。

Reading Exercises (Simplified Characters) 简体字

Now practice reading the new characters and words for this lesson in context in sentences, conversations, and narratives. Be sure to refer to the Notes at the end of this lesson, and make use of the accompanying audio disc to hear and practice correct pronunciation, phrasing, and intonation.

A. SENTENCES 句子

Read out loud each of the following sentences, which include all the new characters of this lesson. The first time you read a sentence, focus special attention on the characters and words that are new to you, reminding yourself of their pronunciation and meaning. The second time, aim to comprehend the overall meaning of the sentence.

一、老白是湖北人，当然会说湖北话。

二、小李说笑话说得每个人都笑个不停。

三、小姐，请问，你知不知道这件衣服是用什么料子做的？

四、除了小林和小方之外，好像其他同学不太愿意再去动物园。

五、那个老外很客气，常常用中文说"您好"、"请"和"谢谢"。

六、谁都不愿意天天只工作、做饭、做家事，那样的生活太没意思。

七、我的主意是这个菜不要加这种调料了，不知道你觉得怎么样？

八、小高不但人长得好看，也很会讲话，还会调酒；女孩子当然特别喜欢他。

九、同学们，你们应当对王老太太客气一点儿，以后别让她生这么大的气。

十、王大海对他的女朋友说："除了你以外，我还有谁呢？"

B. CONVERSATIONS 对话

Read out loud the following conversations, including the name or role of the person speaking. If possible, find a partner or partners and each of you play a role. Then switch roles, so you get practice reading all of the lines.

一、

中国人：你愿意星期六去我那儿做中国菜吗？

美国人：当然愿意！（星期六到了中国人的家之后）这是什么？里头都有什么？

中国人：这个叫"饺子馅儿"。主要是肉和白菜。除了这些之外，还有些调料，像香油什么的。

美国人：真香！能不能先让我吃几个？

中国人：当然可以。请吃吧！

美国人：好吃极了！

中国人：好吃就多吃一点儿！

二、

男生：你明天有事吗？

女生：没什么特别的事。

Street Sign in Hong Kong

男生：你愿意和我一起吃中饭吗？
女生：当然愿意。几点？在哪里？
男生：十二点半在首都饭店门口见，
　　　怎么样？
女生：没问题。先谢谢你！
男生：你谢我什么？我又没说要请你！
女生：什么？我听错了吗？
　　　你……你……你不请我？
男生：放心，我当然要请你！

Street Sign in Beijing

三、
李老师：高老师，真对不起，让您久等了！
高老师：没关系，没关系。我也没等多久。
李老师：实在不好意思，今天交通不太好，路上的车子太多，我应当早
　　　　一点儿出来才对。
高老师：我不是已经跟你说过没关系吗？
李老师：那我得多谢你等我等了这么久了。
高老师：您别这么客气，我们又是老同事，又是老朋友。好吧，那我
　　　　们进去吧，好像刚开始……

C. NARRATIVES 短文

Read the following narratives, paying special attention to punctuation and overall structure. The first time you read a narrative, read it out loud. The second time, read silently and try to gradually increase your reading speed. Always think of the meaning of what you're reading.

一、"各位先生，各位小姐，大家好！我叫何万里，我想你们大概都认
　　识我吧？你们每一位我差不多都认识，可能有两、三位还不太认
　　识。非常高兴大家都能来参加今晚的这个酒席。饭店的人刚刚跟
　　我讲，很快就要上菜了。等一会儿菜上了桌子，请大家别客气，一定
　　要多吃一点儿，多喝一点儿，好不好？现在我请大家一起先来喝点
　　儿酒！"

二、最近几年，张太太为了她的先生，差不多什么事都愿意做。她天天
　　除了上班以外，回家还给他先生做饭、做家事什么的，忙得不得了。
　　可是最近几个月她的先生对她越来越冷了，后来有人说张先生在
　　外面还交了女朋友，常常跟他的女朋友在一起。张太太知道了这件
　　事，气得好几天都不能上班，什么事都做不了，心里非常难过。现
　　在张太太对张先生也不那么客气了。除了不跟他说话、不给他做
　　饭、不给他做家事之外，她根本不让他的先生回家！如果你是张
　　太太的话，你会怎么办？

Eating with a Colleague in a Restaurant

不好意思。改天我做东吧。
(不好意思。改天我做東吧。)

今天我请客。
(今天我請客。)

 New Characters and Words

Study the six characters below and the common words written with them, paying careful attention to each character's pronunciation, meaning, and structure, as well as similar-looking characters. After you've studied a character, turn to the *Practice Essentials* volume and practice writing it on the practice sheet, making sure to follow the correct stroke order and direction as you pronounce it out loud and think of its meaning.

---

409 而   **ér**   also, and, yet, but

This character is itself a radical. Originally, 而 was a pictograph of a beard, with the horizontal stroke 一 representing the mouth. Distinguish 而 from 西 **xī** (35), 两 (兩) **liǎng** (99), 百 **bǎi** (113), 面 **miàn** (168), and 雨 **yǔ** (279).

◉ 而   **ér**   and, yet, but, moreover [CJ]

···而已   **...éryǐ**   only; and that is all [PT]

---

410 且   **qiě**   moreover, and

Radical is 一 **yī** "one" (1). This character is itself a phonetic, e.g., in 姐 **jiě** (72). Distinguish 且 from 日 **rì** (132), 白 **bái** (328), 百 **bǎi** (113), 自 **zì** (379), 直 **zhí** (243), 真 **zhēn** (173), and 首 **shǒu** (225).

而且   **érqiě**   moreover, and, also [CJ]

不但···而且   **búdàn...érqiě**   not only...but also [PT]

---

411 鱼 (魚)   **yú**   fish

This character, which itself is a radical, is a pictograph of a fish. 鱼 (魚) is also a common radical at the left side of characters, typically indicating various types of fish. It can also sometimes serve as a phonetic, e.g., in 渔 (漁) **yú** "to fish."

鱼 (魚)	yú	fish [N]
一条鱼 (一條魚)	yìtiáo yú	a fish
⊙鱼肉 (魚肉)	yúròu	the flesh of a fish [N]
⊙金鱼 (金魚)	jīnyú	goldfish [N]

412 改   **gǎi**   change; correct

Radical is 攴 **pū** "tap" or "strike," which on the right side of a character appears as 攵. Phonetic is 己 **jǐ** "self" (380). Distinguish 改 from 己.

⊙改	gǎi	change; correct [V]
⊙改错 (改錯)	gǎicuò	correct mistakes [VO]
改天	gǎitiān	on some other day [TW]
改行	gǎiháng	change one's line of work [VO] (Note that 行 is here pronounced **háng**.)

413 务 (務)   **wù**   be engaged in; matter, affair

Radical is 力 **lì** "strength" (478). The other component is 攵 **pū** "rap" or "tap." The traditional character also includes 矛 **máo** "spear" on the left-hand side. The whole character 务 (務) can serve as a phonetic, e.g., in 雾 (霧) **wù** "fog."

| 务 (務) | Wù | Wu [SN] |
| 服务 (服務) | fúwù | serve [V] |

414 员 (員)   **yuán**   a person engaged in some field of activity; member

Radical is 口 **kǒu** "mouth" (140). The other component is 贝 (貝) **bèi** "cowry shell."

服务员 (服務員)	fúwùyuán	attendant, waiter, waitress [N]
⊙专员 (專員)	zhuānyuán	specialist [N]
⊙学员 (學員)	xuéyuán	student [N]

💿 New Words in ISC 16-1 Written with Characters You Already Know

便饭 (便飯)	biànfàn	simple meal [N]
刚才 (剛才)	gāngcái	just now [TW]
过 (過)	-guo	(expresses completed action) [P] (e.g., 你吃过饭了吗？[你吃過飯了嗎？] "Have you eaten?")
老	lǎo	be tough (of food) [SV]
买单 (買單)	mǎidān	"figure up the bill" [IE]; bill [N]
满…的 (滿…的)	mǎn...-de	quite [PT] (Note that some writers write this as 蛮…的 [蠻…的] **mán...-de**.)
请客 (請客)	qǐngkè	invite; treat (someone to something) [VO]

一块 (一塊)	**yíkuài(r)**	together [A/PW]
早点 (早點)	**zǎodiǎn**	breakfast [N]
做东 (做東)	**zuòdōng**	serve as host [VO]

Reading Exercises (Simplified Characters) 简体字

Now practice reading the new characters and words for this lesson in context in sentences, conversations, and narratives. Be sure to refer to the Notes at the end of this lesson, and make use of the accompanying audio disc to hear and practice correct pronunciation, phrasing, and intonation.

A. SENTENCES 句子

Read out loud each of the following sentences, which include all the new characters of this lesson. The first time you read a sentence, focus special attention on the characters and words that are new to you, reminding yourself of their pronunciation and meaning. The second time, aim to comprehend the overall meaning of the sentence.

一、我刚才给校长打了一个电话，可是她不在。

二、服务员，买单！也请你把这些菜包起来，谢谢！

三、没关系，你如果今天太忙的话，我可以改天再来找你。

四、那家书店的服务非常好，我很喜欢去那儿买书，买报纸什么的。

五、服务员，请你把菜单拿来，好吗？我们已经等了很久了！

六、我的表姐以前在工厂里工作，后来改行了，现在做一点儿小买卖。

七、你不应该让白老师请你，她只是一位小学老师而已，又不是什么很有钱
　　的人。

八、水里本来有两条金鱼，可是大的把小的给吃了，所以现在只有一条了。

九、我觉得一个老师应该常常改学生的错，不过学生不应该改别的学生
　　的错。

十、王大海不但不喜欢吃肉，而且也不喜欢吃鱼。

B. CONVERSATIONS 对话

Read out loud the following conversations, including the name or role of the person speaking. If possible, find a partner or partners and each of you play a role. Then switch roles, so you get practice reading all of the lines.

一、

台湾人：吃过饭没有？

美国人：还没。刚才有点事。你呢？

台湾人：我也还没吃。要不要一块儿去吃？

美国人：好！

服务员：（在饭店）几位？

台湾人：两位。（开始吃饭以后）鱼怎么样？好不好吃？

美国人：味道满好的，就是肉老了一点。

台湾人：买单。

美国人：多少钱？
台湾人：不，今天我请客。
美国人：还是我来吧。
台湾人：别客气。只是便饭而已。
美国人：不好意思，每次都让你请客。改天我做东吧。

二、
张东山：你去过和平饭店吗？
关雨中：我自己没去过，可是我表姐夫每次到北京来都住那家饭店。
张东山：他觉得那里的服务怎么样？
关雨中：他说服务不错，还说他们的早点特别好吃！
张东山：你表姐夫觉得那家的价钱怎么样？
关雨中：他说和平饭店不但服务好，而且价钱不贵。
张东山：那太好了！我下个月要定一桌酒席。那我大概就在和平饭店定吧。

三、
王先生：何小姐，你这里好像写错了一个字。
何小姐：让我看看。
王先生：是这个句子，第二个字。
何小姐：我看看。对不起，我真的写错了！我已经不习惯用手写中国字了！
　　　　我来改一下吧。
王先生：好，谢谢你。
何小姐：不客气，这是我的错。以后我会小心一点。

C. NARRATIVES 短文

Read the following narratives, paying special attention to punctuation and overall structure. The first time you read a narrative, read it out loud. The second time, read silently and try to gradually increase your reading speed. Always think of the meaning of what you're reading.

一、有一次，一个美国人想请他的中国朋友王先生、王太太到家里来吃饭。他知道中国人讲话很客气，也听说中国话有时候前头加一个"小"字，那句话就更客气了。像"小姓"比"我姓"客气，"小儿"比"我儿子"客气，"小女"比"我女儿"客气。所以那个美国人把他在中文班上学的"请你们到家里来吃便饭"说成了"请你们到家里来吃小便饭"！当然，他的中国朋友听了，不太高兴。王先生还好，只是觉得有一点儿可笑，可是王太太真的生气了。

二、中国人的生活习惯跟美国不太一样。美国人请客，客人来了，先请他坐，然后主人大概会问客人："Would you like something to drink?"就是"你想不想喝点儿什么？"。而在中国，如果你那样问一位中国客人，他就是想喝东西，大概也会说"不用了！"所以，如果请了中国客人到家里来，根本不用问他想不想喝什么，你就拿给他一些喝的就行了。

Notes 注解

A8. 大的把小的给吃了 (大的把小的給吃了) lit. "The big one took the little one and ate it," or in idiomatic English, "The big one ate the little one." As you learned in ISC 15-3: 1C, the coverb 把 serves to move the object of the verb to a position before the verb and indicates that the object is being disposed of or handled in a certain way. Placing a 给 (給) before the main verb, as here, is optional but common. The 给 (給) strengthens the sense that something is being taken and handled in a certain way (here, that the little fish has been eaten).

B3. Because Chinese people now often write characters by computer or mobile device, they are beginning to forget how to write the less common characters by hand.

C1a. 像 here means "like." The writer is giving examples of Chinese expressions where adding the character 小 at the beginning renders the expression politer or more modest. The expression 小姓 is rarely used nowadays.

C1b. 把A说成B (把A說成B) lit. "take A and say it so that it becomes B."

C2a. 他就是想喝东西，大概也会说"不用了！"（他就是想喝東西，大概也會說"不用了！"）lit. "Even if he wants to drink something, he'll probably say, 'It's not necessary!'" The pattern 就是……也 means "even if" or "even."

C2b. 你就拿给他一些喝的就行了 (你就拿給他一些喝的就行了) "Just bring him some things to drink and that will do." 喝的 here means 喝的东西 (喝的東西) "things to drink" or "beverages."

"**Jìnzhǐ Diàoyú, Bǔyú**" (sign in Taipei park)

A Dinner Party at Home

今天我们替Larry 接风。
(今天我們替Larry 接風。)

谢谢，实在不敢当。
(謝謝，實在不敢當。)

New Characters and Words

Study the six characters below and the common words written with them, paying careful attention to each character's pronunciation, meaning, and structure, as well as similar-looking characters. After you've studied a character, turn to the *Practice Essentials* volume and practice writing it on the practice sheet, making sure to follow the correct stroke order and direction as you pronounce it out loud and think of its meaning.

415 替 **tì**   replace, substitute; for

Radical is 曰 **yuē** "speak." At the top of this character are two 夫 **fū** "men." As a mnemonic, remember: "two men" 夫夫 "speak" 曰 "for" 替 someone.

替	**tì**	for [CV]

416 接 **jiē**   receive, meet, welcome

Radical is 手 **shǒu** "hand" (305), which at the left side of a character is written as 扌 and is referred to colloquially as 提手 **tíshǒu** "raised hand." Phonetic is 妾 **qiè** "concubine."

接风 (接風)	**jiēfēng**	give a welcome dinner [VO]
替…接风 (替…接風)	**tì…jiēfēng**	give a welcome dinner for... [PT]
◉接电话 (接電話)	**jiē diànhuà**	receive or take a phone call [PH]

417 敢 (敢) **gǎn**   dare; be bold

Radical is 攴 **pū** "tap" or "strike," which on the right side of a character is written 攵. This character is itself a phonetic, e.g., in the character 橄 as it is used in the word 橄榄 (橄欖) **gǎnlǎn** "olive."

| 敢 (敢) | **gǎn** | dare [V/AV] |
| 不敢当 (不敢當) | **bù gǎn dāng** | "don't dare accept" [IE] |

Note that the difference between the official simplified form and the official traditional form of this character does not show up in all fonts; in some fonts, they both look the same.

....

418 量 **liàng** capacity, amount

Radical is 里 **lǐ** "mile" (163). The other components are 日 **yuē** "speak" and 一 **yī** "one" (1). The whole character sometimes occurs as a phonetic in other characters, e.g., in the traditional character 糧 as it is used in 糧食 **liángshí** "grain" or "cereal." Distinguish 量 from 里 **lǐ** (163).

海量	**hǎiliàng**	lit. "ocean capacity" (meaning a great capacity for drinking liquor) [IE]
雨量	**yǔliàng**	rainfall [N]
◉ 酒量	**jiǔliàng**	capacity for drinking alcohol [N]

....

419 深 **shēn** deep

Radical is 水 **shuǐ** "water" (333), which is written 氵 and is referred to colloquially as 三点水 (三點水) **sāndiǎn shuǐ** "three drops of water" when it occurs at the left-hand side of a character. The right-hand component of the character is the phonetic, which is usually pronounced **-en** or **-an**.

深	**shēn**	be deep; dark (of colors) [SV]
深色	**shēnsè**	dark in color, dark-colored [AT]
深水	**shēn shuǐ**	deep water

....

420 石 **shí** rock, stone

This character is itself a radical. Distinguish 石 from 右 **yòu** (166).

石	**Shí**	Shi [SN]
石头 (石頭)	**shítou**	stone [N]
一块石头 (一塊石頭)	**yíkuài shítou**	a stone

New Words in ISC 16-2 Written with Characters You Already Know

不如	**bù rú**	not as good as; it would be better to [PT]
海	**hǎi**	ocean, sea [N]
河	**hé**	river [N]
湖	**hú**	lake [N]
回到	**huídào**	come back to [V+PV]
回来 (回來)	**huílai**	come back [RC]
回去	**huíqu**	go back [RC]
随意 (隨意)	**suíyì**	at will; as one pleases; "as you like" [IE]

Reading Exercises (Simplified Characters) 简体字

Now practice reading the new characters and words for this lesson in context in sentences, conversations, and narratives. Be sure to refer to the Notes at the end of this lesson, and make use of the accompanying audio disc to hear and practice correct pronunciation, phrasing, and intonation.

A. SENTENCES 句子

Read out loud each of the following sentences, which include all the new characters of this lesson. The first time you read a sentence, focus special attention on the characters and words that are new to you, reminding yourself of their pronunciation and meaning. The second time, aim to comprehend the overall meaning of the sentence.

一、"简开石先生，简开石先生，请快到前面来接电话！"

二、那位法国老太太的先生死了以后，她天天都穿深色的衣服。

三、小石，你先别着急，那件事我替你办就是了，你可以放心。

四、时间不早了，而且家里还有好多事得做，不如早点儿回去吧！

五、林夫人刚回国，我们星期六晚上替她跟她先生接风，你能参加吗？

六、我们学校前边的那条河很深，不过好像水里头没有什么鱼，只有很多石头！

七、我每到一个新地方，都喜欢随意走走看看，多认识儿个本地人，交几个新朋友。

八、一个学习外语的学生如果不敢开口说话，那么他一定学不好。

九、中国东边和南方各省雨量都很多，比较起来北方雨量就少得多，所以中国北方各省都特别干。

十、工大海不喝酒，可是他爸爸很会喝，王老先生的酒量根本就是海量。

B. CONVERSATIONS 对话

Read out loud the following conversations, including the name or role of the person speaking. If possible, find a partner or partners and each of you play a role. Then switch roles, so you get practice reading all of the lines.

一、

白先生　　：今天我们替 Larry 接风。Larry，我们都好高兴你这次回到台湾来了！大家也都是老朋友。来，我们敬 Larry！

美国主客：谢谢，谢谢，实在不敢当。

石先生　　：Larry，来，我敬你！干杯怎么样？

美国主客：量浅，量浅。你干，我随意吧。

石先生　　：你是海量！来，干杯，干杯！

美国主客：恭敬不如从命。那我先干为敬了！

二、

文老师：石老师，后天您有什么事吗？

石老师：我想一想，后天是星期五，应该没什么事吧。

文老师：我们要替张老师接风，您能来参加吗？

石老师：没问题。几点钟？在什么地方？

文老师：首都饭店。时间还没决定，不过大概是六点或是六点一刻。
我明天再给您打电话通知您时间，行吗？

石老师：行。

C. NARRATIVES 短文

Read the following narratives, paying special attention to punctuation and overall structure. The first time you read a narrative, read it out loud. The second time, read silently and try to gradually increase your reading speed. Always think of the meaning of what you're reading.

一、我的女朋友金金已经二十二岁了，可是她还不会开车。她不会开车是因为她根本不敢学！金金今年七月要开始在一家离她家很远的公司工作，每天上下班都需要开车，因为从她家到那家公司根本没有公共汽车，当然也不可能每天都打的。金金也知道，她得在两、三个月之内学会开车。我刚才跟她说，不如早一点开始学，别再等了。现在已经四月了，她还没开始学，我真替她着急！

二、老简去了加拿大好几个月，刚回北京，所以我星期六晚上替他接风。我打算请他跟我们公司的一些同事到阳明饭店吃饭。阳明饭店刚开不久，听说满高级的，他们的山东菜做得特别好。当然，我们一定会喝不少酒，我已经通知了饭店多为我们准备一些酒。老简本来就是海量，所以我想没有人敢跟他比酒量。我叫大家那天晚饭后千万别开车，打的比较好，因为我们都知道，"酒后不开车，开车不喝酒！"

三、我姓石，石京生。我是北京人，今年二十六岁，在美国西北大学留学，我的专业是比较文学。我原来打算今年七月回中国看看我的家人和我的男朋友，可是因为七月的机票很难定，也太贵，而且我在这边的事儿还很多，所以我最后决定十二月再回国。前天刚好是七月四号，我跟一些中国同学先做了中饭，都是中国菜，好吃极了，然后一块儿到湖边随意走走看看。那天有太阳，天气特别好。有一点小风，气温正好，不冷也不热。湖看起来很深，但水很清，我们在湖里还看到好多大大小小的鱼。那天大家都特别高兴！

"Běiyī Bǔxíbān" (Beiyi Cram School, Taipei)

Reading Exercises (Traditional Characters) 繁體字

A. SENTENCES 句子

Read out loud each of the following sentences, which include all the new characters of this lesson. The first time you read a sentence, focus special attention on the characters and words that are new to you, reminding yourself of their pronunciation and meaning. The second time, aim to comprehend the overall meaning of the sentence.

一、「簡開石先生,簡開石先生,請快到前面來接電話!」

二、那位法國老太太的先生死了以後,她天天都穿深色的衣服。

三、小石,你先別着急,那件事我替你辦就是了,你可以放心。

四、時間不早了,而且家裡還有好多事得做,不如早點兒回去吧!

五、林夫人剛回國,我們星期六晚上替她跟她先生接風,你能參加嗎?

六、我們學校前邊的那條河很深,不過好像水裡頭沒有甚麼魚,只有很多石頭!

七、我每到一個新地方,都喜歡隨意走走看看,多認識幾個本地人,交幾個新朋友。

八、一個學習外語的學生如果不敢開口說話,那麼他一定學不好。

九、中國東邊和南方各省雨量都很多,比較起來北方雨量就少得多,所以中國北方各省都特別乾。

十、王大海不喝酒,可是他爸爸很會喝,王老先生的酒量根本就是海量。

B. CONVERSATIONS 對話

Read out loud the following conversations, including the name or role of the person speaking. If possible, find a partner or partners and each of you play a role. Then switch roles, so you get practice reading all of the lines.

一、

白先生 ：今天我們替 Larry 接風。Larry,我們都好高興你這次回到台灣來了!大家也都是老朋友。來,我們敬 Larry!

美國主客 ：謝謝,謝謝,實在不敢當。

石先生 ：Larry,來,我敬你!

美國主客 ：量淺,量淺。你乾,我隨意吧。

石先生 ：你是海量!來,乾杯,乾杯!

美國主客 ：乾杯怎麼樣?

美國主客 ：恭敬不如從命。那我先乾為敬了!

A Dinner Party at Home (cont.)

没什么菜，实在简单得很。(沒什麼菜，實在簡單得很。)

您今天预备了这么多菜啊！(您今天預備了這麼多菜啊！)

New Characters and Words

Study the six characters below and the common words written with them, paying careful attention to each character's pronunciation, meaning, and structure, as well as similar-looking characters. After you've studied a character, turn to the *Practice Essentials* volume and practice writing it on the practice sheet, making sure to follow the correct stroke order and direction as you pronounce it out loud and think of its meaning.

421 预 (預) **yù** prepare; in advance

Radical is 页 (頁) **yè** "page." Phonetic is 予 **yǔ** "give." Distinguish 预 (預) from traditional 頭 **tóu** (120).

预备 (預備)	**yùbei**	prepare [V]
⊙预备中学 (預備中學)	**yùbei zhōngxué**	preparatory high school, prep school [PH]
预报 (預報)	**yùbào**	forecast [N]
天气预报 (天氣預報)	**tiānqi yùbào**	weather forecast [PH]

422 爱 (愛) **ài** love, like

Radical of the simplified form is 爪 **zhuǎ** "claw," which certainly does not seem very "loving," but fortunately the character for "friend" (友 **yǒu**) appears at the bottom. Radical of the traditional form is 心 **xīn** "heart" (262), indicating that an emotion is involved. Distinguish 爱 (愛) from 要 **yào** (137) and 受 **shòu** (367).

爱 (愛)	**ài**	love, like [V]
爱人 (愛人)	**àiren**	spouse, husband, wife [N]
可爱 (可愛)	**kě'ài**	be loveable, cute [SV]
⊙最爱 (最愛)	**zuì'ài**	favorite [N]

423 步　**bù**　step, pace

Radical is 止 **zhǐ** "stop." This character is a picture of a right foot and a left foot taking one "step" after another. Distinguish 步 from simplified 岁 **suì** (107).

步	**bù**	step, pace [M]
走一步	**zǒu yíbù**	walk one step, take a step
先走一步	**xiān zǒu yíbù**	lit. "take one step first," meaning leave before others [IE]
⊙饭后百步走，活到九十九 (飯後百步走，活到九十九)	**Fàn hòu bǎi bù zǒu, huódào jiǔshíjiǔ.**	"Walk a hundred paces after eating and live to be 99." [EX]

424 数（數）　**shù**　number, figure; several

Radical is 攴 **pū** "tap" or "strike," which at the right side of a character is written 攵. The other component is 娄（婁）**lóu** "weak."

多数（多數）	**duōshù**	majority [N]
大多数（大多數）	**dà duōshù**	great majority [PH]
数学（數學）	**shùxué**	mathematics [N]
⊙算数（算數）	**suànshù**	count [VO]
⊙岁数（歲數）	**suìshu**	age (of a person) [N]
⊙您多大岁数了？ (您多人歲數了？)	**Nín duō dà suìshu le?**	"How old are you?"

425 紧（緊）　**jǐn**　tight, tense

Radical is 丝（絲）**sī** "silk," which is here at the bottom of the character. The sense is that something has been tied "tightly" 紧（緊）with "silk" 丝（絲）.

紧张（緊張）	**jǐnzhāng**	be nervous, intense [SV]
要紧（要緊）	**yàojǐn**	be important [SV]
不要紧（不要緊）	**bú yàojǐn**	be unimportant; "never mind" [IE]

426 啊　**a**　(particle that softens the sentence)

Radical is 口 **kǒu** "mouth" (140). This radical is referred to colloquially as 口字旁 **kǒuzìpáng** "side made up of the character 口." Phonetic is 阿 **ā**.

啊	**a**	(softens the sentence) [P]
你好啊！	**Nǐ hǎo a!**	"How are you?"
慢走啊！	**Màn zǒu a!**	"Take it easy!"

New Words in ISC 16-3 Written with Characters You Already Know

便当 (便當)	**biàndāng**	box lunch [N]
不要客气 (不要客氣)	**búyào kèqi**	"don't be polite" [IE]
吃到	**chīdào**	succeed in eating [RC]
够 (夠)	**gòu**	reach (by stretching) [V]
够得着 (夠得著)	**gòudezháo**	be able to reach [RC]
够不着 (夠不著)	**gòubuzháo**	be unable to reach [RC]
慢用	**màn yòng**	"take your time eating" [IE]
内人 (內人)	**nèirén**	one's wife (polite) [N]
特地	**tèdì**	especially [A]
为 (爲)	**wèi**	for [CV]
味儿 (味兒)	**wèir**	smell, fragrance, aroma [N]
小吃	**xiǎochī**	snack [N]
SV+ 得很	**SV + de hěn**	very SV [PT] (e.g., 我最近忙得很。 "I've been very busy recently.")

Reading Exercises (Simplified Characters) 简体字

Now practice reading the new characters and words for this lesson in context in sentences, conversations, and narratives. Be sure to refer to the Notes at the end of this lesson, and make use of the accompanying audio disc to hear and practice correct pronunciation, phrasing, and intonation.

A. SENTENCES 句子

Read out loud each of the following sentences, which include all the new characters of this lesson. The first time you read a sentence, focus special attention on the characters and words that are new to you, reminding yourself of their pronunciation and meaning. The second time, aim to comprehend the overall meaning of the sentence.

一、你如果现在不方便跟我讲话，不要紧，我可以改天再来。

二、不好意思，我有一点儿急事，得先走一步，各位请慢用！

三、听说你的数学特别好，我能问你一个跟数学有关系的问题吗？

四、王老先生，您好啊？好久不见了！能不能问您个问题，您今年多大岁数了？

五、你别紧张！一步一步地来吧。你要是太紧张的话，什么事儿都办不好。

六、天气预报说今天会下毛毛雨，不过天气预报只是预报而已，不一定准！

七、这是我爱人特地为您预备的小吃和菜，您爱吃什么就吃什么吧，不要客气了！

八、我姐姐、姐夫有一个儿子，今年四岁，非常可爱，因为他是牛年生的，所以大家都叫他"牛牛"。

九、在中国请客的时候，主人常常给客人拿菜；可是大多数美国人不
　　喜欢你给他拿菜，他们习惯自己拿。

十、王大海，你快来接电话，校长说他有一件非常要紧的事找你！

B. CONVERSATIONS 对话

Read out loud the following conversations, including the name or role of the person speaking. If possible, find a partner or partners and each of you play a role. Then switch roles, so you get practice reading all of the lines.

一、

美国主客：您今天预备了这么多菜啊！

白太太　：没什么菜，实在简单得很。不要客气！来，这是糖醋里脊，
　　　　　我记得你最爱吃的。

美国主客：味儿真香啊！真是两、三年没吃到了。

白太太　：我也记得你爱吃辣的。我特地为你做了麻辣杂拌儿。你够
　　　　　得着吧？我给你加一点儿。

美国主客：够得着，够得着，我自己来。

林先生　：对不起，我们有一点儿事，得先走一步。我跟内人敬各位！
　　　　　各位慢用。

二、

谢国平：表姐，你们家住在哪儿啊？

李爱文：我们住在通县，在北京城的东边儿。

谢国平：你们家都有什么人啊？

李爱文：我们一家三口。我和你表姐夫，还有一个女儿。

谢国平：表姐，您在哪儿工作啊？

李爱文：我在一家进出口公司做事。

谢国平：表姐夫呢？

李爱文：你表姐夫原来在一家工厂工作。因为太忙，所以他最近改行了，
　　　　现在做点儿小买卖。

三、

外国学生：老师，请问，"饭后百步走，活到九十九"这句话是什么意思？

中文老师：这句话的意思就是吃饭以后应该多走一走，才会活到比较大
　　　　　的岁数。也就是说，要是你吃了饭以后都不动，就会老得很
　　　　　快，可能活不到很大的年纪。

四、

小学老师：你跟你弟弟写的作文《我的狗》怎么完全一样？是不是抄的？

明明：不是抄的。老师，您知道，我们写的是同一条狗啊！

C. NARRATIVE 短文

Read the following narrative, paying special attention to punctuation and overall structure. The first time you read the narrative, read it out loud. The second time, read silently and try to gradually increase your reading speed. Always think of the meaning of what you're reading.

我的同屋小东今年大三，不过他才十七岁。他十一岁就开始上一个预备中学，十四岁就进大学了。小东的数学特别好，他妈妈说他两岁还不太会说话，可是已经会算数了！不过除了数学以外，其他很多事小东都不会。他不敢开车，坐别人开的车他也很紧张。他也不会做饭，更不会做家务什么的。穿衣服他也不知道什么衣服跟什么衣服一起穿好看。他走路想数学，吃饭也想数学，每天只想数学，因为数学就是他的最爱。我想小东的头和别人的头一定不太一样。不过，小东是个好人，对同学很好，他愿意替我们做我们的数学作业！

Reading Exercises (Traditional Characters) 繁體字

A. SENTENCES 句子

Read out loud each of the following sentences, which include all the new characters of this lesson. The first time you read a sentence, focus special attention on the characters and words that are new to you, reminding yourself of their pronunciation and meaning. The second time, aim to comprehend the overall meaning of the sentence.

一、你如果現在不方便跟我講話，不要緊，我可以改天再來。

二、不好意思，我有一點兒急事，得先走一步，各位請慢用！

三、聽說你的數學特別好，我能問你一個跟數學有關係的問題嗎？

四、王老先生，您好啊！好久不見了！能不能問您一個問題，您今年多大歲數了？

五、你別緊張！一步一步地來吧。你要是太緊張的話，什麼事兒都辦不好。

六、天氣預報說今天會下毛毛雨，不過天氣預報只是預報而已，不一定準！

七、這是我愛人特地為您預備的小吃和菜，您愛吃甚麼就吃甚麼吧，不要客氣了！

八、我姐姐、姐夫有一個兒子，今年四歲，非常可愛，因為他是牛年生的，所以大家都叫他「牛牛」。

九、在中國請客的時候，主人常常給客人拿菜；可是大多數美國人不喜歡你給他拿菜，他們習慣自己拿。

十、王大海，你快來接電話，校長說他有一件非常要緊的事找你！

B. CONVERSATIONS 對話

Read out loud the following conversations, including the name or role of the person speaking. If possible, find a partner or partners and each of you play a role. Then switch roles, so you get practice reading all of the lines.

一、

美國主客：您今天預備了這麼多菜啊！

白太太：沒什麼菜，實在簡單得很。不要客氣！來，這是糖醋裡脊，我記得你最愛吃的。

美國主客：味兒真香啊！真是兩、三年沒吃到了。

白太太：我也記得你愛吃辣的。我特地為你做了麻辣雜拌兒。你夠得著嗎？我給你加一點兒。

美國主客：夠得著，夠得著，我自己來。

林先生：對不起，我有一點兒事，得先走一步。我跟內人敬各位！各位慢用。

二、

李愛文：你表姐夫原來在一家工廠工作。因為太忙，所以他最近改行了，現在做點兒小買賣。

謝國平：表姐夫呢？

李愛文：我在一家進出口公司做事。

謝國平：表姐，您在哪兒工作啊？

李愛文：我們住在通縣，在北京城的東邊兒。

謝國平：表姐，你們家住在哪兒啊？

李愛文：我們一家三口。我和你表姐夫，還有一個女兒。

謝國平：你們家都有甚麼人啊？

三、

外國學生：老師，請問，「飯後百步走，活到九十九」這句話是甚麼意思？

中文老師：這句話的意思就是吃飯以後應該多走一走，才會活到比較大的歲數。也就是說，要是你吃了飯以後都不動，就會老得很快，可能活不到很大的年紀。

四、

小學老師：你跟你弟弟寫的作文《我的狗》怎麼完全一樣？是不是抄的？

明明：不是抄的。老師，您知道，我們寫的是同一條狗啊！

C. NARRATIVE 短文

Read the following narrative, paying special attention to punctuation and overall structure. The first time you read the narrative, read it out loud. The second time, read silently and try to gradually increase your reading speed. Always think of the meaning of what you're reading.

我的同屋小東今年大三，不過他才十七歲。他十一歲就開始上一個預備中學，十四歲就進大學了。小東的數學特別好，他媽媽說他兩歲還不太會說話，可是已經會算數了！不過除了數學以外，其他很多事小東都不會。他不敢開車，坐別人開的車他也很緊張。他也不會做飯，更不會做家務什麼的。穿衣服他也不知道甚麼衣服跟甚麼衣服一起穿好看。他走路想數學，吃飯也想數學，每天只想數學，因為數學，就是他的最愛。我想小東的頭和別人的頭一定不太一樣。不過，小東是個好人，對同學很好，他願意替我們做我們的數學作業！

Notes 注解

A3. ⊙A跟B有关系 (A跟B有關係) **A gēn B yǒu guānxi** "A is related to B" [PT]

B1a. ◆糖醋里脊 (糖醋裡脊) **Tángcù Lǐjī** "Sweet and Sour Pork" [PH]. 糖 means "sugar" or "candy" and 醋 means "vinegar," so this refers to a sweet and sour sauce. 里脊 (裡脊) means "tenderloin" or "filet."

B1b. ◆辣 **là** "be peppery hot" [SV]

B1c. ◆麻辣杂拌儿 (麻辣雜拌兒) **Málà Zábànr** "Sesame Hot Spicy Medley" [PH]. 麻辣 means "peppery and spicy," while 杂半儿 (雜半兒) refers to a mixture of something.

B1d. ◆敬 **jìng** "toast" or "drink to" [V]

B3a. ⊙老 **lǎo** "become old, age" [V]

B3b. 活不到很大的年纪 (活不到很大的年紀) "won't be able to live to an old age"

B4a. ⊙作文 **zuòwén** "essay" or "composition" [N]

B4b. ◆狗 **gǒu** "dog" [N]. There are two common measure words for 狗. One is 条 (條), which is the measure word used in this narrative, since dogs are long and "strip-like." Snakes, fish, and crocodiles also use 条 (條) as a measure word. The other measure word for 狗 is 只 (隻) **zhī**, which is the measure word used for many animals.

B4c. ◆抄 **chāo** "copy" [V]

B4d. ⊙同 **tóng** "the same" [SP]. 同一条狗 (同一條狗) means "the same dog."

C1a. ⊙进大学 (進大學) **jìn dàxué** "enter a university" [PH]

C1b. ⊙家务 (家務) **jiāwù** "household duties" or "housework" [N]

C1c. ⊙头 (頭) **tóu** "head" [N]

A Dinner Party at Home (cont.)

我已经喝得太多了，实在是不能
再喝了。我以茶代酒好吧。
(我已經喝得太多了，實在是不能
再喝了。我以茶代酒好吧。)

New Characters and Words

Study the six characters below and the common words written with them, paying careful attention to each character's pronunciation, meaning, and structure, as well as similar-looking characters. After you've studied a character, turn to the *Practice Essentials* volume and practice writing it on the practice sheet, making sure to follow the correct stroke order and direction as you pronounce it out loud and think of its meaning.

427 代 **dài** substitute for, take the place of; generation

Radical is 人 **rén** "person" (30), which is written 亻 when occurring at the left-hand side of a character so as not to get in the way of the component at the right. The colloquial name for this radical is 人字旁 **rénzìpáng** "side made up of the character 人." This whole character can serve as a phonetic, e.g., in the character 袋 as in the word 袋子 **dàizi** "bag." Distinguish 代 from 什 **shén** (127) and 他 **tā** (55).

代	**dài**	substitute for, take the place of [V/CV]
以A代B	**yǐ A dài B**	take A to substitute for B; substitute A for B [PT]
以汽水代酒	**yǐ qìshuǐ dài jiǔ**	"substitute soda for liquor"
◉代替	**dàitì**	replace, substitute [V]

428 课（課） **kè** lesson; class

Radical is 讠（言）**yán** "speech" (336). The colloquial name for this radical is 言字旁 **yánzìpáng** "side made up of the character 言." Phonetic is 果 **guǒ** "fruit" or "result" (334). A "lesson" 课（課）involves the use of 言 "words" of instruction to bear fruit and produce results 果. Distinguish 课（課）from 果 **guǒ** (334).

课 (課)	kè	class; lesson [N]
上课 (上課)	shàngkè	have class [VO]
下课 (下課)	xiàkè	end class [VO]
中文课 (中文課)	Zhōngwén kè	Chinese class
第一课 (第一課)	dìyīkè	lesson one
代课 (代課)	dàikè	teach in place of someone [VO]
代课老师 (代課老師)	dàikè lǎoshī	substitute teacher [PH]

429 馆 (館)   guǎn   establishment; hotel; restaurant

Radical is 食 **shí** "eat" (341), which is written as 饣 (飠) when occurring at the left-hand side of a character as a radical. The colloquial name for this radical is 食字旁 **shízìpáng** "side made up of the character 食." Phonetic is 官 **guān** "official" (589). Where else would an "official" 官 "eat" 食 than in an expensive "restaurant" 馆 (館)?

饭馆 (飯館)	fànguǎn(r)	restaurant [PW]
馆子 (館子)	guǎnzi	restaurant [PW]
◉川菜馆子 (川菜館子)	Chuāncài guǎnzi	Sichuan-style restaurant [PH]

430 虽 (雖)   suī/suí   though, although

Radical of the simplified character is 口 **kǒu** "mouth" (140). Radical of the traditional character is 隹 **zhuī** "short-tailed bird." Most mainland Chinese speakers pronounce this character **suī**, while most Taiwanese speakers pronounce it **suí**.

虽然 (雖然)	suīrán	although..., though... [PT]
虽然…可是… (雖然…可是…)	suīrán...kěshi...	although..., though... [PT]
虽然…但是… (雖然…但是…)	suīrán...dànshi...	although..., though... [PT]

431 茶   chá   tea

Radical is 艹 **cǎo** "grass," which is written 草 when it occurs as an independent word (456). When it occurs as a radical at the top of a character, as here, the "grass" radical is written as ⁺⁺ and is then known as 草字头 (草字頭) **cǎozìtóu** "top made up of the character 草." The rest of the character 茶 consists of 人 **rén** (30), which here looks like a big canopy or cover, over 木 **mù** "tree." "Tea" 茶 is picked from a "tree"-like 木 plant and is dried under a "cover" 人 before being sold and brewed. Distinguish 茶 from 菜 **cài** (327).

茶	chá	tea [N]
喝茶	hēchá	drink tea [VO]
以茶代酒	yǐ chá dài jiǔ	"substitute tea for liquor" [EX]
◉茶馆 (茶館)	cháguǎn(r)	teahouse [PW]

432 乐 (樂) **lè**   cheerful, happy, joyful

Radical of the simplified form is 丿 **piě** "left-falling stroke." Radical of the traditional form is the pictograph 木 **mù** "tree." Distinguish simplified 乐 from simplified 东 **dōng** (29) and simplified 车 **chē** (224).

快乐 (快樂)	**kuàilè**	be happy [SV]
生日快乐 (生日快樂)	**shēngrì kuàilè**	"birthday happiness," happy birthday [PH]
可乐 (可樂)	**kělè**	cola [N]
可口可乐 (可口可樂)	**Kěkǒu Kělè**	Coca-Cola® [N]
百事可乐 (百事可樂)	**Bǎishì Kělè**	Pepsi-Cola® [N]

New Words in ISC 16-4 Written with Characters You Already Know

比不上	**bǐbushàng**	not be able to compare [RC]
家常菜	**jiācháng cài**	home-style cooking [PH]
开水 (開水)	**kāishuǐ**	boiled water [N]
老	**lǎo**	very [A] (e.g., 大老远地来 (大老遠地來) "come from very far away")
门前清 (門前清)	**ménqiánqīng**	lit. "clear before the door," finish drinking alcoholic beverages before leaving [EX]
七喜	**Qīxǐ**	Seven-Up® [N]
色香味	**sè xiāng wèi**	color, aroma, and taste [PH]
水	**shuǐ**	water [N]
汽水	**qìshuǐ(r)**	soda [N]
算	**suàn**	consider as; be considered as being [V]
以	**yǐ**	take [CV] (e.g., 以茶代酒 "substitute tea for liquor")

Reading Exercises (Simplified Characters) 简体字

Now practice reading the new characters and words for this lesson in context in sentences, conversations, and narratives. Be sure to refer to the Notes at the end of this lesson, and make use of the accompanying audio disc to hear and practice correct pronunciation, phrasing, and intonation.

A. SENTENCES 句子

Read out loud each of the following sentences, which include all the new characters of this lesson. The first time you read a sentence, focus special attention on the characters and words that are new to you, reminding yourself of their pronunciation and meaning. The second time, aim to comprehend the overall meaning of the sentence.

一、张老师明天有一点事不能来上课，所以何老师要替她代课。

二、小李虽然长得好看，也很有钱，可是他一点儿都不快乐。

On the Telephone

COMMUNICATIVE OBJECTIVES

Once you've mastered this unit, you'll be able to use Chinese to read and write about:

1. Making and taking telephone calls.

2. Telephone talk.

3. Leaving a message for someone who isn't there.

4. Calling on the telephone to inquire about an apartment that has been advertised.

5. The Yellow River of China.

6. Chinese tea.

7. Common Chinese sayings containing the verb 怕 "be afraid of."

"Want to Go to the Show?"

小王，这个星期六晚上有
音乐会，不知道你有没有空儿？
(小王，這個星期六晚上有音樂會，
不知道你有沒有空兒？)

 New Characters and Words

Study the six characters below and the common words written with them, paying careful attention to each character's pronunciation, meaning, and structure, as well as similar-looking characters. After you've studied a character, turn to the *Practice Essentials* volume and practice writing it on the practice sheet, making sure to follow the correct stroke order and direction as you pronounce it out loud and think of its meaning.

433 坏(壞)   **huài**   bad

Radical is 土 **tǔ** "earth" (343). The colloquial name for this radical is 土字旁 **tǔzìpáng** "side made up of the character 土." Notice that the top horizontal line of 土 is shorter than the bottom line. Also notice that when used as a radical, the bottom line of 土 slants up toward the right, so as not to get in the way of the other component. Phonetic of the traditional character is 裹 **huái**. Distinguish 坏 (壞) from 不 **bù** (63) and 让 (讓) **ràng** (406).

坏 (壞)	**huài**	be bad [SV]
坏人 (壞人)	**huài rén**	bad person
坏事 (壞事)	**huài shì**	bad thing, evil deed
坏 (壞)	**-huài**	bad; extremely [RE]
忙坏 (忙壞)	**mánghuài**	become extremely busy [RC]
把我忙坏了 (把我忙壞了)	**bǎ wǒ mánghuàile**	made me extremely busy

434 提   **tí**   mention

Radical is 手 **shǒu** "hand" (305), which at the left side of a character is written as 扌 and is referred to colloquially as 提手 **tíshǒu** "raised hand." The other component is 是 **shì** (76). Distinguish 提 from 是 and 题 (題) **tí** (291).

提	**tí**	mention [V]
别提了 (別提了)	**Bié tíle!**	"Don't mention it!" [IE]
提前	**tíqián**	move up (a time or date) [V]

435 际 (際)   **jì**   border, boundary, edge

Radical is 阜 **fù** "mound," which is written 阝 when occurring at the left-hand side of a character. This radical is referred to colloquially as 左耳旁 **zuǒ'ěrpáng** "side made up of a left ear."

国际 (國際)	**guójì**	international [AT]
国际关系 (國際關係)	**guójì guānxi**	international relations [PH]
国际学校 (國際學校)	**guójì xuéxiào**	international school
国际和平 (國際和平)	**guójì hépíng**	international peace

436 音   **yīn**   sound

This character is itself a radical and a phonetic. Distinguish 音 from 言 **yán** (336), 意 **yì** (347), and 高 **gāo** (62).

音乐 (音樂)	**yīnyuè**	music [N] (Note that 乐 [樂] is here pronounced **yuè**, not **lè**.)
音乐会 (音樂會)	**yīnyuèhuì**	musical performance, concert [N]

437 空   **kōng**   empty; air, sky

　　　　　kòng   free time

Radical is 穴 **xué** "cave" or "hole." Phonetic is 工 **gōng** (154). The whole character can serve as a phonetic in other characters, e.g., in the character 控 as used in the word 控告 **kònggào** "accuse." Distinguish 空 from 工 and 穿 **chuān** (353).

空气 (空氣)	**kōngqì**	air, atmosphere [N]
空	**kòng(r)**	free time [N]
有空	**yǒukòng(r)**	have free time, be free [VO]

438 趣   **qù**   interest; interesting

Radical is 走 **zǒu** "walk" (70). The colloquial name for this radical is 走字旁 **zǒuzìpáng** "side made up of the character 走." When 走 serves as the radical in another character, its last stroke is lengthened, with the component on the right side placed above the last stroke of 走. Phonetic is 取 **qǔ** "take." Distinguish 趣 from 走, 起 **qǐ** (177), and 越 **yuè** (265).

兴趣 (興趣)	**xìngqu**	interest [N]
对⋯有兴趣 (對⋯有興趣)	**duì...yǒu xìngqu**	be interested in... [PT]
对⋯感兴趣 (對⋯感興趣)	**duì...gǎn xìngqu**	be interested in... [PT]

New Words in ISC 17-1 Written with Characters You Already Know

打通	dǎtōng	call and get through [RC]
打不通	dǎbutōng	call but not be able to get through [RC]
定	dìng	settle; decide [V]
感	gǎn	feel [V]
会 (會)	huì	gathering, meeting [N]
没人接 (沒人接)	méi rén jiē	no one is answering [PH]
市内电话 (市內電話)	shìnèi diànhuà	local telephone call [PH]
一言为定 (一言爲定)	yì-yán-wéi-dìng	be agreed with one word [EX]
总机 (總機)	zǒngjī	switchboard [N]

Reading Exercises (Simplified Characters) 简体字

Now practice reading the new characters and words for this lesson in context in sentences, conversations, and narratives. Be sure to refer to the Notes at the end of this lesson, and make use of the accompanying audio disc to hear and practice correct pronunciation, phrasing, and intonation.

A. SENTENCES 句子

Read out loud each of the following sentences, which include all the new characters of this lesson. The first time you read a sentence, focus special attention on the characters and words that are new to you, reminding yourself of their pronunciation and meaning. The second time, aim to comprehend the overall meaning of the sentence.

一、老高对音乐很有兴趣，一个月去听好几次音乐会。

二、最近几年，北京市的空气越来越坏了，一定要想个办法。

三、那位法国文学专家对中国解放后的文学特别感兴趣。

四、下个星期四在北京有一个国际大会，听说有三百多人打算参加。

五、我知道我做错了，可是还是请你不要跟别人提这件事，好吗？

六、今天晚上的音乐会是八点钟开始，我们应该提前一个钟头到比较好。

七、他们的儿子是小留学生，听说在美国交了坏朋友，自己也学坏了。

八、小方，我有一件事想请你替我办，不知道你这个星期日早上有没有空？

九、北京的国际机场叫"首都机场"，离北京市中心大概有三十公里左右。

十、王大海又把我给气坏了，你以后别跟我提他的名字，我真受不了他！

Calling About an Advertisement for an Apartment

我在报上看到你们的广告……（我在報上看到你們的廣告……）

 New Characters and Words

Study the six characters below and the common words written with them, paying careful attention to each character's pronunciation, meaning, and structure, as well as similar-looking characters. After you've studied a character, turn to the *Practice Essentials* volume and practice writing it on the practice sheet, making sure to follow the correct stroke order and direction as you pronounce it out loud and think of its meaning.

445 声（聲）　**shēng**　　sound; tone

Radical of the simplified form is 士 **shì** "scholar." Radical of the traditional form is 耳 **ěr** "ear."

声音（聲音）	**shēngyīn**	sound; voice [N]
大声（大聲）	**dà shēng**	in a loud voice [PH]
小声（小聲）	**xiǎo shēng**	in a low voice; quietly [PH]
四声（四聲）	**sìshēng**	the four tones (of Mandarin Chinese) [N]
第一声（第一聲）	**dìyīshēng**	first tone [N]
第二声（第二聲）	**dì'èrshēng**	second tone [N]
第三声（第三聲）	**dìsānshēng**	third tone [N]
第四声（第四聲）	**dìsìshēng**	fourth tone [N]
轻声（輕聲）	**qīngshēng**	neutral tone [N]
声调（聲調）	**shēngdiào**	tone [N] (Note that 调 [調] [407], which you learned as **tiáo**, is here pronounced **diào**.)

446 立   **lì**   stand; establish

This character is both a radical and a phonetic. It represents a person "standing" 立 on the ground. It is a radical in 站 **zhàn** "stand" (248), a phonetic in 粒 **lì** (measure for grains of rice), and a component of 位 **wèi** (polite measure for people) (98). Distinguish 立 from 位 and 站.

立刻	**lìkè**	immediately [A]

447 红（紅）   **hóng**   red

Radical is 纟（絲）**sī** "silk." When at the left side of a character, this radical is referred to colloquially as 绞丝旁（絞絲旁）**jiǎosīpáng** "side made up of twisted silk" and is written as 纟（糹）. Phonetic is 工 **gōng** "work" (154). Distinguish 红（紅）from 工 and 空 **kōng** (437).

红（紅）	**hóng**	be red [SV]
红色（紅色）	**hóngsè**	the color red [N]
⊙红酒（紅酒）	**hóngjiǔ**	red wine [N]

448 黄（黃）   **huáng**   yellow

This character is itself both a radical and a phonetic. It occurs as a phonetic in various characters, e.g., in the character 磺 as it is used in the word 硫磺 **liúhuáng** "sulphur." Distinguish 黄（黃）from 由 **yóu** (383).

黄（黃）	**Huáng**	Huang [SN]
黄（黃）	**huáng**	be yellow [SV]
黄色（黃色）	**huángsè**	the color yellow [N]
⊙黄河（黃河）	**Huáng Hé**	Yellow River [PW]
⊙黄海（黃海）	**Huáng Hǎi**	Yellow Sea (between China and the Korean Peninsula) [PW]

449 图（圖）   **tú**   drawing, illustration, map, chart

Radical is 囗 **wéi** "enclose." This radical is referred to colloquially as 围字框（圍字框）**wéizìkuàng** "frame made up of the character 围（圍）." The other part of the simplified form is 冬 **dōng** "winter." Distinguish simplified 图 from simplified 因 **yīn** (181).

地图（地圖）	**dìtú**	map [N]
一张地图（一張地圖）	**yìzhāng dìtú**	a map
图书馆（圖書館）	**túshūguǎn**	library [PW]
⊙图（圖）	**tú**	diagram, chart; illustration [N]

450 领（領）   **lǐng**   lead; head

Radical is 页（頁）**yè** "page." Phonetic is 令 **lìng** "order." Distinguish 领（領）from 冷 **lěng** (272).

领事（領事）	**lǐngshì**	consul [N]
总领事（總領事）	**zǒnglǐngshì**	consul general [N]
领事馆（領事館）	**lǐngshìguǎn**	consulate [PW]
总领事馆（總領事館）	**zǒnglǐngshìguǎn**	consulate general [PW]

New Words in ISC 17-3 Written with Characters You Already Know

报 (報)	**bào**	newspaper [N]
出去	**-chūqu**	out [RE] (e.g., 走出去 "go out")
广告 (廣告)	**guǎnggào**	advertisement [N]
间 (間)	**jiān**	(measure for rooms) [M]
客房	**kèfáng**	living room [PW]
空调 (空調)	**kōngtiáo**	air conditioning [N]
是的	**shìde**	"yes" [IE]
清楚	**-qīngchu**	clear [RE]
听清楚 (聽清楚)	**tīngqīngchu**	hear clearly [RC]
听不清楚 (聽不清楚)	**tīngbuqīngchu**	can't hear clearly [RC]
阳台 (陽台)	**yángtái**	porch [PW]
最好	**zuìhǎo**	it would be best; had better [MA]

Reading Exercises (Simplified Characters) 简体字

Now practice reading the new characters and words for this lesson in context in sentences, conversations, and narratives. Be sure to refer to the Notes at the end of this lesson, and make use of the accompanying audio disc to hear and practice correct pronunciation, phrasing, and intonation.

A. SENTENCES 句子

Read out loud each of the following sentences, which include all the new characters of this lesson. The first time you read a sentence, focus special attention on the characters and words that are new to you, reminding yourself of their pronunciation and meaning. The second time, aim to comprehend the overall meaning of the sentence.

一、为什么中国的中国地图和台湾的中国地图不一样？

二、领事告诉她最好两、三天之内回领事馆再办那件事。

三、那位美国领事中国话讲得好极了，他的四声也特别准。

四、广州的广东话有七个声调，不过香港的广东话只有六个声调。

五、我需要买书、报、几百张白纸、两个本子和一张北京市地图。

六、图书馆的空调冷死了；外头一点儿也不热，根本不需要开空调。

七、这个房子只有两个房间；我们是不是应该换一个大一点儿的房子
　　住呢？

八、那是什么声音？你听到了没有？好像是什么小动物的样子，最好
　　小心一点儿！

九、对不起，这儿是图书馆，请您让您的儿子小声一点儿说话，要不然
　　我们就得请你们立刻出去！

十、王大海说晚上要请客，叫我立刻去买汽水、红酒、白酒、水果和
　　一些小吃。

B. CONVERSATIONS 对话

Read out loud the following conversations, including the name or role of the person speaking. If possible, find a partner or partners and each of you play a role. Then switch roles, so you get practice reading all of the lines. In the first conversation, notice the backchannel comments (cf. BSC 7-4: 6C).

一、

美国人：我在报上看到你们的广告……

台湾人：对不起，听不清楚。请你说大声一点。

美国人：我说我在报上看到你们的广告（是的。），有家具要卖（对，对。）。不知道卖了没有？

台湾人：还没有，但是有人来看过，好像满有兴趣的。如果你想来看的话，最好早一点。

二、

黄美金：我在找房子住。你觉得这个广告怎么样？

林　会：我看……我觉得看起来满不错的。离大学很近，客房特别大，而且还有书房、阳台什么的。带家具跟电话，每个月五千块，其实这也不算贵。

黄美金：那，你觉得我现在应该怎么办？

林　会：你应该立刻打电话问还有没有。要是还有的话，最好早一点去看，然后再决定。如果房东说还有的话，我愿意跟你一起去看。

三、

毛小姐：你觉得我穿黄色的鞋好看还是穿红色的好看？

简小姐：我觉得黄色的、红色的都不太好看。

毛小姐：是吗？那你说我应当穿什么鞋呢？

简小姐：我看你还不如买一双黑色的鞋。

毛小姐：好吧，我就听你的了。（对鞋店的店员）先生，我需要买一双黑色的高跟鞋，我穿三七号，不知道你们有没有？

店　员：有，这双刚上市，您穿穿看。

Chinese University of Hong Kong

453 怕   **pà**   fear

Radical is 心 **xīn** "heart" (262), since "fear" is an emotion. When at the left side of a character, this radical is referred to colloquially as 心字旁 **xīnzìpáng** "side made up of the character 心" and is written as 忄. Phonetic is 白 **bái** "white" (328). Distinguish 怕 from 白.

怕	**pà**	be afraid; fear [V]
可怕	**kěpà**	be frightful, terrible, horrible [SV]

454 树（樹）   **shù**   tree

Radical is the pictograph 木 **mù** "tree." This radical is referred to colloquially as 木字旁 **mùzìpáng** "side made up of the character 木." Note that when 木 is written at the left of a character as a radical, its last stroke is shortened so that it doesn't collide with the component to its right. Contrast simplified 树 with simplified 对 **duì** (108).

树（樹）	**shù**	tree [N]
◉ 茶树（茶樹）	**cháshù**	tea tree, tea plant [N]
◉ 树林（樹林）	**shùlín**	woods, forest [N]

455 花   **huā**   flower

Radical is 艹 **cǎo** "grass," which is written 草 when it occurs as an independent word (456). When it occurs as a radical at the top of a character, the "grass" radical is written as ⁺⁺ and is then known as 草字头（草字頭）**cǎozìtóu** "top made up of the character 草." Phonetic is 化 **huà** "change" (479).

花	**huā(r)**	flower [N]
菜花	**càihuā**	cauliflower [N]

456 草   **cǎo**   grass

This character itself involves a common radical. The radical is 艹 **cǎo** "grass," which is written 草 when it occurs as an independent word. When it occurs as a radical at the top of a character, the "grass" radical is written as ⁺⁺ and is then known as 草字头（草字頭）**cǎozìtóu** "top made up of the character 草." Phonetic is 早 **zǎo** "early" (259). Distinguish 草 from 早.

草	**cǎo**	grass [N]
一根草	**yìgēn cǎo**	a blade of grass
花草	**huācǎo**	flowers and grass [N]

New Words in ISC 17-4 Written with Characters You Already Know

别人（別人）	**biérén**	another person; others [PR]
电（電）	**diàn**	electricity [N]
方便	**fāngbian**	be convenient [SV]
书桌（書桌）	**shūzhuō(r)**	desk [N]
一些	**yìxiē**	some [NU+M]
种（種）	**zhòng**	plant [V] (Note that 320 种 [種] is here pronounced **zhòng**, not **zhǒng**.)

Reading Exercises (Simplified Characters) 简体字

Now practice reading the new characters and words for this lesson in context in sentences, conversations, and narratives. Be sure to refer to the Notes at the end of this lesson, and make use of the accompanying audio disc to hear and practice correct pronunciation, phrasing, and intonation.

A. SENTENCES 句子

Read out loud each of the following sentences, which include all the new characters of this lesson. The first time you read a sentence, focus special attention on the characters and words that are new to you, reminding yourself of their pronunciation and meaning. The second time, aim to comprehend the overall meaning of the sentence.

一、学校门口儿最近种了好多红花儿，实在是好看！

二、你怕不怕晚上一个人在对面的那片树林里走路？我可不敢！

三、菜单上的菜，每道二十五元，米饭和酒另外算，茶水不要钱。

四、那个大城不怎么好看，应该在路上多种一些树、花儿跟草。

五、那个房子好像十年没有人住了，外面的草长得这么高，有一点儿可怕。

六、有时候有中国人说"不太方便"，其实他的意思是"根本不可能"。

七、听说在香港有的男人很坏，在家里有太太，在外面还另外有"小太太"。

八、那个房间只有一张单人床，不过我们需要的是一张双人床，能不能换另
外一个房间？

九、我们家人最喜欢吃的两道家常菜一个是用菜花做的，另外一个是用白菜
做的。

十、王大海的同学小林实在很可怕，他喝酒以后常常大声叫，有时候还会
打人。

B. CONVERSATIONS 对话

Read out loud the following conversations, including the name or role of the person speaking. If possible, find a partner or partners and each of you play a role. Then switch roles, so you get practice reading all of the lines.

一、

美国人：房子有没有家具、电话？

台湾人：有一些简单的家具，像床、饭桌、书桌什么的。没有电话。

美国人：一个月大概是多少？

台湾人：一个月三万块，水电另外算。

美国人：那我什么时候来比较方便？

台湾人：你可以今天晚上过来，明天早上也可以。再晚就怕别人已经决
定了。

美国人：我今天晚上六点左右到，方不方便？

台湾人：没问题。贵姓？

美国人：我姓黄，黄京文。

台湾人：好的，黄小姐，六点钟见。

美国人：再见。

Notes 注解

A2. ⊙片 **piàn** "section," "stretch" or "expanse" **[M]**. 那片树林里 (那片樹林裡) means "in that expanse of woods." 一片大海 would mean "a broad expanse of ocean."

A3. ⊙茶水 **cháshuǐ** "brewed tea" **[N]**

A4. 不怎么好看 (不怎麼好看) "not particularly attractive"

C1. ⊙热带 (熱帶) **rèdài** "tropical zone" or "the tropics" **[PW]**

C3. ⊙品种 (品種) **pǐnzhǒng** "variety" or "species" **[N]**

C4. ⊙红茶 (紅茶) **hóngchá** "black tea" **[N]**. What people in the West call "black tea" is known as "red tea" in China.

C5. ◆绿 (綠) **lǜ** "be green" **[SV]**

C6. ⊙花茶 **huāchá** "flower-scented green tea" **[N]**. A common example of this would be jasmine tea.

C7. ⊙花草茶 **huācǎo chá** "herbal tea" **[N]**

C8. ⊙特点 (特點) **tèdiǎn** "characteristic" or "trait" **[N]**

C9. ⊙香味 **xiāngwèi** "aroma," "fragrance" or "scent" **[N]**

D1. There is a whole series of sayings in Chinese that begin 天不怕, 地不怕, 就怕…… "(I/We/They) don't fear heaven, don't fear earth, only fear…" that end with whatever it is that one is really concerned about or wishes to emphasize. Sometimes, instead of 就怕, the words 只怕—which have the same meaning— are used instead. Many of these sayings (D1-D7 above) poke fun at the poor Mandarin spoken by Chinese from other parts of China, or by foreigners. In fact, there used to be a saying 天不怕，地不怕，就 怕洋鬼子说中国话！(天不怕，地不怕，就怕洋鬼子說中國話！) "Fear neither heaven nor earth, fear only foreign devils speaking Chinese!" However, that saying, containing the noun 洋鬼子 **yángguǐzi** "foreign devil," is now considered crude and is generally no longer used except humorously.

D5. ⊙温州 (溫州) **Wēnzhōu** "Wenzhou" (city in Zhejiang Province) **[PW]**. The dialect of 温州 (溫州), which is a subdialect of the Wu dialect, is notorious for its difficulty for Mandarin speakers.

D8. The Roman letter abbreviations CFO (Chief Financial Officer) and CEO (Chief Executive Officer) are fairly widely used in Chinese newspapers, magazines, and business reports (cf. BWC 2-4, note A5).

D9. ⊙停电 (停電) **tíngdiàn** "the power stops," "power failure" **[VO]**. The whole saying above makes fun of the younger generation of Chinese, many of whom—like their counterparts in other countries—possess no end of electronic devices, which cease operating in case of prolonged power failure.

D10. ◆辣 **là** "be peppery hot" **[SV]**. The provinces listed above are some of the ones whose cuisines are particularly spicy hot. There are various versions of this saying, some also including the province of Jiangxi (IWC 14-2: 2B).

Visiting People (I)

COMMUNICATIVE OBJECTIVES

Once you've mastered this unit, you'll be able to use Chinese to read and write about:

1. Making an informal visit to a Chinese friend's home.

2. Paying a formal call on someone at their residence to request a favor.

3. Apologizing for being late for an appointment.

4. Accepting or declining invitations.

5. The famous story of Kong Rong, who let his brothers have the best pears, as well as other passages on the Gang of Four, Sino-Japanese relations, parenting, driving, smoking, learning Chinese, and various aspects of Chinese culture.

Visiting a Friend at Home

小牛，你进来坐吧。
他马上就来。
（小牛，你進來坐吧。
他馬上就來。）

小李在家吗？
（小李在家嗎？）

 New Characters and Words

Study the six characters below and the common words written with them, paying careful attention to each character's pronunciation, meaning, and structure, as well as similar-looking characters. After you've studied a character, turn to the *Practice Essentials* volume and practice writing it on the practice sheet, making sure to follow the correct stroke order and direction as you pronounce it out loud and think of its meaning.

457 孩   **hái**   child

Radical is 子 **zǐ** "son" (155). Phonetic is 亥 **hài** , which is the last of the twelve earthly branches. Distinguish 孩 from 刻 **kè** (116) and 该 (該) **gāi** (356).

孩子	**háizi**	child [N]
男孩子	**nánháizi**	boy [N]
女孩子	**nǚháizi**	girl [N]
男孩儿 (男孩兒)	**nánhái r**	boy [N]
女孩儿 (女孩兒)	**nǚhái r**	girl [N]
小孩	**xiǎohái**	child [N]
小孩儿 (小孩兒)	**xiǎohái r**	child [N]
小孩子	**xiǎo háizi**	small child [PH]
坏孩子 (壞孩子)	**huài háizi**	bad child

458 马(馬)   **mǎ**   horse

This character is itself a radical. It is a picture of a horse with four feet. Distinguish simplified 马 from simplified 写 **xiě** "write" (202), and distinguish traditional 馬 from traditional 魚 **yú** (411).

马 (馬)	**Mǎ**	Ma [SN]
司马 (司馬)	**Sīmǎ**	Sima (one of the few common two-syllable Chinese surnames) [SN]
马上 (馬上)	**mǎshàng**	immediately, right away [A]

459 相   **xiāng**   mutually

Radical is 目 **mù** "eye" (543). The character 相 frequently occurs as a phonetic within other characters, e.g., 想 **xiǎng** (319). Distinguish 相 from 想 and 怕 **pà** (453).

| ◉相当 (相當) | **xiāngdāng** | rather, pretty, quite [A] |

460 管   **guǎn**   control; manage

Radical is 竹 **zhú** "bamboo." The colloquial name for this radical is 竹字头 (竹字頭) **zhúzìtóu** "top made up of the character 竹." When it is a radical, the third and sixth strokes of 竹 are shortened. Phonetic is 官 **guān** "official" (589). Distinguish 管 from 馆 (館) **guǎn** (429).

管	**Guǎn**	Guan [SN]
管	**guǎn**	control, manage, administer [V]
别管我！(別管我！)	**Bié guǎn wǒ!**	"Don't bother me!", "Leave me alone!"

461 严(嚴)   **yán**   stern, severe

Radical of the simplified form is 一 **yī** "one" (1). Radical of the traditional form is 口 **kǒu** "mouth" (140). Distinguish simplified 严 from simplified 广 **guǎng** (27), simplified 问 **wèn** (75), and 向 **xiàng** (493).

| ◉严 (嚴) | **Yán** | Yan (also Om or Eom, a Korean surname) [SN] |

462 重   **zhòng**   heavy; weight

Radical is 里 **lǐ** "mile" (163). The whole character 重 occurs as a phonetic in other characters, e.g., in 种 (種) **zhǒng** "kind" (320). Distinguish 重 from 种 (種).

重	**zhòng**	be heavy [SV]
你有多重？	**Nǐ yǒu duō zhòng?**	"How much do you weigh?"
◉严重 (嚴重)	**yánzhòng**	be serious, grave [SV]

New Words in ISC 18-1 Written with Characters You Already Know

急	**jí**	be in a hurry [SV]
忙	**máng**	be busy with (something) [V]
牛	**Niú**	Niu (lit. "cow") [SN]
外公	**wàigōng**	grandfather (maternal) [N]
问好 (問好)	**wènhǎo**	send one's regards to [RC]

屋子	**wūzi**	room [N]
小朋友	**xiǎo péngyou**	child [PH]
这 (這)	**zhè**	right away [A]
住	**-zhù**	firm [RE] (e.g., 拿不住 **nábuzhù** "can't hold on to firmly")
总是 (總是)	**zǒngshi**	always [A]

Reading Exercises (Simplified Characters) 简体字

Now practice reading the new characters and words for this lesson in context in sentences, conversations, and narratives. Be sure to refer to the Notes at the end of this lesson, and make use of the accompanying audio disc to hear and practice correct pronunciation, phrasing, and intonation.

A. SENTENCES 句子

Read out loud each of the following sentences, which include all the new characters of this lesson. The first time you read a sentence, focus special attention on the characters and words that are new to you, reminding yourself of their pronunciation and meaning. The second time, aim to comprehend the overall meaning of the sentence.

一、司马，你回国请别忘了替我问你爸爸、妈妈好！

二、有的人总是爱管别人，其实他们应该先管好自己。

三、我们往前走了没有几步，就到了一条相当深的河。

四、这件行李怎么这么重啊！好像里头放了很多石头的样子！

五、虽然其他人都把这件事看得很严重，但是司马先生一点儿也不紧张。

六、这么严重的问题需要马上解决！你怎么还先上茶馆跟朋友喝茶去了呢？

七、老白和他爱人住的房子很小，只有两间屋子，他们根本不可能生两、三个孩子。

八、虽然中美关系最近几年好像相当不错，但还有不少问题，有的问题不太要紧，有的相当严重。

九、虽然大多数人总是说生男生女都一样，其实不少人还是觉得如果只能生一个孩子，那么生男孩子比较好。

十、除了王大海之外，其他参加酒席的客人，就是严东山、李想、管二妹、司马红、马立国和牛小花，已经全来了。

B. CONVERSATIONS 对话

Read out loud the following conversations, including the name or role of the person speaking. If possible, find a partner or partners and each of you play a role. Then switch roles, so you get practice reading all of the lines.

一、

小牛　：小李在家吗？

李太太：在，在。小牛，你进来坐吧，他马上就来。先喝点儿茶吧。

小李　：小牛，对不起，我正忙着呢，这就完了。我马上就来。

小牛　：小李，你忙你的，别急。

二、
小严: 小马, 我问你, 你有多高?
小马: 我一米八二。
小严: 你有多重?
小马: 我九十八公斤, 可是……你为什么问我这些问题?

三、
小学一年级的管老师: 小朋友们, 校长来了, 快问校长好!
小朋友们: 校长好!
严校长　: 管老师早, 小朋友们好!

四、
严小姐: 你觉得这儿的气候怎么样?
马先生: 这儿的气候啊? 我觉得……相当好, 还可以吧。
严小姐: 真的吗? 我觉得这个地方最近几个星期热得要死, 又那么干,
　　　　我真受不了!
马先生: 没有你说的那么严重吧!

C. NARRATIVES 短文

Read the following narratives, paying special attention to punctuation and overall structure. The first time you read a narrative, read it out loud. The second time, read silently and try to gradually increase your reading speed. Always think of the meaning of what you're reading.

一、最近几年, 越来越多的孩子不好好儿地在学校里学习, 这是不是已经成了相当严重的问题了呢? 可能会有人说, 这根本不是什么问题, 大家都想得太多, 管得也太多了。但是我就觉得如果我们这些做爸爸、妈妈的不管自己孩子的事儿, 那么还有谁会去管呢? 我觉得, 孩子学习的问题不能不管。孩子一有问题, 就要马上解决!

二、我的外公六十九岁了, 马上就要七十岁了。他老人家住在台湾台南市, 离台南火车站不太远。我平常每年六月都回台湾去看他。我最爱我的外公, 因为他对我相当好。记得我小时候, 外公常常带我去菜市场买菜。他不管有多忙, 总是会找时间请我吃一点儿台南的小吃或是给我买一点儿美国没有的小东西。我非常高兴我有那么好的一位外公!

三、孔融让梨

差不多一千九百年以前有个小孩子叫孔融。他有五个哥哥，一个弟弟。有一天，孔融的爸爸买了一些梨。回到家，他叫孩子们过来吃。他爸爸说："让孔融先选吧！"孔融走过去，拿了一个最小的梨。大家都觉得很奇怪。他爸爸问他："你为什么选了小的呢？"孔融说："我年纪小，应该吃小的，大的让给哥哥们吃吧！"他爸爸听了以后很高兴，又问："那弟弟比你还小啊？"孔融说："我比弟弟大，我是哥哥，我应该把一个大的留给弟弟吃。"那一年，孔融才四岁。后来孔融成为了一个很有学问的人。

Reading Exercises (Traditional Characters) 繁體字

A. SENTENCES 句子

Read out loud each of the following sentences, which include all the new characters of this lesson. The first time you read a sentence, focus special attention on the characters and words that are new to you, reminding yourself of their pronunciation and meaning. The second time, aim to comprehend the overall meaning of the sentence.

一、司馬，你回國請別忘了替我問你爸爸、媽媽好！

二、有的人總是愛管別人，其實他們應該先管好自己。

三、我們往前走了沒有幾步，就到了一條相當深的河。

四、這件行李怎麼這麼重啊！好像裡頭放了很多石頭的樣子！

五、雖然其他人都把這件事看得很嚴重，但是司馬先生一點兒也不緊張。

六、這麼嚴重的問題需要馬上解決！你怎麼還先上茶館跟朋友喝茶去了呢？

七、老白和他愛人住的房子很小，只有兩間屋子，他們根本不可能生兩、三個孩子。

八、雖然中美關係最近幾年好像相當不錯，但還有不少問題，有的問題不太要緊，有的相當嚴重。

九、雖然大多數人總是說生男生女都一樣，其實不少人還是覺得如果只能生一個孩子，那麼生男孩子比較好。

十、除了王大海之外，其他參加酒席的客人，就是嚴東山、李想、管二妹、司馬紅、馬立國和牛小花，已經全來了。

B. CONVERSATIONS 對話

Read out loud the following conversations, including the name or role of the person speaking. If possible, find a partner or partners and each of you play a role. Then switch roles, so you get practice reading all of the lines.

一、

小牛：小李在家嗎？

李太太：在，在。小牛，你進來坐吧，他馬上就來。先喝點兒茶吧。

小李：小牛，對不起，我正忙著呢，這就完了。我馬上就來。

小牛：小李，你忙你的，別急。

二、

小嚴：小馬，我問你，你有多高？

小馬：我一米八二。

小嚴：你有多重？

小馬：我九十八公斤，可是⋯⋯你為什麼問我這些問題？

三、

小學一年級的管老師：小朋友們，校長來了，快問校長好！

小朋友們：校長好！

嚴校長：管老師早，小朋友們好！

四、

嚴小姐：你覺得這兒的氣候怎麼樣？

馬先生：這兒的氣候啊？我覺得⋯⋯相當好，還可以吧。

嚴小姐：真的嗎？我覺得這個地方最近幾個星期熱得要死，又那麼乾，我真受不了！

馬先生：沒有你說的那麼嚴重吧！

C. NARRATIVES 短文

Read the following narratives, paying special attention to punctuation and overall structure. The first time you read a narrative, read it out loud. The second time, read silently and try to gradually increase your reading speed. Always think of the meaning of what you're reading.

一、

最近幾年，越來越多的孩子不好好兒地在學校裡學習，這是不是已經成了相當嚴重的問題了呢？可能會有人說，這根本不是甚麼問題，大家都想得太多，管得也太多了。但是我就覺得如果我們這些做爸爸、媽媽的不管自己孩子的事兒，那麼還有誰會去管呢？我覺得，孩子學習的問題不能不管。那孩子一有問題，就要馬上解決！

二、

我的外公六十九歲了，馬上就要七十歲了。他老人家住在台灣台南市，離台南火車站不太遠。我平常每年六月都回台灣去看他。我最愛我的外公，因為他對我相當好。記得我小時候，外公常常帶我去菜市場買菜。他不管有多忙，總是會找時間請我吃一點兒台南的小吃或是給我買一點兒美國沒有的小東西。我非常高興我有那麼好的一位外公！

三、孔融讓梨

差不多一千九百年以前有個小孩子叫孔融。他有五個哥哥，一個弟弟。有一天，孔融的爸爸買了一些梨。回到家，他叫孩子們過來吃。他爸爸說：「讓孔融先選吧！」孔融走過去，拿了一個最小的梨。大家都覺得很奇怪。他爸爸問他：「你為什麼選了小的呢？」孔融說：「我年紀小，應該吃小的，大的讓給哥哥們吃吧！」他爸爸聽了以後很高興，又問：「那弟弟比你還小啊？」孔融說：「我比弟弟大，我是哥哥，我應該把一個大的留給弟弟吃。」那一年，孔融才四歲。後來孔融成為了一個很有學問的人。

Notes 注解

A3. 没有几步 (沒有幾步) "a couple of steps"

A9. 生男生女都一样 (生男生女都一樣) lit. "Giving birth to boys or giving birth to girls is all the same", which in more idiomatic English means "It is all the same whether you give birth to a boy or give birth to a girl."

C1a. 不好好儿地在学校里学习 (不好好兒地在學校裡學習) "don't learn well in school." The use of reduplicated stative verbs, such as 好好儿地 (好好兒地) "well", as adverbs is taken up in ISC 19-2: 2B.

C1b. ⦿成 chéng "become" [V]

C1c.   ◉ 做 **zuò** "be," "act as," or "serve as" [V]. 我们这些做爸爸、妈妈的 (我們這些做爸爸、媽媽的) lit. "We, these who serve as dads and moms," or more colloquially "We, as parents."

C2a.   ◉ 老人家 **lǎorenjia** "elderly person" [N]. 老人家 is a polite way of referring to an older person, especially one's parent or grandparent. 他老人家 here could be translated rather literally as "He, elderly gentleman that he is."

C2b.   记得我小时候 (記得我小時候) "I remember when I was small." The verb 记得 (記得) is often used this way, without an explicit subject 我.

C2c.   ◉ 不管 **bùguǎn** "no matter, regardless" [PT].

C3a.   ◉ 孔 **Kǒng** [SN]. 孔 is the surname of several famous people in Chinese history, including 孔子 **Kǒngzǐ** "Confucius" and 孔融 **Kǒng Róng**, the main character in this narrative. Kong Rong (153–208), a direct descendant of Confucius, was a famous scholar, politician, and warlord of the Eastern Han Dynasty. The story about an episode during Kong Rong's childhood that you read here, known as 孔融让梨 (孔融讓梨) "Kong Rong Gives Up A Pear," is still read today by elementary school children in mainland China, Hong Kong, Taiwan, and Singapore to teach children the importance of modesty and kindness toward others.

C3b.   You have learned 让 (讓) (406) with the meaning "let" or "cause." In this narrative, 让 (讓) occurs a total of three times: twice with a new meaning of "give up," "yield," or "let someone else have something"; and once in the sense of "let," which you are already familiar with.

C3c.   ◆ 梨 **lí(r)** "pear" [N]

C3d.   孩子们 (孩子們) "children." 孩子 is one of the relatively few nouns referring to people that frequently occurs with the pluralizing suffix 们 (們). Other nouns that commonly take 们 (們) include 朋友们 (朋友們) "friends" and 同学们 (同學們) "classmates." Later in this narrative you'll also encounter 哥哥们 (哥哥們) "older brothers." We have previously discussed the relatively new Chinese word 人们 (人們) (IWC 16-4: A7b).

C3e.   ◆ 选 (選) **xuǎn** "choose" or "select" [V]

C3f.   ◆ 奇怪 **qíguài** "be strange" [SV]

C3g.   那弟弟比你还小啊？(那弟弟比你還小啊？) "In that case, your little brother is even smaller than you (so why didn't you leave the smallest pear for him)?"

C3h.   ◉ 才 **cái** "only" [A]

C3i.   ◉ 成为 (成為) **chéngwéi** "become" [V+PV]

C3j.   ◉ 学问 (學問) **xuéwèn** "learning," "knowledge," or "scholarship" [N]

PART 2

Visiting a Friend at Home (cont.)

小牛，在这儿吃饭吧！
(小牛，在這兒吃飯吧！)

不用了。等会儿我跟
小李谈完了，就回去。
(不用了。等會兒我跟小李
談完了，就回去。)

New Characters and Words

Study the six characters below and the common words written with them, paying careful attention to each character's pronunciation, meaning, and structure, as well as similar-looking characters. After you've studied a character, turn to the *Practice Essentials* volume and practice writing it on the practice sheet, making sure to follow the correct stroke order and direction as you pronounce it out loud and think of its meaning.

463 谈 (談)　　**tán**　　chat, talk

Radical is 讠 (言) **yán** "speech" (336). The colloquial name for this radical is 言字旁 **yánzìpáng** "side made up of the character 言." Phonetic is 炎 **yán** "hot."

谈 (談)	**tán**	chat, talk [V]
谈话 (談話)	**tánhuà**	talk, speak [VO]; conversation; statement [N]
谈完话 (談完話)	**tánwán huà**	finish talking

464 既　　**jì**　　since

Radical is 无 **wú** "not have" (621). Distinguish 既 from 概 **gài** (222).

既然	**jìrán**	since [MA]
既然…就…	**jìrán…jiù…**	since… [PT]

465 送 sòng give (as a present); deliver; see someone out

Radical is 辶 **chuò** "walk" or "go." The colloquial name for this radical is 走之 **zǒu zhī** "the walking 之," because of its meaning "walk" and its resemblance to the particle 之. Distinguish 送 from simplified 关 **guān** (124).

送	sòng	give (as a present); deliver; see someone off or out [V]
送给 (送給)	sònggěi	give someone as a present [V+PV]
买二送一 (買二送一)	mǎi èr sòng yī	"buy two, get one free" (lit. "[you] buy two, [we] give one as a gift")

466 使 shǐ send; envoy; use

Radical is 人 **rén** "person" (30), which is written 亻 when occurring at the left side of a character so as not to get in the way of the component at the right. The colloquial name for this radical is 人字旁 **rénzìpáng** "side made up of the character 人." Phonetic is 史 **shǐ** "history," but note that the right side of 使 consists of 史 plus an additional stroke above it, so it forms the character 吏 **lì** "official." An "envoy" 使 (a person "sent" some place) is an "official" 吏 "person" 人. Distinguish 使 from 更 **gèng** (401) and 便 **biàn** (362).

大使	dàshǐ	ambassador [N]
大使馆 (大使館)	dàshǐguǎn	embassy [PW]
使用	shǐyòng	use, employ [N]

467 希 xī hope

Radical is 巾 **jīn** "towel." Distinguish 希 from 市 **shì** (47).

468 望 (望) wàng hope; watch

Radical is 月 **yuè** "moon" (130), which has been "squeezed" into the upper right-hand quadrant so that it looks almost like 夕 (plus one extra stroke). The colloquial name for this radical is 月字旁 **yuèzìpáng** "side made up of the character 月." Phonetic is 亡 **wáng** "die," "flee," or "destroyed." Distinguish 望 from 忘 **wàng** (190) and 忙 **máng** (59).

希望 (希望)	xīwàng	hope [V/N]

Note that the difference between the official simplified form and the official traditional form of this character does not show up in all fonts; in some fonts, they both look the same.

New Words in ISC 18-2 Written with Characters You Already Know

等会儿 (等會兒)	děng huǐr	in a little while [PH] (Note that 会 [會] is here pronounced as **huǐ** by many speakers.)
街	jiē	street [N]
上街	shàngjiē	go out on the street [VO]
一边 (一邊)	yìbiān(r)	on the one hand [PW]
一边 A 一边 B (一邊 A 一邊 B)	yìbiān(r) A yìbiān(r) B	on the one hand A on the other hand B; do B while doing A [PT]

Reading Exercises (Simplified Characters) 简体字

Now practice reading the new characters and words for this lesson in context in sentences, conversations, and narratives. Be sure to refer to the Notes at the end of this lesson, and make use of the accompanying audio disc to hear and practice correct pronunciation, phrasing, and intonation.

A. SENTENCES 句子

Read out loud each of the following sentences, which include all the new characters of this lesson. The first time you read a sentence, focus special attention on the characters and words that are new to you, reminding yourself of their pronunciation and meaning. The second time, aim to comprehend the overall meaning of the sentence.

一、我已经把我的爱给你了，你还要我送给你什么呢？

二、我还没去过中国，真希望以后能有机会去中国留学。

三、你既然时间很紧张，那么我们就一边吃饭一边谈话吧。

四、已经下了一个多星期雨了，大家都希望明天能出太阳！

五、下面是习近平主席2013年8月17日和外国记者谈话的全文。

六、你怎么没有早一点儿告诉我，你等会儿还需要上街买东西？

七、张先生打算改天去大使馆找李大使谈话，因为大使是他的老朋友。

八、既然那家饭馆菜不怎么样，而且服务很差，我们这次就换一家饭馆吧。

九、我想学习怎么使用iPhone手机，请问，谁能给我讲一讲iPhone的使用方法？

十、明天是王大海妈妈的五十岁生日，所以大海要送她一些花儿。

B. CONVERSATIONS 对话

Read out loud the following conversations, including the name or role of the person speaking. If possible, find a partner or partners and each of you play a role. Then switch roles, so you get practice reading all of the lines.

一、

小李：我来了，我来了！小牛，对不起，让你久等了。

小牛：没关系，没关系。

李太太：小牛，在这儿吃饭吧！

小牛：不用了。等会儿我跟小李谈完了，就回去。

小李：不，小牛，你就在这儿吃吧。我们一边儿吃一边儿谈。

小牛：那也好。简单点儿！

二、

小牛：小李，时候不早了，我该走了。

小李：再坐一会儿吧！

小牛：不了，我还得上街买点东西。

小李：好吧。既然你还有事，我就不留你了。以后有空儿再来吧。
小牛：我走了。小李，明天学校见！
小李：明天见。我不送了，慢走！

三、
高大林：小万，我先走了。公司那边还有点儿事我得办。
万小京：好吧。你既然还有事儿，我就不留你了。
高大林：好，再见！明天见！
万小京：好，我们改天再谈吧。我不送你了，慢走！

C. NARRATIVE 短文

Read the following narrative, paying special attention to punctuation and overall structure. The first time you read the narrative, read it out loud. The second time, read silently and try to gradually increase your reading speed. Always think of the meaning of what you're reading.

上个星期，我在美国南加州大学的同屋司米文从美国到北京来看我。我已经十多年没看见他了，不过他还是老样子，看起来跟二十几岁的时候差不多一样。因为是米文第一次到中国来，所以白天我带他到很多地方去看了看，像天安门、长城、北海公园、后海和北京动物园。因为我女儿美美很想以后到美国去留学，所以米文有一天也到美国大使馆去问了美美应该怎么样准备去美国的事。每天晚上我跟米文都谈到一、两点钟，谈得非常高兴，也喝了不少酒。米文在我们家住了一个多星期才回美国。他既然从这么远的地方来看我们，我们就在他走的时候送了他很多北京的小吃，希望他会喜欢。我们也希望米文以后有空还能再来我们家住。他也请我们全家有时间到美国去看他，还说如果美美去美国留学的话，可以住在他家。他那样说，我跟我太太特别感谢他，因为美美住在他家不但能省钱，而且女儿住在朋友家，我们这些做爸爸、妈妈的当然也比较放心。

Street Sign in Qingdao

Calling on Someone to Request a Favor

New Characters and Words

Study the six characters below and the common words written with them, paying careful attention to each character's pronunciation, meaning, and structure, as well as similar-looking characters. After you've studied a character, turn to the *Practice Essentials* volume and practice writing it on the practice sheet, making sure to follow the correct stroke order and direction as you pronounce it out loud and think of its meaning.

469 抽 **chōu** take out, draw out

Radical is 手 **shǒu** "hand" (305), which at the left side of a character is written as 扌 and is referred to colloquially as 提手 **tíshǒu** "raised hand." The other component is 由 **yóu** "from" (383). Use your "hand" 扌 to "take something out" 抽 "from" 由 somewhere. Distinguish 抽 from 由 and 油 **yóu** (308).

抽	**chōu**	take out, draw out [V]
抽空	**chōukòng**	find time (to do something) [VO]

470 烟 (煙) **yān** tobacco; cigarette; smoke

Radical is 火 **huǒ** "fire" (566). This radical is referred to colloquially as 火字旁 **huǒzìpáng** "side made up of the character 火." When 火 is written at the left of a character as a radical, its last stroke is shortened so that it doesn't collide with the component to its right. Phonetic of the simplified form is 因 **yīn** (181). The traditional form contains 西 **xī** (35) and 土 **tǔ** (343). Distinguish simplified 烟 from 因 **yīn** (181).

烟 (煙)	**yān**	tobacco, cigarette; smoke [N]
抽烟 (抽煙)	**chōuyān**	smoke (cigarettes, etc.) [VO]
⊙ 香烟 (香煙)	**xiāngyān**	cigarette [N]
一根烟 (一根煙)	**yìgēn yān**	a cigarette

| 一包烟 (一包煙) | **yìbāo yān** | a pack of cigarettes |
| 一条烟 (一條煙) | **yìtiáo yān** | a carton of cigarettes |

471 吸   **xī**   inhale, breathe in

Radical is 口 **kǒu** "mouth" (140). This radical is referred to colloquially as 口字旁 **kǒuzìpáng** "side made up of the character 口." Phonetic is 及 **jí** (400). Distinguish 吸 from 及 and 级 (級) **jí** (174).

| 吸 | **xī** | inhale, breathe in [V] |
| 吸烟 (吸煙) | **xīyān** | smoke (cigarettes, etc.) [VO] |

472 区 (區)   **qū**   area, district, region

Radical is 匸 **xǐ** "cover." The simplified form contains 乂 **yì** "govern," while the traditional form contains 品 **pǐn** (342). This character is itself a phonetic, e.g., in the character 躯 (軀) as used in the word 身躯 (身軀) **shēnqū** "body." Distinguish simplified 区 from 四 **sì** (4), 回 **huí** (161), and 因 **yīn** (181).

区 (區)	**qū**	area, district, region [N]
吸炳区 (吸煙區)	**xīyān qū**	smoking section [PH]
非吸烟区 (非吸煙區)	**fēixīyān qū**	non-smoking section [PH]
◉地区 (地區)	**dìqū**	area, district, region, zone [N]
◉山区 (山區)	**shānqū**	mountain region [PW]
◉林区 (林區)	**línqū**	forest region [PW]

473 情   **qíng**   sentiment; situation, condition

Radical is 心 **xīn** "heart" (262). When at the left side of a character, this radical is referred to colloquially as 心字旁 **xīnzìpáng** "side made up of the character 心" and is written as 忄. Phonetic is 青 **qīng** "blue-green." Distinguish 情 from 請 **qǐng** (67) and 清 **qīng** (245).

事情	**shìqing**	thing, matter [N]
一件事情	**yíjiàn shìqing**	a thing, a matter
◉心情	**xīnqíng**	mood, state of mind [N]
◉爱情 (愛情)	**àiqíng**	love [N]

474 帮 (幫)   **bāng**   help; gang, clique

Radical is 巾 **jīn** "cloth." Phonetic of the simplified form is 邦 **bāng** "nation." Phonetic of the traditional form is 封 **fēng** "seal." The other component in the traditional form is 帛 **bó** "silk." "Silk cloth" 巾 was formerly used as currency and was therefore recognized as being the biggest "help" 帮 to the "nation" 邦. Distinguish 帮 (幫) from 市 **shì** (47).

帮 (幫)	**bāng**	help [V]
帮忙 (幫忙)	**bāngmáng**	help [VO]
◉帮 (幫)	**bāng**	gang, clique, group [N/M]
◉四人帮 (四人幫)	**Sìrénbāng**	Gang of Four [N]

New Words in ISC 18-3 Written with Characters You Already Know

换句话说 (換句話說)	**huàn jù huà shuō**	in other words [PH]
看	**kàn**	visit, call on [V]
看朋友	**kàn péngyou**	visit a friend
看法	**kànfǎ**	way of looking at something, opinion [N]
晚	**-wǎn**	late [RE]
来晚 (來晚)	**láiwǎn**	come late [RC]
习惯 (習慣)	**xíguàn**	custom, habit [N]
意思	**yìsi**	intention [N]
一点小意思 (一點小意思)	**yìdiǎn(r) xiǎo yìsi**	"a little something," a gift [PH]
这个 (這個)	**zheige**	(pause filler) [I]
直	**zhí**	be straightforward [SV]
直说 (直說)	**zhí shuō**	speak frankly [PH]

Reading Exercises (Simplified Characters) 简体字

Now practice reading the new characters and words for this lesson in context in sentences, conversations, and narratives. Be sure to refer to the Notes at the end of this lesson, and make use of the accompanying audio disc to hear and practice correct pronunciation, phrasing, and intonation.

A. SENTENCES 句子

Read out loud each of the following sentences, which include all the new characters of this lesson. The first time you read a sentence, focus special attention on the characters and words that are new to you, reminding yourself of their pronunciation and meaning. The second time, aim to comprehend the overall meaning of the sentence.

一、爱情要紧还是面包要紧？不知道大家的看法是什么？

二、你百忙之中还抽空来看我，真是让我感到很不好意思！

三、这儿是非吸烟区，不是吸烟区，那些人为什么还抽烟呢？

四、我们两点开会，现在已经两点四十了，换句话说，他一定不来了。

五、对不起，我不是不愿意帮你的忙，可是这件事情我还真办不到。

六、老张说话很直，心里想什么就说什么，他以后大概不能做大使！

七、中国西北边的山区，交通不方便，很多地区小孩子还是走路去上学。

八、小张，你又来晚了。我们不是说过9:00开会吗？现在已经9:20了。
　　你这个习惯一定要改！

九、中国有句老话说"笑一笑，十年少"，意思是常常笑、心情好的人可以
　　比不喜欢笑、心情不好的人活得更长。

十、王大海很难过地问："为什么我觉得自己还行，但是总是找不到
　　爱情？"

B. CONVERSATIONS 对话

Read out loud the following conversations, including the name or role of the person speaking. If possible, find a partner or partners and each of you play a role. Then switch roles, so you get practice reading all of the lines.

一、

美国留学生：对不起，我因为有点事，所以来晚了。

简太太　　　：没关系。

美国留学生：这是一点小意思。

简太太　　　：您太客气了。请进，请坐。

简先生　　　：请抽烟。

美国留学生：我不会抽，谢谢。

简先生　　　：您在电话里说有点事要找我？

美国留学生：不好意思。有点小事情，想请您
　　　　　　帮个忙。

Sign in Hong Kong Park

简太太　　　：请喝茶。

美国留学生：谢谢。

简先生　　　：不要客气，请直说。

美国留学生：这个，这个，事情是这样子的……

二、

小王：老高，您能帮我一个忙吗？

老高：是什么事情？

小王：我有一个好朋友下星期五要来看我，但是我们家里没有地方让他
　　　住。不知道有没有可能让他住在你们家？只是一个晚上而已。

老高：当然可以，这根本不成问题。我跟你是老同学，这种事情不用客气。

小王：真是非常感谢你愿意帮我这么大的忙！

老高：没事儿，没事儿。

三、

张明：小马，你后天忙不忙？

马清：好像没什么特别的事情。

张明：我星期六晚上要办酒席，那天是我外公的一百岁生日。
　　　你一定要抽空来参加！

马清：你外公的一百岁生日？不简单！我怎么敢不来啊？几点？在哪里？

张明：时间大概是六点钟，饭店还没决定。我明天再给你打电话。

马清：好，一言为定！

C. NARRATIVES 短文

Read the following narratives, paying special attention to punctuation and overall structure. The first time you read a narrative, read it out loud. The second time, read silently and try to gradually increase your reading speed. Always think of the meaning of what you're reading.

Notes 注解

A6. ⊙全长 (全長) **quáncháng** "total length" [N]

A7a. ◆大陆 (大陸) **dàlù** "mainland" or "continent" [PW]. Learn the expression 中国大陆 (中國大陸) "mainland China."

A7b. ⊙A跟B之间 (A跟B之間) **A gēn B zhījiān** "between A and B" [PT]. The phrase 中国大陆跟台湾之间的交流 (中國大陸跟台灣之間的交流) means "interaction between mainland China and Taiwan."

A7c. ⊙两岸 (兩岸) **liǎng'àn** "the two shores" (of the Taiwan Straits) [N]. This is a politically neutral way of referring to mainland China and Taiwan.

A8. ⊙留言 **liúyán** "recorded message" (N)

A10a. 长得不高 (長得不高) **zhǎngde bù gāo** lit. "grew up in such a way that he is not tall" or, in better English, simply "is not tall."

A10b. 人也不重 lit. "As a person he is not heavy" or, in more idiomatic English, "He's not heavy."

B3. ⊙说话算话 (說話算話) **shuōhuà suàn huà** "do as one says one will do" or "mean what one says" [IE]

C1a. 十五、六岁 (十五、六歲) "15 or 16 years old"

C1b. The verb 叫, which often means "call," here means "tell" (someone to do something).

C1c. ◆练习 (練習) **liànxí** "practice" [V]

C1d. 她说开多了，就好了 (她說開多了，就好了) lit. "She says when I have driven more, it'll be better."

C1e. 你现在要到哪里去吗？(你現在要到哪裡去嗎？) "Do you want to go someplace now?" This sentence is already a question on account of the 吗 (嗎) at the end, so the question word 哪里 (哪裡) does not mean "Where?" but instead means "somewhere" or "someplace" (IWC 12-2: 10).

C2a. ⊙日常 **rìcháng** "daily," "everyday" or "routine" [AT]. 日常生活 means "daily life." Another common collocation is 日常工作 "routine work."

C2b. Pay careful attention to the grammatical structure of the long, complex sentence that begins with 虽然 (雖然). Everything before the 但是 goes with 虽然 (雖然). An English translation of the kernel of the sentence would be: "Although for many years…, I still feel that…."

C2c. 多年以来 (多年以來) "for many years." This means the same as 很多年以来 (很多年以來), but has here been shortened for stylistic reasons. As we have noted before, according to the rules of Chinese prosody, there is often a preference for groups of four syllables or characters.

C2d. 中日之间 (中日之間) "between China and Japan." This is an abbreviated, more formal way of writing 中国跟日本之间 (中國跟日本之間). Cf. A7b above.

C2e. 两国之间 (兩國之間) "between the two countries." Again, cf. A7b above.

C2f. ⊙进行 (進行) **jìnxíng** "conduct," "carry out," or "do" [V]. 进行语言交流 (進行語言交流) means "conduct a language exchange."

Visiting People (II)

COMMUNICATIVE OBJECTIVES

Once you've mastered this unit, you'll be able to use Chinese to read and write about:

1. Visiting a friend or classmate who is ill.

2. Explaining why you didn't come to visit your sick friend or classmate earlier.

3. Asking someone how they're feeling and urging them to get enough rest and take good care of themselves.

4. Offering to help someone if they need assistance.

5. Paying a formal call on a teacher at her or his home.

6. Your progress in learning Chinese in the areas of pronunciation, grammar, vocabulary, accuracy, and fluency.

7. Different kinds of tests, your impressions of a test, how you did, etc.

8. Academic life: reports, term papers, theses, courses, grades, credits, and semesters.

9. A passage on simplified and traditional characters.

10. A passage involving a pun that is a reflection of modern Chinese society.

Visiting a Sick Classmate

谢谢你还跑来看我。
(謝謝你還跑來看我。)

听说你病了，给你带了一点儿水果。(聽說你病了，給你帶了一點兒水果。)

New Characters and Words

Study the six characters below and the common words written with them, paying careful attention to each character's pronunciation, meaning, and structure, as well as similar-looking characters. After you've studied a character, turn to the *Practice Essentials* volume and practice writing it on the practice sheet, making sure to follow the correct stroke order and direction as you pronounce it out loud and think of its meaning.

481 考 **kǎo** test, take a test

Radical is 老 **lǎo** "old" (61). This character is itself a phonetic, e.g., 烤 **kǎo** "bake." Note that 考 has an alternate form written 攷. Distinguish 考 from 老 **lǎo** (61) and 者 **zhě** (298).

考	**kǎo**	test, take a test [V]
小考	**xiǎokǎo**	quiz [N]
大考	**dàkǎo**	final examination [N]
⊙月考	**yuèkǎo**	monthly test [N]
⊙期中考	**qīzhōngkǎo**	mid-term examination [N]

482 试 (試) **shì** try; test

Radical is 讠(言) **yán** "speech" (336). The colloquial name for this radical is 言字旁 **yánzìpáng** "side made up of the character 言." Phonetic is 式 **shì** (598) as in 方式 **fāngshì** "way."

试 (試)	**shì**	try [V]
试试 (試試)	**shìshi**	try
试试看 (試試看)	**shìshi kàn**	try and see

| 考试 (考試) | **kǎoshì** | test, examination [N]; take a test [VO] |
| 期中考试 (期中考試) | **qīzhōng kǎoshì** | mid-term examination [PH] |

---

483 病   **bìng**   get sick; illness

Radical is 疒 **chuáng** "disease" [BF]. Phonetic is 丙 **bǐng**, which is third of the heavenly stems.

病	**bìng**	get sick [V]; illness, disease [N]
大病	**dà bìng**	major illness
小病	**xiǎo bìng**	minor illness
生病	**shēngbìng**	become sick [VO]

---

484 跑   **pǎo**   run

Radical is 足 **zú** "foot" (546), since you "run" 跑 with your "feet" 足. Phonetic is 包 **bāo** (332). Distinguish 跑 from 包.

跑	**pǎo**	run [V]
跑来 (跑來)	**pǎolái**	run over here, come over
跑去	**pǎoqù**	run over there
跑来跑去 (跑來跑去)	**pǎolái pǎoqù**	run all over the place
跑步	**pǎobù**	run paces, run [VO]; running [N]
慢跑	**mànpǎo**	jog [V]; jogging [N]

---

485 飞 (飛)   **fēi**   fly

This character is itself a radical. The traditional form is a pictograph of a crane in flight, with the two 飞 depicting the crane's wings, and the straight line in the middle depicting the crane's body and tail.

◉飞 (飛)	**fēi**	fly [V]
◉飞机 (飛機)	**fēijī**	airplane [N]
◉飞机场 (飛機場)	**fēijīchǎng**	airport [PW]
◉开飞机 (開飛機)	**kāi fēijī**	fly an airplane
◉坐飞机 (坐飛機)	**zuò fēijī**	take an airplane, travel by plane

---

486 船 (船)   **chuán**   boat, ship

Radical is 舟 **zhōu** "boat." The simplified form 船 consists of a "boat" 舟 with "several" 几 survivors or "mouths" 口. Distinguish simplified 船 from simplified 没 **méi** (92).

| ◉船 (船) | **chuán** | boat, ship [N] |
| ◉坐船 (坐船) | **zuò chuán** | take a boat, travel by boat |

C. NARRATIVES 短文

Read the following narratives, paying special attention to punctuation and overall structure. The first time you read a narrative, read it out loud. The second time, read silently and try to gradually increase your reading speed. Always think of the meaning of what you're reading.

一、

我習慣每天早上去慢跑，可是已經有一個多星期沒有跑步了。我這幾天真是忙得很！不但學校裡有很多考試得準備，而且家裡還有很多事情得做。我覺得要是再這樣，一定會生病的。我下個星期要坐飛機去香港替一人人公司一開一個很要緊的會，我一定得參加，怎麼也不能生病！

二、

我去年六月本來要坐飛機去上海，可是去機場的路上有很多車子。我本來應該提前兩個小時就到機場，但在路上花了很長時間，好不容易提前半個小時才到。等我從停車場跑到機場的時候，小姐說飛機已經要飛走了。時間太晚了，她不讓我上飛機。所以我現在坐飛機一定會早三個小時到機場，這樣不會那麼緊張。

Notes 注解

A4. ⊙班 **bān** (for scheduled trips of a plane, bus, or train) **[M]**. 最早的一班飞机 (最早的一班飛機) means "the earliest plane."

A5. 这一生 (這一生) "(in) this life"

A6. 好大工夫 "a lot of time"

A8. 我没有那工夫 (我沒有那工夫) "I don't have that/so much time." Here 那工夫 means 那个工夫 (那個工夫). In colloquial conversation, the measure 个 (個) is sometimes omitted after the specifiers 这 (這) and 那.

B2a. 我刚到城里去买票去了 (我剛到城裡去買票去了) "I just went into town to buy a ticket." The first 去 in this sentence is optional and could be omitted, but such usage is common in colloquial Beijing speech.

B2b. 最近 "in the near future" or "soon." Though 最近 usually means "in the recent past" or "recently," it can also mean "in the near future." From the Chinese point of view, the meaning is the same: that is, at a time point very close to the present, whether moving back in time or moving ahead in time.

C2a. 好不容易提前半个小时才到 (好不容易提前半個小時才到) "barely arrived half an hour in advance"

C2b. 早三个小时 (早三個小時) lit. "early by three hours," or in idiomatic English, "three hours early"

Visiting a Sick Classmate (cont.)

 **New Characters and Words**

Study the six characters below and the common words written with them, paying careful attention to each character's pronunciation, meaning, and structure, as well as similar-looking characters. After you've studied a character, turn to the *Practice Essentials* volume and practice writing it on the practice sheet, making sure to follow the correct stroke order and direction as you pronounce it out loud and think of its meaning.

---

487 身　　**shēn**　　body; oneself

This character is itself a radical. Distinguish 身 from 谢（謝）**xiè** (66).

---

488 体（體）　**tǐ**　　body

Radical of the simplified form is 人 **rén** "person" (30), which is written 亻 when occurring at the left side of a character so as not to get in the way of the component at the right. The colloquial name for this radical is 人字旁 **rénzìpáng** "side made up of the character 人." Radical of the traditional form is 骨 **gǔ** "bone." Distinguish simplified 体 from 本 **běn** (242) and 保 **bǎo** (329).

> 身体（身體）　　**shēntǐ**　　body; health [N]
>
> ⊙简体字（簡體字）　　**jiǎntǐzì**　　simplified Chinese character [N]

---

489 绩（績）　**jī**　　achievement, accomplishment; merit

Radical is 丝（絲）**sī** "silk." When at the left side of a character, this radical is referred to colloquially as 绞丝旁（絞絲旁）**jiǎosīpáng** "side made up of twisted silk" and is written as 纟（糸）. Phonetic is 责（責）"responsibility" (499).

| 成绩 (成績) | **chéngjī** | grade (e.g., on a test or in a course); results; achievements [N] |
| ⊙成绩单 (成績單) | **chéngjīdān(r)** | transcript [N] |

---

490 注   **zhù**   concentrate on

Radical is 水 **shuǐ** "water" (333), which is written 氵 and is referred to colloquially as 三点水 (三點水) **sāndiǎn shuǐ** "three drops of water" when it occurs at the left-hand side of a character. Phonetic is 主 **zhǔ** "primary" or "main" (346). Distinguish 注 from 王 **wáng** (6), 主, 住 **zhù** "live" (138) and 往 **wǎng** "go to" (218).

| 注意 | **zhùyì** | pay attention (to) [V/VO] |
| ⊙注解 (注解) | **zhùjiě** | annotation, explanatory note [N] |

---

491 于 (於)   **yú**   be located at, in, on, to

Radical of the simplified form is 二 **èr** "two" (2). Radical of the traditional form is 方 **fāng** "place" (158). The other components of the traditional form are 人 **rén** (30) and 仌 **bīng** "ice." Both simplified 于 and traditional 於 are phonetics, e.g., in the character 宇, which is used in the word 宇宙 **yǔzhòu** "universe"; and in the character 淤, which is used in the word 淤泥 **yūní** "silt." Distinguish simplified 于 from simplified 干 **gān** (275) and 千 **qiān** (114).

于	**Yú**	Yu (also Woo, a Korean surname) [SN]
		(Note that the surname Yu is written as 于 in both simplified and traditional script.)
关于 (關於)	**guānyú**	about, concerning [CV]

---

492 论 (論)   **lùn**   discuss, debate

Radical is 讠 (言) **yán** "speech" (336). The colloquial name for this radical is 言字旁 **yánzìpáng** "side made up of the character 言." Phonetic is 仑 (侖) **lún**.

| 论文 (論文) | **lùnwén** | thesis, dissertation [N] |

New Words in ISC 19-2 Written with Characters You Already Know

报告 (報告)	**bàogào**	report [N/V]
学期 (學期)	**xuéqī**	semester, term [N]
学期报告 (學期報告)	**xuéqī bàogào**	term paper [PH]
好好儿的 (好好兒的)	**hǎohāorde**	well [PT]
来电话 (來電話)	**lái diànhuà**	call on the telephone [PH]
门 (門)	**mén**	(measure for courses at school) [M]
		(e.g., 一门课 (一門課) "a course")
学分 (學分)	**xuéfēn**	credit, credit hour [N]

Reading Exercises (Simplified Characters) 简体字

Now practice reading the new characters and words for this lesson in context in sentences, conversations, and narratives. Be sure to refer to the Notes at the end of this lesson, and make use of the accompanying audio disc to hear and practice correct pronunciation, phrasing, and intonation.

A. SENTENCES 句子

Read out loud each of the following sentences, which include all the new characters of this lesson. The first time you read a sentence, focus special attention on the characters and words that are new to you, reminding yourself of their pronunciation and meaning. The second time, aim to comprehend the overall meaning of the sentence.

一、这位同学，请问，你的学期报告是关于什么的？

二、小李的论文是关于天文的；我的论文是关于语言学的。

三、学中文的学生一定得注意他们的声调，特别是第三声。

四、这本书是关于国际关系的，特别是中美关系，写得非常有意思。

五、小张，你这学期的学期报告得好好儿地准备，这样成绩才会好。

六、你们学校一门课算几个学分？一个学期最多可以上几门课呢？

七、我跟你讲，身体要紧！一定要注意身体，可别把自己的身体忙坏了！

八、要注意看那本书的注解，注解可以帮你很清楚地了解每个句子的意思。

九、我男朋友从前有抽烟的坏习惯，可是因为很多朋友都告诉他抽烟对身体不好，所以他现在不抽了。

十、王大海上学期的成绩很差，所以他不敢让爸爸妈妈看他的成绩单。

B. CONVERSATIONS 对话

Read out loud the following conversations, including the name or role of the person speaking. If possible, find a partner or partners and each of you play a role. Then switch roles, so you get practice reading all of the lines.

一、

中国女生：考得怎么样？

美国女生：还可以吧。成绩还没出来呢。（过了一会儿）我不多坐了。过几天再来看你。

中国女生：吃了饭再走吧。

美国女生：不了，不了，谢谢你，我得走了。你多注意身体。有什么事的话，来个电话，大家都可以帮你。

中国女生：太谢谢你了。有事我会说的。

美国女生：再见！

中国女生：再见！

Notes 注解

A7.   把自己的身体忙坏了 (把自己的身體忙壞了) lit. "take your own body and make it busy to the extent that it goes bad," or in idiomatic English, "be so busy that you ruin your health"

A8.   ⊙了解 **liǎojiě** "understand" [V]. Note that the character 了 here represents the syllable **liǎo**, not **le**.

B3a.   还算可以 (還算可以) lit. "still can be considered as being all right," or in more idiomatic English, "O.K." or "not too bad"

B3b.   差一点儿没 (差一點兒沒) "nearly didn't" or "almost didn't"

B3c.   ⊙通过 (通過) **tōngguò** "pass (an examination or inspection)" [RC]

C1.   ◆压力 (壓力) **yālì** "pressure" [N]

C2a.   ◆繁体字 (繁體字) **fántǐzì** "complex characters" or "traditional characters" [N]

C2b.   ⊙文字 **wénzì** "script," "written language," or "writing system" [N]

C2c.   ◆大陆 (大陸) "mainland" [PW]. Learn the common expression 中国大陆 (中國大陸) "mainland China."

C2d.   ◆新加坡 **Xīnjiāpō** "Singapore" [PW]

C2e.   ⊙同样地 (同樣地) **tóngyàngde** "in the same way," "similarly" [A]

C2f.   ⊙流行 **liúxíng** "be prevalent, popular, widespread" [SV]

C2g.   ⊙草书 (草書) **cǎoshū** "cursive script" (in calligraphy) [N]

C2h.   ◆例如 **lìrú** "for instance" or "for example" [CJ]

C2i.   ⊙既…又 **jì...yòu** "both...and" [PT]

C2j.   ⊙提出来 (提出來) **tíchūlái** "bring up" or "mention" [RC]

C2k.   ⊙差别 (差別) **chābié** "difference" [N]. Note that 差 (差) is here pronounced **chā** and not **chà**.

C2l.   分清楚 lit. "separate so that something is clear" or "distinguish"

C2m.   只差一点点 (只差一點點) "differ by only a very little bit"

C2n.   ◆例子 **lìzi** "example" [N]

C2o.   ⊙认 (認) **rèn** "recognize" [V]

C2p.   ⊙认为 (認為) **rènwéi** "think," "be of the opinion," or "consider" [V]

A Farewell Call on a Favorite Teacher

记得你刚来的时候，
连一句简单的中国话都不会说。
(記得你刚來的時候，連 一句簡單
的中國話都不會說。)

New Characters and Words

Study the six characters below and the common words written with them, paying careful attention to each character's pronunciation, meaning, and structure, as well as similar-looking characters. After you've studied a character, turn to the *Practice Essentials* volume and practice writing it on the practice sheet, making sure to follow the correct stroke order and direction as you pronounce it out loud and think of its meaning.

493 向 **xiàng** toward, to

Radical is 凵 **kǒu** "mouth" (140). Distinguish 向 from 何 **Hé** (19) and simplified 问 **wèn** (75).

向	**xiàng**	toward, to, from [CV]
向前走	**xiàng qián zǒu**	go forward
向东走 (向東走)	**xiàng dōng zǒu**	go east
向…告别 (向…告別)	**xiàng…gàobié**	bid farewell to [PT]
⊙内向 (內向)	**nèixiàng**	be introverted [SV]
⊙外向	**wàixiàng**	be extroverted [SV]

494 眼 **yǎn** eye

Radical is the pictograph 目 **mù** "eye." Phonetic is 艮 **gèn**. Distinguish 眼 from 很 **hěn** (58), 跟 **gēn** (302), and 根 **gēn** (313).

眼	**yǎn**	eye [N]
左眼	**zuǒyǎn**	left eye [N]

右眼	**yòuyǎn**	right eye [N]
看他一眼	**kàn tā yì yǎn**	look at him (lit. "look at him with one eye")
转眼 (轉眼)	**zhuǎnyǎn**	blink the eyes; glance [VO]; in the blink of an eye [A]

495 连(連)   **lián**   even; link, connect

Radical is 辶 **chuò** "walk, go." The colloquial name for this radical is 走之 **zǒu zhī** "the walking 之," because of its meaning "walk" and its resemblance to the particle 之. The other component is 车 (車) **chē** (224). Distinguish 连 (連) from 车 (車).

连 (連)	**Lián**	Lian [SN]
连 (連)	**lián**	even [CV]
连…都… (連…都…)	**lián...dōu...**	even... [PT]
连…也… (連…也…)	**lián...yě...**	even... [PT]
◉大连 (大連)	**Dàlián**	Dalian (city in Liaoning Province) [PW]

496 利   **lì**   sharp (e.g., a knife); benefit

Radical is 刀 **dāo** "knife," which is written 刂 when occurring at the right-hand side of a character. This radical is referred to colloquially as 立刀 **lìdāo** "standing knife." The other component is 禾 **hé** "growing grain." Cutting "grain" 禾 with a "knife" 刀 results in "benefits" 利. The character 利 also serves as a phonetic in other characters, e.g., 梨 **lí** "pear." Distinguish 利 from 到 **dào** (205) and 刻 **kè** (116).

流利	**liúlì**	be fluent [SV]
意大利	**Yìdàlì**	Italy [PW]
意大利语 (意大利語)	**Yìdàlìyǔ**	Italian language [N]

497 产(產)   **chǎn**   produce

Radical of the simplified form is 亠 **tóu** "head." Radical of the traditional form is 生 **shēng** "be born" (22). This whole character can itself serve as a phonetic, e.g., in the character 铲 (鏟), which is used in the word 铲子(鏟子) **chǎnzi** "shovel." There are two variants for the traditional form of this character: 產 and 産.

生产 (生產)	**shēngchǎn**	produce, manufacture, make [V]
◉出产 (出產)	**chūchǎn**	produce, manufacture, make [V]
◉产品 (產品)	**chǎnpǐn**	product [N]

498 义(義)   **yì**   righteousness

Radical of the simplified form is 丶 **zhǔ** "dot." Radical of the traditional form is 羊 **yáng** "goat," the last stroke of which has here been shortened, with the other component being 我 **wǒ** (51). The whole character 义(義) can serve as a phonetic, e.g., in the character 议 (議), which is used in the word 建议(建議) **jiànyì** "suggest." Distinguish simplified 义 from 又 **yòu** (210).

| ◉主义 (主義) | **zhǔyì** | doctrine [N] |
| ◉共产主义 (共產主義) | **Gòngchǎn Zhǔyì** | Communism [PH] |

New Words in ISC 19-3 Written with Characters You Already Know

告别 (告別)	**gàobié**	bid farewell, take leave [V]
没少… (沒少…)	**méi shǎo...**	"not a little...," ...a lot [PT] (e.g., 她也没少花钱。[她也沒少花錢。] "She sure spent a lot of money.")
语法 (語法)	**yǔfǎ**	grammar [N]

Reading Exercises (Simplified Characters) 简体字

Now practice reading the new characters and words for this lesson in context in sentences, conversations, and narratives. Be sure to refer to the Notes at the end of this lesson, and make use of the accompanying audio disc to hear and practice correct pronunciation, phrasing, and intonation.

A. SENTENCES 句子

Read out loud each of the following sentences, which include all the new characters of this lesson. The first time you read a sentence, focus special attention on the characters and words that are new to you, reminding yourself of their pronunciation and meaning. The second time, aim to comprehend the overall meaning of the sentence.

一、请问，你们的工厂生产一些什么样的产品呢？

二、小马的左眼正常，可是右眼从小就有点儿毛病。

三、现在在中国还有多少人主张毛主席主张的那种共产主义？

四、四川是中国出产米最多的一个省，而成都平原又是四川省内出产米的中心。

五、常州离南京很近，离上海也不太远，人口有差不多四百万，出产的鱼和米特别多。

六、我认为内向的学生可能看书、写作比较好，但是外向的学生可能口语比较流利。

七、有很多种主义；除了共产主义以外，还有爱国主义、和平主义、自由主义、个人主义什么的。

八、最好把不如意的事情给忘了，一个人不可能完全没有问题，但是我们还是得向前走，对不对？

九、饭馆儿的那位中国服务员告诉我，她一转眼已经来美国二十年了，在这二十年里头，连一次国也没回过。

十、王大海的中文说得很流利，可是他的语法还有一些小错。

Notes 注解

A8. ⊙只不过 (只不過) **zhǐbúguò** "only," "merely" [PH]

B1. ◆丁 **Dīng** Ding [SN]. Chinese elementary school students with this surname are often the envy of their class-mates, since this character is so easy to write! There also exists a *chengyu* (idiom) with this character, written with characters which you have learned: 目不识丁 (目不識丁) **mù-bù-shí-Dīng** meaning lit. "eyes not recognize (even the character) Ding," or in more idiomatic English, "illiterate."

B2a. ⊙A跟B没什么两样 (A跟B沒什麼兩樣) **A gēn B méi shénme liǎngyàng** "A is no different from B" or "A is the same as B" [PT]. The sentence 老师看起来跟十年前没什么两样 (老師看起來跟十年前沒什麼兩樣) means "Teacher, you look no different from ten years ago."

B2b. ⊙北一女 **Běiyī'nǚ** "Taipei Municipal First Girls' Senior High School" [PW]. This is an abbreviation for 台北市立第一女子高级中学 (台北市立第一女子高級中學). Notice which syllables are retained in the abbreviation.

B2c. ⊙当年 (當年) **dāngnián** "at that time" or "in those days" [TW]

B2d. ⊙向A学到B (向A學到B) **xiàng A xuédào B** "to learn B from A" [PT]

B2e. ⊙多保重 **duō bǎozhòng** "take good care of yourself" [IE]

B3a. 这工作 (這工作) means the same as 这个工作 (這個工作) "this job." In rapid, colloquial conversation, the measure 个 (個) is sometimes dropped after the specifiers 这 (這) and 那.

B3b. ⊙说的也是 (說的也是) **shuōde yě shì** "that's right" or "of course" [IE]

B3c. ⊙交 **jiāo** "hand over" or "deliver" [V]. 父母把孩子交给我们 (父母把孩子交給我們) lit. "Parents take children and hand them over to us," or in idiomatic English, "Parents give us their kids."

B3d. 我们责任重大 (我們責任重大) lit. "Our responsibility is weighty," or in idiomatic English, "We have a heavy responsibility."

B3e. 要把学生教好了 (要把學生教好了) lit. "(We) are supposed to teach students so they turn out well."

B3f. ◆昨天 **zuótiān** "yesterday" [TW]

B3g. ◆夜里 (夜裡) **yèli** "at night" [TW]

B3h. ◆睡觉 (睡覺) **shuìjiào** "sleep" [VO]

B3i. ◆辛苦 **xīnkǔ** "hardship," "toil," or "hard work" [N]. This word also functions as a stative verb meaning "to be hard," "toilsome," or "laborious," and is used as an idiomatic expression meaning "You've worked hard!"

C1a. ⊙应城 (應城) **Yìngchéng** [PW]. This is a city of about 600,000 in eastern Hubei province. Notice that the character 应 (應) is here pronounced **yìng**, not **yīng**.

C1b. ◆小镇 (小鎮) **xiǎozhèn** "small town" [PW]

C1c. 很多人不知道老师有多忙 (很多人不知道老師有多忙) "Lots of people don't know how busy a teacher is."

C1d. ⊙工作量 **gōngzuòliàng** "amount of work" or "workload" [N]

C2. 管我管得很严 (管我管得很嚴) "(They) control me very strictly."

Leisure Time Activities (I)

COMMUNICATIVE OBJECTIVES

Once you've mastered this unit, you'll be able to use Chinese to read and write about:

1. Hobbies.

2. Watching a film or attending a Peking opera performance.

3. Your future career plans.

4. Fractions, percents, and decimals.

5. Several amusing stories.

6. The Taiwanese language or dialect.

中國字畫

社團
法人
中華玉器藝術文化交

台北市建國段日日所

Hobbies

你有什么爱好吗？
（你有什麼愛好嗎？）

我喜欢音乐。
（我喜歡音樂。）

New Characters and Words

Study the six characters below and the common words written with them, paying careful attention to each character's pronunciation, meaning, and structure, as well as similar-looking characters. After you've studied a character, turn to the *Practice Essentials* volume and practice writing it on the practice sheet, making sure to follow the correct stroke order and direction as you pronounce it out loud and think of its meaning.

505 唱 **chàng**   sing

Radical is 口 **kǒu** "mouth" (140). This radical is referred to colloquially as 口字旁 **kǒuzìpáng** "side made up of the character 口." Phonetic is 昌 **chāng** "prosperous." Distinguish 唱 from 品 **pǐn** (342).

| 唱 | **chàng** | sing [V] |

506 歌 **gē**   song

Radical is 欠 **qiàn** "owe." Phonetic is 可 **kě** "can" (145). Distinguish 歌 from 哥 **gē** (187).

歌	**gē(r)**	song [N]
一首歌	**yìshǒu gē**	a song
唱歌	**chànggē(r)**	sing songs [VO]

507 怪 **guài**   blame; strange

Radical is 心 **xīn** "heart" (262), which indicates that an emotion is involved. When at the left side of a character, this radical is referred to colloquially as 心字旁 **xīnzìpáng** "side made up of the character 心" and is written as 忄. Distinguish 怪 from 惯（慣）**guàn** (394).

难怪 (難怪)	**nánguài**	no wonder [MA]
怪不得	**guàibudé**	no wonder that [MA] (得 is here pronounced **dé**, not **děi** or **de**)
◉怪	**guài**	blame [V]; be strange [SV]

508 观(觀) **guān**   look at

Radical is 见 (見) **jiàn** "see" (300). The other component of the simplified form is 又 **yòu** (210). Phonetic of the traditional form is 藋 **guān**. Distinguish 观 (觀) from 欢 (歡) **huān** (170).

参观 (參觀)	**cānguān**	visit (as a tourist or observer) [V]

509 画(畫) **huà**   paint; painting

Radical of the simplified form is 一 **yī** (1). Radical of the traditional form is 田 **tián** "field." Distinguish simplified 画 from simplified 国 **guó** (74), and distinguish traditional 畫 from traditional 書 **shū** (321).

画 (畫)	**huà**	paint [V]; painting [N]
一张画 (一張畫)	**yìzhāng huà(r)**	a painting
画画 (畫畫)	**huàhuà(r)**	paint a painting [VO]
国画 (國畫)	**guóhuà(r)**	traditional Chinese painting [N]
◉山水画 (山水畫)	**shānshuǐ huà(r)**	landscape painting [PH]

510 照 **zhào**   shine; illuminate

Radical is 火 **huǒ** "fire" (566), which is written 灬 and is referred to colloquially as 四点火 (四點火) **sìdiǎn huǒ** "four dots of fire" when it occurs at the bottom of a character. Phonetic is 召 **zhào** "call together." The third component is 日 **rì** "sun" (132), which also gives a hint as to the meaning. Distinguish 照 from traditional 魚 **yú** (411).

照	**zhào**	shine; illuminate; take (photographs) [V]
照相	**zhàoxiàng**	take a photograph [VO] (相 is here pronounced **xiàng**, not **xiāng**)
◉照相机 (照相機)	**zhàoxiàngjī**	camera [N]
◉照相馆 (照相館)	**zhàoxiàngguǎn**	photo studio, photo shop [PW]

🔘 **New Words in ISC 20-1 Written with Characters You Already Know**

爱好 (愛好)	**àihào**	hobby, interest [IE] (好 is here pronounced **hào**, not **hǎo**)
调子 (調子)	**diàozi**	tune, melody [N] (Note that 调 [調] is here pronounced **diào**, not **tiáo**.)
好听 (好聽)	**hǎotīng**	be nice-sounding, pretty [SV]
看书 (看書)	**kànshū**	read books, read [VO]
书法 (書法)	**shūfǎ**	calligraphy [N]

是吗？（是嗎？）	**Shì ma?**	"Really?" [IE]
下	**xià**	play (chess or checkers) [V]
小说（小說）	**xiǎoshuō(r)**	novel [N]
写东西（寫東西）	**xiě dōngxi**	write things, write [PH]

 ## Reading Exercises (Simplified Characters) 简体字

Now practice reading the new characters and words for this lesson in context in sentences, conversations, and narratives. Be sure to refer to the Notes at the end of this lesson, and make use of the accompanying audio disc to hear and practice correct pronunciation, phrasing, and intonation.

A. SENTENCES 句子

Read out loud each of the following sentences, which include all the new characters of this lesson. The first time you read a sentence, focus special attention on the characters and words that are new to you, reminding yourself of their pronunciation and meaning. The second time, aim to comprehend the overall meaning of the sentence.

一、我的爱好是画画儿、照相、以及看小说儿。

二、这个照相机是在哪儿买的？价钱怎么这么贵？

三、白老太太不但喜欢画画儿，而且也很喜欢唱歌儿。

四、这首歌的调子太高了，我唱不了这么高的调子！

五、我们今天要参观的第一家工厂做鞋子，第二家工厂做手表。

六、老张从小只喜欢一个人在家看书，怪不得他没有什么朋友。

七、中国人非常喜欢天安门，每天都有好几万人到那里去参观。

八、那个意大利人从小就住在北京，难怪他的中国话讲得那么流利。

九、你说你的专业是音乐，是吗？怪不得我常看你一边儿走，一边儿唱歌儿！

十、王大海告诉大家他的爱好是唱歌儿，可是大家都觉得他唱得很难听。

B. CONVERSATIONS 对话

Read out loud the following conversations, including the name or role of the person speaking. If possible, find a partner or partners and each of you play a role. Then switch roles, so you get practice reading all of the lines.

一、

张爱红：李文，你有什么爱好吗？

李文　：我喜欢音乐。从小在美国学唱歌儿。

张爱红：怪不得我常看你一边走一边唱歌儿。

李文　：是吗？

张爱红：除了音乐，你还有其他的爱好吗？

李文　：还喜欢看小说儿或是写东西。你呢？你的爱好是什么？

张爱红：画画儿，特别是国画儿，还有书法。

二、

中国同学：好，现在请每位同学给我们唱一首歌儿！

美国同学：要唱歌儿啊？我们在美国很少唱歌儿，我不太会唱。一定得
　　　　　唱吗？

中国同学：你随便唱一首，大家都是好朋友，没关系。

美国同学：这样子。好吧，可是我真的不太会唱。如果唱得不好听，你们
　　　　　可别笑我！

中国同学：不会的。

美国同学：好，一、二、三、唱："王老先生有块地"。对不起，这个调子太
　　　　　高了！我再来一次吧……

三、

严小姐：小管，你今天早上是不是出去了一会儿？

管先生：是的，我到对面很快地参观了一下最近开的公共图书馆，不过我
　　　　只去了差不多十五分钟而已。

严小姐：怪不得！我差不多十点钟的时候找你，可是怎么找也找不到你。

管先生：对不起，不好意思。有什么事情吗？

严小姐：有，事情是这样子的……

四、

美国人：您好！对不起，不好意思，请您帮我们照一张相，好吗？

中国人：好，没问题。不过，等一下，这个照相机怎么用？

美国人：我教您……奇怪，好像坏了。怎么办？

中国人：离这儿不远有一家照相馆，我带您去。

五、

女儿：妈妈，我这学期的成绩不太好，你别生气。

妈妈：来，成绩单拿给妈妈看看。什么？你这个孩子！平常不去上课，也不
　　　做作业，也不好好准备考试，难怪成绩会不好。妈妈怎么能不生气？

C. NARRATIVE 短文

Read the following narrative, paying special attention to punctuation and overall structure. The first time you read the narrative, read it out loud. The second time, read silently and try to gradually increase your reading speed. Always think of the meaning of what you're reading.

"你好吗？"

　　我听过这样一个笑话。有一个男的外国大学生到中国去学中文。他很
想多找机会讲中国话。有一天，他的中文老师的一个朋友请客，老师就带
他一块儿去吃饭。去以前，老师提醒他，看见其他的中国客人，可以说一
句："你好吗？"

老师和学生到了饭店，坐下了。外国学生左手边坐着一位中国老太太。他就开口问老太太："你妈好？"老太太觉得很奇怪，就问那位老师："我妈已经死了很多年了，这个老外为什么会问我的妈怎么样？"

外国男生右手边坐着一位年轻小姐，年纪跟他差不多。他想再试一次，就跟那位小姐说："妈，你好！"小姐听他这样说，很不高兴，就对他说："我不是你妈！"说完站起来就走了。这个外国大学生觉得中文实在是太难了，决定回国去，不再学中文了。

从这个笑话，我们可以知道，在中文里，语法特别要紧："你好吗？"、"你妈好？"、"妈，你好！"这三句话的意思太不一样！所以外国人要学好中文，一定得注意中文的语法。

Reading Exercises (Traditional Characters) 繁體字

A. SENTENCES 句子

Read out loud each of the following sentences, which include all the new characters of this lesson. The first time you read a sentence, focus special attention on the characters and words that are new to you, reminding yourself of their pronunciation and meaning. The second time, aim to comprehend the overall meaning of the sentence.

一、我的愛好是畫畫兒、照相、以及看小說兒。

二、這個照相機是在哪兒買的？價錢怎麼這麼貴？

三、白老太太不但喜歡畫畫兒，而且也很喜歡唱歌兒。

四、這首歌的調子太高了，我唱不了這麼高的調子！

五、我們今天要參觀的第一家工廠做鞋子，第二家工廠做手表。

六、老張從小只喜歡一個人在家看書，怪不得他沒有甚麼朋友。

七、中國人非常喜歡天安門，每天都有好幾萬人到那裡去參觀。

八、那個意大利人從小就住在北京，難怪他的中國話講得那麼流利。

九、你說你的專業是音樂，是嗎？怪不得我常看你一邊兒走，一邊兒唱歌兒！

十、王大海告訴大家他的愛好是唱歌兒，可是大家都覺得他唱得很難聽。

B. CONVERSATIONS 對話

Read out loud the following conversations, including the name or role of the person speaking. If possible, find a partner or partners and each of you play a role. Then switch roles, so you get practice reading all of the lines.

一、

張愛紅：李文，你有甚麼愛好嗎？

李文：我喜歡音樂。從小在美國學唱歌兒。

張愛紅：怪不得我常看你一邊走一邊唱歌兒。

李文：是嗎？

張愛紅：除了音樂，你還有其他的愛好嗎？

李文：還喜歡看小說兒或是寫東西。你呢？你的愛好是甚麼？

張愛紅：畫畫兒，特別是國畫兒，還有書法。

二、

中國同學：好，現在請每位同學給我們唱一首歌兒！

美國同學：要唱歌兒啊？我們在美國很少唱歌兒，我不太會唱。

中國同學：你隨便唱一首，大家都是好朋友，沒關係。

美國同學：這樣子。好吧，可是我真的不太會唱。如果唱得不好聽，你們可別笑我！

中國同學：不會的。

美國同學：好，一、二、三、唱：「王老先生有塊地」。對不起，這個調子太高了！我再來一次吧⋯⋯

三、

嚴小姐：小管，你今天早上是不是出去了一會兒？

管先生：是的，我到對面很快地參觀了一下最近開的公共圖書館，不過我只去了差不多十五分鐘而已。

嚴小姐：怪不得！我差不多十點鐘的時候找你，可是怎麼找也找不到。

管先生：對不起，不好意思。有什麼事情嗎？

嚴小姐：有，事情是這樣子的⋯⋯

四、

美國人：您好！對不起，不好意思，請您幫我們照一張相，好嗎？

中國人：好，沒問題。不過，等一下，這個照相機怎麼用？

美國人：我教您⋯⋯奇怪，好像壞了。怎麼辦？

中國人：離這兒不遠有一家照相館，我帶您去。

五、

女兒：媽媽，我這學期的成績不太好，你別生氣。

媽媽：來，成績單拿給媽媽看看。甚麼？你這孩子！平常不去上課，也不做作業，也不好好準備考試，難怪成績會不好。媽媽怎麼能不生氣？

C. NARRATIVE 短文

Read the following narrative, paying special attention to punctuation and overall structure. The first time you read the narrative, read it out loud. The second time, read silently and try to gradually increase your reading speed. Always think of the meaning of what you're reading.

「你好嗎?」

我聽過這樣一個笑話。有一個男的外國大學生到中國去學中文。他很想多找機會講中國話。有一天,他的中文老師的一個朋友請客,老師就帶他一塊兒去吃飯。去以前,老師提醒他,看見其他的中國客人,可以說一句:「你好嗎?」

老師和學生到了飯店,坐下了。外國學生左手邊坐著一位中國老太太。他就開口問老太太:「你媽好?」老太太覺得很奇怪,就問那位老師:「我媽已經死了很多年了,這個老外為什麼會問我的媽怎麼樣?」

外國男生右手邊坐著一位年輕小姐,年紀跟他差不多。他想再試一次,就跟那位小姐說:「媽,你好!」小姐聽他這樣說,很不高興,就對他說:「我不是你媽!」說完站起來就走了。這個外國大學生覺得中文實在是太難了,決定回國去,不再學中文了。

從這個笑話,我們可以知道,在中文裡,語法特別要緊:「你好嗎?」、「你媽好?」、「媽,你好!」這三句話的意思太不一樣!所以外國人要學好中文,一定得注意中文的語法。

Notes 注解

B2. 王老先生有块地 (王老先生有塊地) "Old Mr. Wang had a plot of land." This is the first line of the Chinese translation of the American song "Old MacDonald Had a Farm." Note that the noun 地 "land," "ground" takes the measure 块 (塊) "piece of," "plot of."

B4. ◆奇怪 qíguài "be strange" [SV]. The character 怪 is one of the new characters for this lesson. Note that the word 奇怪 reoccurs in the Narrative for this lesson.

C1. ◆提醒 tíxǐng "remind" [V]. The character 醒 by itself is how one writes the verb xǐng "awaken" or "wake up."

"Chinese Calligraphy and Paintings"
(store sign in Taipei)

 New Characters and Words

Study the six characters below and the common words written with them, paying careful attention to each character's pronunciation, meaning, and structure, as well as similar-looking characters. After you've studied a character, turn to the *Practice Essentials* volume and practice writing it on the practice sheet, making sure to follow the correct stroke order and direction as you pronounce it out loud and think of its meaning.

511 研 **yán** grind; study

Radical is 石 **shí** "stone" (420). One "grinds" 研 with a "stone" 石. It's interesting to note that in colloquial English, the verb "grind" can also—just like Chinese 研—sometimes mean "study"! Distinguish 研 from 石 and simplified 开 **kāi** (122).

512 究 **jiū** study

Radical is 穴 **xué** "cave" or "hole." Phonetic is 九 **jiǔ** "nine" (10). Distinguish 究 from 空 **kòng/kōng** (437).

研究	**yánjiū**	study, research [V/N]
中国研究 (中國研究)	**Zhōngguo Yánjiū**	Chinese Studies [PH]
美国研究 (美國研究)	**Měiguo Yánjiū**	American Studies [PH]
近东研究 (近東研究)	**Jìndōng Yánjiū**	Near Eastern Studies [PH]
对⋯有研究 (對⋯有研究)	**duì...yǒu yánjiū**	be an expert in..., have expertise in... [PT]
研究生	**yánjiūshēng**	graduate student [N]
◉研究所	**yánjiūsuǒ**	graduate school [N]

513 懂   **dǒng**   understand

Radical is 心 **xīn** "heart" (262), which here gives a hint as to the meaning. When at the left side of a character, this radical is referred to colloquially as 心字旁 **xīnzìpáng** "side made up of the character 心" and is written as 忄. Phonetic is 董 **Dǒng**, which is a fairly common surname. Distinguish 懂 from 重 **zhòng** (462), traditional 種 **zhǒng** (320), and traditional 動 **dòng** (250).

懂	**dǒng**	understand [V]
听懂 (聽懂)	**tīngdǒng**	understand by hearing [RC]
听得懂 (聽得懂)	**tīngdedǒng**	be able to understand by hearing; understand [RC]
看懂	**kàndǒng**	understand by reading [RC]
看不懂	**kànbudǒng**	not be able to understand by reading; can't read [RC]

514 民   **mín**   people

Radical is 氏 **shì** "name," "clan." Distinguish 民 from 及 **jí** (400), 很 **hěn** (58) and 眼 **yǎn** (494).

人民	**rénmín**	people [N]
⊙人民日报 (人民日報)	**Rénmín Rìbào**	People's Daily (name of a newspaper) [N]
民国…年 (民國…年)	**Mínguó...nián**	in the...year of the Republic [PT]
原住民	**yuánzhùmín**	native people [N]
美国的原住民 (美國的原住民)	**Měiguóde yuánzhùmín**	Native American [PH]
⊙三民主义 (三民主義)	**Sān Mín Zhǔyì**	The Three Principles of the People (consisting of nationalism, democracy, and the people's livelihood, as proposed by Sun Yat-sen) [N]

515 华 (華)   **huá**   China
　　　　　　　 Huà   Hua (as a surname)

Radical of the simplified form is 十 **shí** "ten" (11). Phonetic of the simplified form is 化 **huà** "change" (479). Radical of the traditional form is 艸 **cǎo** "grass" (as an independent word this is written 草). When it occurs as a radical at the top of a character, the "grass" radical is written as ⁺⁺ and is then known as 草字头 (草字頭) **cǎozìtóu** "top made up of the character 草." Distinguish simplified 华 from 化 and 花 **huā** (455).

华 (華)	**Huà**	Hua [SN] (Note the tone here is Tone Four.)
华人 (華人)	**Huárén**	Chinese person; Chinese people [N]
中华人民共和国 (中華人民共和國)	**Zhōnghuá Rénmín Gònghéguó**	People's Republic of China [PW]
中华民国 (中華民國)	**Zhōnghuá Mínguó**	Republic of China (official name of Taiwan, and from 1912–49 the name for all of China) [PW]

516 亲 (親) **qīn** parent, relative; to kiss

Radical of the simplified form is 立 **lì** "stand" (446). Radical of the traditional form is 见 (見) **jiàn** "see" (300). Distinguish 亲 (親) from 立, 见, 来 (來) **lái** (135), 平 **píng** (241), and 本 **běn** (242).

父亲 (父親)	**fùqīn**	father [N]
母亲 (母親)	**mǔqīn**	mother [N]
父母亲 (父母親)	**fùmǔqīn**	parents [N]
◉亲人 (親人)	**qīnrén**	family member [N]

New Words in ISC 20-2 Written with Characters You Already Know

分	**fēn**	part, fraction [M]
…分之…	**…fēnzhī…**	(pattern for fractions) [PT]
百分之…	**bǎifēnzhī…**	…percent [PT]
…点… (…點…)	**…diǎn…**	(pattern for decimals) [PT]
共和国 (共和國)	**gònghéguó**	republic [N]
用	**yòng**	need to [V]
有用	**yǒuyòng**	be useful [SV]
没有用 (沒有用)	**méiyou yòng**	not have any use [PH]
这还用谢？(這還用謝？)	**Zhè hái yòng xiè?**	"What are you thanking me for?"
们 (們)	**-men**	(plural suffix) [BF] (e.g., 朋友们 [朋友們] "friends")
正好	**zhènghǎo(r)**	just; as it happens [MA]
传 (傳)	**zhuàn**	chronicle; biography [N] (Note that the character 传 [傳] is here pronounced **zhuàn**, not **chuán**.)

Reading Exercises (Simplified Characters) 简体字

Now practice reading the new characters and words for this lesson in context in sentences, conversations, and narratives. Be sure to refer to the Notes at the end of this lesson, and make use of the accompanying audio disc to hear and practice correct pronunciation, phrasing, and intonation.

A. SENTENCES 句子

Read out loud each of the following sentences, which include all the new characters of this lesson. The first time you read a sentence, focus special attention on the characters and words that are new to you, reminding yourself of their pronunciation and meaning. The second time, aim to comprehend the overall meaning of the sentence.

一、《人民日报》是中华人民共和国的第一大报。

二、华国树的父亲对天文很有研究，他的母亲对数学很有研究。

三、母亲大声地叫："孩子们！晚饭预备好了，快下来吃饭吧！"

四、"王爱华，女，民国三十七年出生于中华民国台湾省台东市。"

五、这个研究报告说美国的原住民占美国总人口的百分之一点七。

六、对不起，我没有完全听懂您刚才说的话，您能不能再讲一次？

七、听说在马来西亚，华人占总人口的四分之一，马来人占总人口的四分之三。

八、一个外国人如果认识差不多两千个中国字，就应该可以看懂《人民日报》了。

九、中华人民共和国的首都是北京，中华民国的首都是台北，不过也有人说中华民国
　　的首都是南京。

十、大海，我们今天一共是五个人，所以米饭你只能拿五分之一，懂不懂？

B. CONVERSATIONS 对话

Read out loud the following conversations, including the name or role of the person speaking. If possible, find a partner or partners and each of you play a role. Then switch roles, so you get practice reading all of the lines.

一、

张爱红：对了，你对京剧感兴趣吗？

李文　：京剧啊？我虽然不太懂，但是很爱看。

张爱红：这个星期六晚上我要跟父母一起去人民剧场看《白蛇传》。正好
　　　　多一张票，你愿意跟我一起去吗？

李文　：太好了！几点开始？

张爱红：八点。我星期六晚上七点一刻来找你。

李文　：好，真谢谢你！

张爱红：这还用谢？星期六见！

二、

李天乐：请问，你是华人吗？

高利民：是啊，我是华人。你呢？

李天乐：我也是华人。你在哪里出生的？

高利民：我在马来西亚出生的。你呢？

李天乐：我在新加坡出生的。

C. NARRATIVES 短文

Read the following narratives, paying special attention to punctuation and overall structure. The first time you read a narrative, read it out loud. The second time, read silently and try to gradually increase your reading speed. Always think of the meaning of what you're reading.

一、我的同学们都是研究生物和化学的，只有我一个人是研究文学的。
　　他们常常笑我说文学没有什么用。可是没办法，我真的只对文学感
　　兴趣。

二、一九七一年中华人民共和国和美国开始了对话，但是那时候，对话是不公开的，所以知道这件事情的人很少。

三、我父亲在一个研究所服务，母亲是一位中学教员。我们一家都是华人。我们的老家是上海，但是现在全家都住在美国。虽然我已经学了很久的中文了，说得也还算流利，但还是有一些话我听不太懂。中国字当然不用说，除了那些最简单的字之外，我都看不太懂。

四、何老头

从前，可能是民国二十年左右吧，我们家对面住着一个老头姓何，大家都叫他何老头。何老头很喜欢唱歌儿。记得有一天早上，何老头走到街上，站在一张桌子上，跟很多人说："我想人人都知道我很会唱歌儿。我也知道有很多朋友都喜欢听我唱。现在我要给你们唱几首最好听的歌儿，你们听一听！"他还说了很多别的话，说了半天。何老头说话，听的人真不少，大概有一百多个人。何老头就开始唱了。唱了一会儿，人就都走了，只有我跟我父亲没走。何老头跟我父亲说："先生，我唱的歌儿就是您和您的女儿懂。他们都不懂，所以都走了。"我父亲说："先生，您唱的歌儿我们也不懂。我们没走，是因为那张桌子是我们的，我们还需要用！"

 ## Reading Exercises (Traditional Characters) 繁體字

A. SENTENCES 句子

Read out loud each of the following sentences, which include all the new characters of this lesson. The first time you read a sentence, focus special attention on the characters and words that are new to you, reminding yourself of their pronunciation and meaning. The second time, aim to comprehend the overall meaning of the sentence.

一、《人民日報》是中華人民共和國的第一大報。

二、華國樹的父親對天文很有研究，他的母親對數學很有研究。

三、母親大聲地叫："孩子們！晚飯預備好了，快下來吃飯吧！"

四、「王愛華」女，民國三十七年出生於中華民國台灣省台東市。」

五、這個研究報告說美國的原住民佔美國總人口的百分之一點七。

六、對不起，我沒有完全聽懂您剛才說的話，您能不能再講一次？

七、聽說在馬來西亞，華人佔總人口的四分之一，馬來人佔總人口的四分之三。

八、一個外國人如果認識差不多兩千個中國字，就應該可以看懂《人民日報》了。

九、中華人民共和國的首都是北京，中華民國的首都是台北，不過也有人說中華民國的首都是南京。

十、大海，我們今天一共是五個人，所以米飯你只能拿五分之一，懂不懂？

B. CONVERSATIONS 對話

Read out loud the following conversations, including the name or role of the person speaking. If possible, find a partner or partners and each of you play a role. Then switch roles, so you get practice reading all of the lines.

一、

張愛紅：對了，你對京劇感興趣嗎？

李文：京劇啊？我雖然不太懂，但是很愛看。

張愛紅：這個星期六晚上我要跟父母一起去人民劇場看《白蛇傳》。正好多一張票，你願意跟我一起去嗎？

李文：太好了！幾點開始？

張愛紅：八點。我星期六晚上七點一刻來找你。

李文：好，真謝謝你！

張愛紅：這還用謝？星期六見！

二、

李天樂：請問，你是華人嗎？

高利民：是啊，我是華人。你呢？

李天樂：我也是華人。你在哪裡出生的？

高利民：我在馬來西亞出生的。你呢？

李天樂：我在新加坡出生的。

C. NARRATIVES 短文

Read the following narratives, paying special attention to punctuation and overall structure. The first time you read a narrative, read it out loud. The second time, read silently and try to gradually increase your reading speed. Always think of the meaning of what you're reading.

一、我的同學們都是研究生物和化學的，只有我一個人是研究文學的。他們常常笑我說文學沒有甚麼用。可是沒辦法，我真的只對文學感興趣。

二、一九七一年中華人民共和國和美國開始了對話，但是那時候，對話是不公開的，所以知道這件事情的人很少。

三、我父親在一個研究所服務，母親是一位中學教員。我們一家都是華人。我們的老家是上海，但是現在全家都住在美國。雖然我已經學了很久的中文了，說得也還算流利，但還是有一些話我聽不太懂。中國字當然不用說，除了那些最簡單的字之外，我都看不太懂。

四、何老頭

從前，可能是民國二十年左右吧，我們家，對面住著一個老頭姓何，大家都叫他何老頭。何老頭很喜歡唱歌兒。記得有一天早上，何老頭走到街上，站在一張桌子上，對很多人說：「我想人人都知道我很喜歡唱歌兒。我也知道我很喜歡唱，很多朋友都喜歡聽我唱。現在我要給你們唱幾首最好聽的歌兒，你們聽一聽！」何老頭就開始唱了。何老頭說了很多別的話，說了半天，他還說話，聽的人真不少，大概有一百多個人。唱了一會兒，人就都走了，只有我跟我父親沒走。何老頭跟我父親說：「先生，我唱的歌兒就是您和您的女兒懂。他們都不懂，所以都走了。」我父親說：「先生，您唱的歌兒我們也不懂。我們沒走，是因為那張桌子是我們的，我們還需要用！」

Notes 注解

A1. 第一大报 (第一大報) "biggest newspaper"

A4. This sentence is in formal written register or style. The word 于 (於) corresponds to 在 in spoken register.

A7a. ◆ 马来西亚 (馬來西亞) **Mǎláixīyà** "Malaysia" [PW]

A7b. ◉ 总人口 (總人口) **zǒngrénkǒu** "total population" [N]

A7c. ◉ 马来人 (馬來人) **Mǎlái rén** "Malay" [PH]

A9. Though the majority of people in Taiwan consider Taipei the capital of Taiwan, Republic of China, there are some who argue that, for historical and legal reasons, Nanjing is still the *de jure* capital of the Republic of China.

B1a. ◆ 京剧 (京劇) **Jīngjù** "Peking opera" [N]

B1b. ◆ 人民剧场 (人民劇場) **Rénmín Jùchǎng** "People's Theater" (in Beijing) [PW]

B1c. ◆ 蛇 **shé** "snake" [N]. The measure for 蛇 is 条 (條), so one says 一条蛇 (一條蛇) "one snake." 白蛇传 (白蛇傳) **Bái Shé Zhuàn** is the name of a famous Peking opera which is often translated as "The Chronicle of the White Snake."

B2. ◆ 新加坡 **Xīnjiāpō** "Singapore" [PW]

C2a. ◆ 对话 (對話) **duìhuà** "dialog" [N]

C2b. ◆ 公开 (公開) **gōngkāi** "be public," "be open" [SV]

C4a. ◆ 老头 (老頭) **lǎotóu(r)** "old man" [N]

C4b. 住着一个老头姓何 (住著一個老頭姓何) "there lived an old man with the last name of He"

Going to the Movies

New Characters and Words

Study the six characters below and the common words written with them, paying careful attention to each character's pronunciation, meaning, and structure, as well as similar-looking characters. After you've studied a character, turn to the *Practice Essentials* volume and practice writing it on the practice sheet, making sure to follow the correct stroke order and direction as you pronounce it out loud and think of its meaning.

517 影   **yǐng**   shadow; image; film

Radical is 彡 **shān** "feathers." Phonetic is 景 **jǐng** "view," which in turn consists of 日 **rì** (132) and 京 **jīng** (17). Distinguish 影 from 京.

电影 (電影)	**diànyǐng(r)**	movie [N]
看电影 (看電影)	**kàn diànyǐng(r)**	see a movie
看场电影 (看場電影)	**kàn chǎng diànyǐng(r)**	see a showing of a movie

518 新   **xīn**   new, fresh

Radical is 斤 **jīn** "catty" (326). Distinguish 新 from 亲 (親) **qīn** (516).

新	**xīn**	be new, fresh [SV]
◉新年	**xīn nián**	New Year [TW]
◉新年好！	**Xīn nián hǎo!**	"Happy New Year!" [IE]
◉新年快乐！(新年快樂！)	**Xīn nián kuàilè!**	"Happy New Year!" [IE]

519 故   **gù**   cause, reason; therefore

Radical is 攴 **pū** "tap" or "strike," which at the right side of a character is written 攵. Phonetic is 古 **gǔ** "old." Distinguish 故 from 做 **zuò** (378).

故事	**gùshi**	story [N]
说故事 (說故事)	**shuō gùshi**	tell a story [PH]
讲故事 (講故事)	**jiǎng gùshi**	tell a story [PH]

520 将 (將)   **jiāng**   will, be about to; take

Radical is 寸 **cùn** "inch." The whole character can serve as a phonetic, e.g. in 桨 (槳) **jiǎng** "oar." Distinguish 将 (將) from 特 **tè** (310).

将来 (將來)	**jiānglái**	in the future [TW]

521 计 (計)   **jì**   calculate; plan

Radical is 讠 (言) **yán** "speech" (336). The colloquial name for this radical is 言字旁 **yánzìpáng** "side made up of the character 言." The other component is 十 **shí** "ten" (11). If you can "speak" 言 or count from one to "ten" 十, then you can "plan" 计 (計). Distinguish 计 (計) from 什 **shén** (127).

计 (計)	**Jì**	Ji [SN]
计算机 (計算機)	**jìsuànjī**	computer; calculator [N]

522 划 (劃)   **huà**   plan

Radical is 刀 **dāo** "knife," which is written 刂 when occurring at the right-hand side of a character. This radical is referred to colloquially as 立刀 **lìdāo** "standing knife." Phonetic of the traditional form is 畫 **huà** (509). Distinguish traditional 劃 from traditional 畫 **huà** (509) and traditional 書 **shū** (321).

计划 (計劃)	**jìhua**	plan [N/V]

New Words in ISC 20-3 Written with Characters You Already Know

场 (場)	**chǎng**	(measure for a showing of a movie) [M]
当 (當)	**dāng**	serve as, work as [V]
家	**-jiā**	(noun suffix indicating professions) [BF]
画家 (畫家)	**huàjiā**	painter (artist) [N]
小说家 (小說家)	**xiǎoshuōjiā**	novelist [N]
音乐家 (音樂家)	**yīnyuèjiā**	musician [N]
讲 (講)	**jiǎng**	tell the story of; be about [V]
名叫	**míng jiào**	be named [PH]
年代	**niándài**	decade [N]
片子	**piānzi**	film, movie [N] (片 is here pronounced **piān**, not **piàn**)

生意	**shēngyì**	business [N]
做生意	**zuò shēngyì**	engage in business, do business [PH]
月	**yuè**	moon [N]

 Reading Exercises (Simplified Characters) 简体字

Now practice reading the new characters and words for this lesson in context in sentences, conversations, and narratives. Be sure to refer to the Notes at the end of this lesson, and make use of the accompanying audio disc to hear and practice correct pronunciation, phrasing, and intonation.

A. SENTENCES 句子

Read out loud each of the following sentences, which include all the new characters of this lesson. The first time you read a sentence, focus special attention on the characters and words that are new to you, reminding yourself of their pronunciation and meaning. The second time, aim to comprehend the overall meaning of the sentence.

一、最近有一个新片子,讲的是五十年代法国一个画家的故事。

二、一九七六年,毛主席死了以后,中国走上了一条全新的道路。

三、中国的新年不是一月一号,有的时候在一月,有的时候在二月。

四、今晚的电影名叫《活着》,是关于中国人民五十年代生活的电影。

五、五十、六十年代在中国,大人、小孩儿、男人、女人穿的衣服都一样。

六、听说王先生以前是小说家;他每次到我们家都会讲很多有意思的故事。

七、我的同屋差不多每天晚上都看一场电影,我真不懂他什么时候做作业!

八、白小姐在一家新开的进出口公司做事,听说那家公司的生意做得很
不错。

九、张新民的老大是画家,老二是音乐家,老三做生意;所以做爸爸的他现
在可以放心了。

十、王大海最怕有人问他"你将来有什么计划?",因为他还没有计划,也不
知道将来要做什么。

B. CONVERSATIONS 对话

Read out loud the following conversations, including the name or role of the person speaking. If possible, find a partner or partners and each of you play a role. Then switch roles, so you get practice reading all of the lines.

一、

小牛:进来。小李!

小李:做什么呢?

小牛:学习呢。

小李:是吗?你晚上有空吗?想不想去看场电影儿?

小牛:可以啊。有什么好片子吗?

小李:最近有一个新片子,名叫《月的主人》,听说不错。讲的是三十年代中国一
个音乐家的故事。

二、(中国新年的时候)
张老师：校长，新年快乐！
校长　　：张老师，新年好！

三、
班立新：小班，我不会用这个计算机。你可不可以教我怎么用？
计国明：我看看。这个计算机好像坏了。你最好换一个新的吧！

四、
女生：你将来有什么计划？
男生：我喜欢小孩子，所以将来想当小学老师。你呢？
女生：我从小就对音乐感兴趣，所以将来打算当音乐家。
男生：你这个计划不错！

C. NARRATIVES 短文

Read the following narratives, paying special attention to punctuation and overall structure. The first time you read a narrative, read it out loud. The second time, read silently and try to gradually increase your reading speed. Always think of the meaning of what you're reading.

一、我哥哥特别喜欢看电影。每次有新片子出来，他就一定得去看。他有时候也带我去看，可是我不懂电影有什么好看的。我觉得花钱去看电影还不如花钱去书店买书。

二、我小的时候非常喜欢看故事书，我什么样的故事都喜欢看。我也很喜欢画画儿，可是画得不太好。很多人常问我将来有什么计划，我告诉他们长大了以后想做小说家或画家。现在我已经长大了，可是如果有人问我将来打算做什么，我会有一点儿紧张，也不知道该说什么，因为说真的，我还没决定我将来的计划。

三、牛吃草
王大川先生是一位非常好的画家，人人都听过他的名字。他最近画了一张新画儿叫"牛吃草"，所以我跟我父亲、母亲都去看了。我们看他的这张画儿看了很久，是一大张白纸，上面什么都没有。所以我就问王先生："这张画儿为什么叫'牛吃草'？草在哪儿呢？"王先生告诉我们说牛把草吃完了，所以没有草了。后来别人问王先生："那，牛呢？牛在哪儿？"王先生先看了画儿，然后看了那个人，就告诉他因为没有草了，所以牛也走了。

New Town Plaza, Hong Kong

Reading Exercises (Traditional Characters) 繁體字

A. SENTENCES 句子

Read out loud each of the following sentences, which include all the new characters of this lesson. The first time you read a sentence, focus special attention on the characters and words that are new to you, reminding yourself of their pronunciation and meaning. The second time, aim to comprehend the overall meaning of the sentence.

一、最近有一個新片子，講的是五十年代法國一個畫家的故事。

二、一九七六年，毛主席死了以後，中國走上了一條全新的道路。

三、中國的新年不是一月一號，有的時候在一月，有的時候在二月。

四、今晚的電影名叫《活着》，是關於中國人民五十年代生活的電影。

五、五十、六十年代在中國，大人、小孩兒、男人、女人穿的衣服都一樣。

六、聽說王先生以前是小說家；他每次到我們家都會講很多有意思的故事。

七、我的同屋差不多每天晚上都看一場電影，我真不懂他什麼時候做作業！

八、白小姐在一家新開的進出口公司做事，聽說那家公司的生意做得很不錯。

九、張新民的老大是畫家，老二是音樂家，老三做生意；所以做爸爸的他現在可以放心了。

十、王大海最怕有人問他「你將來有甚麼計劃？」，因為他還沒有計劃，也不知道將來要做什麼。

B. CONVERSATIONS 對話

Read out loud the following conversations, including the name or role of the person speaking. If possible, find a partner or partners and each of you play a role. Then switch roles, so you get practice reading all of the lines.

一、

小牛：進來。小李！

小李：做什麼呢？

小牛：學習呢。

小李：是嗎？你晚上有空嗎？想不想去看場電影兒？

小牛：可以啊。有甚麼好片子嗎？

小李：最近有一個新片子，名叫《月的主人》，聽說不錯。講的是三十年代中國一個音樂家的故事。

二、（中國新年的時候）

校長　：張老師，新年好！

張老師：校長，新年快樂！

班立新：小班，我不會用這個計算機。你可不可以教我怎麼用？

計國明：我看看。這個計算機好像壞了。你最好換一個新的吧！

三、

四、

女生：你將來有甚麼計劃？

男生：我喜歡小孩子，所以將來想當小學老師。你呢？

女生：我從小就對音樂感興趣，所以將來打算當音樂家。

男生：你這個計劃不錯！

Street Sign in Taipei

C. NARRATIVES 短文

Read the following narratives, paying special attention to punctuation and overall structure. The first time you read a narrative, read it out loud. The second time, read silently and try to gradually increase your reading speed. Always think of the meaning of what you're reading.

一、

我哥哥特別喜歡看電影。每次有新片子出來，他就一定得去看。他有時候也帶我去看，可是我不懂電影有甚麼好看的。我覺得花錢去看電影還不如花錢去書店買書。

二、

我小的時候非常喜歡看故事書，我什麼樣的故事都喜歡看。我也很喜歡畫畫兒，可是畫得不太好。很多人常問我將來有甚麼計劃，我告訴他們長大了以後想做小說家或畫家。現在我已經長大了，可是如果有人問我將來打算做什麼，我會有一點兒緊張，也不知道該說甚麼，因為說真的，我還沒決定我將來的計劃。

三、

牛吃草

王大川先生是一位非常好的畫家，人人都聽過他的名字。他最近畫了一張新畫兒叫「牛吃草」，所以我跟我父親、母親都去看了。我們看他的這張畫兒看了很久，是一大張白紙，上面甚麼都沒有。所以我就問王先生：「這張畫兒為什麼叫『牛吃草』？草在哪兒呢？」王先生告訴我們說牛把草吃完了，所以沒有草了。後來別人問王先生：「那，牛呢？」王先生先看了畫兒，然後看了那個人，就告訴他因為沒有草了，所以牛也走了。

Notes 注解

A1. 今晚 is an abbreviation of 今天晚上.

A8. 新开的进出口公司 (新開的進出口公司) "a newly opened import-export company"

A9. 做爸爸的他 lit. "he, who is the father"

C1. 我不懂电影有什么好看的 (我不懂電影有什麼好看的) "I don't understand what's so good about watching movies."

 New Characters and Words

Study the six characters below and the common words written with them, paying careful attention to each character's pronunciation, meaning, and structure, as well as similar-looking characters. After you've studied a character, turn to the *Practice Essentials* volume and practice writing it on the practice sheet, making sure to follow the correct stroke order and direction as you pronounce it out loud and think of its meaning.

523 类（類） **lèi**　kind, type

Radical of the simplified form is 米 **mǐ** "hulled rice" (368), the other component being 大 **dà** (13). Radical of the traditional form is 頁 **yè** "page," the other components being 米 and 犬 **quǎn** "dog." Distinguish simplified 类 from 米, and traditional 類 from traditional 頭.

类（類）	**lèi**	kind, type, category [M]
这类（這類）	**zhèilèi**	this kind
那类(那類)	**nèilèi**	that kind
哪类(哪類)	**něilèi**	which kind?
人类学（人類學）	**rénlèixué**	anthropology [N]
⊙人类（人類）	**rénlèi**	mankind, humanity [N]

524 排 **pái**　row, line

Radical is 手 **shǒu** "hand" (305), which at the left side of a character is written as 扌 and is referred to colloquially as 提手 **tíshǒu** "raised hand." Phonetic is 非 **fēi** "not" (385). Distinguish 排 from 非.

排	**pái**	row, line [M]
第八排	**dìbāpái**	Row 8
第几排 (第幾排)	**dìjǐpái**	which row?
排行	**páiháng**	(refers to one's rank or order in a family) [N]

525 楼(樓)   **lóu**   building; floor

Radical is the pictograph 木 **mù** "tree." This radical is referred to colloquially as 木字旁 **mùzìpáng** "side made up of the character 木." Note that when 木 is written at the left of a character as a radical, its last stroke is shortened so that it doesn't collide with the component to its right. Phonetic is 娄 (婁) **lóu** "weak." Distinguish 楼 (樓) from 数 (數) **shù** (424).

楼 (樓)	**lóu**	building [N]; floor [BF]
上楼 (上樓)	**shànglóu**	go upstairs [VO]
下楼 (下樓)	**xiàlóu**	go downstairs [VO]
楼上 (樓上)	**lóushàng**	upstairs [PW]
楼下 (樓下)	**lóuxià**	downstairs [PW]
三楼 (三樓)	**sānlóu**	third floor
专家楼 (專家樓)	**zhuānjiā lóu**	(foreign) experts building [PH]

526 部   **bù**   part, section

Radical is 邑 **yì** "city," which is written 阝 when occurring at the right-hand side of a character. This radical is referred to colloquially as 右耳旁 **yòu'ěrpáng** "side made up of a right ear." Phonetic is 音 **pòu** "spit out." Distinguish 部 from 都 **dōu** (32).

部分	**bùfen**	part, portion [M]
大部分	**dà bùfen**	majority, greater part, most [PH]
外交部	**Wàijiāo Bù**	Foreign Ministry [PH]
部	**bù**	(measure for films) [M] (e.g., 一部片子 **yíbù piānzi** "a film")
◉东部 (東部)	**dōngbù**	eastern part (of an area), the East [PW]
◉南部	**nánbù**	southern part (of an area), the South [PW]
◉西部	**xībù**	western part (of an area), the West [PW]
◉北部	**běibù**	northern part (of an area), the North [PW]
◉中部	**zhōngbù**	central part (of an area) [PW]

527 理   **lǐ**   pay attention to

Radical is 玉 **yù** "jade." Phonetic is 里 **lǐ** "mile." Distinguish 理 from 里.

理	**lǐ**	pay attention to [V]
理解	**lǐjiě**	understand [V]; understanding [N]
经理 (經理)	**jīnglǐ**	manager [N]
总经理 (總經理)	**zǒngjīnglǐ**	general manager [N]

地理	dìlǐ	geography [N]
物理	wùlǐ	physics [N]
心理学 (心理學)	xīnlǐxué	psychology [N]
⊙ 心理学家 (心理學家)	xīnlǐxuéjiā	psychologist [N]

528 它   **tā**   it

Radical is 宀 **mián** "roof." This radical is referred to colloquially as 宝盖头 (寶蓋頭) **bǎogàitóu** "top made up of a canopy." The part that is under the "roof" is 匕 **bǐ**, which is a type of ancient spoon, an object, so we could say that "it" 它 is under the "roof" 宀. The whole character 它 can serve as a phonetic, e.g., in the character 鸵 (鴕), which is used in the word 鸵鸟 (鴕鳥) **tuóniǎo** "ostrich." Distinguish 它 from 他 **tā** "he" (55) and 她 **tā** "she" (56).

它	tā	it [PR]
别管它! (別管它!)	**Bié guǎn ta!**	"Don't concern yourself with it!"
把它放在这儿吧。(把它放在這兒吧。)	**Bǎ ta fàngzai zhèr ba.**	"Put it here."

New Words in ISC 20-4 Written with Characters You Already Know

爱情片 (愛情片)	àiqíngpiàn	romantic movie [N]
北京图书馆 (北京圖書館)	Běijīng Túshūguǎn	Beijing Library [PW]
从来 (從來)	cónglái	all along, always [A]
从来没…过 (從來沒…過)	cónglái méi...-guo	have never ever before... [PT]
电影明星 (電影明星)	diànyǐng míngxīng	movie star [PH]
感	gǎn	touch, move; affect (emotionally) [V]
明白	míngbai	understand [V/RE]
内容 (內容)	nèiróng	content [N]
听不太明白 (聽不太明白)	tīngbutàimíngbai	can't understand very well [RC]
主要	zhǔyào	main, essential [AT]

Reading Exercises (Simplified Characters) 简体字

Now practice reading the new characters and words for this lesson in context in sentences, conversations, and narratives. Be sure to refer to the Notes at the end of this lesson, and make use of the accompanying audio disc to hear and practice correct pronunciation, phrasing, and intonation.

A. SENTENCES 句子

Read out loud each of the following sentences, which include all the new characters of this lesson. The first time you read a sentence, focus special attention on the characters and words that are new to you, reminding yourself of their pronunciation and meaning. The second time, aim to comprehend the overall meaning of the sentence.

一、我今天到书店买了书和地图，可是已经忘了把它放在什么地方了！

二、长白山的林区是中国东北边的主要林区，大概有28万平方公里。

三、我的中国同屋有一次告诉我他希望将来在中国外交部工作。

四、美国老一代的华人，大部分是从广东省来的，他们的母语是台山话。

五、我们的司机老何告诉我他从来没有在大城市开过车，但是他愿意试
　　一试。

六、我在我们家排行老四，我上面有一个哥哥、两个姐姐，下面还有一个
　　弟弟、三个妹妹。

七、我们大二得决定专业，我准备学人类学，我的一个同屋要学心理学，
　　另一个同屋要学物理。

八、美国的中国饭馆，相当一部分都叫"北京楼"，不过他们卖的菜不一
　　定是北京风味儿的菜！

九、北京市西部、北部和东北部都有山，西部的山叫西山，各位听说过的
　　香山也就是西山的一部分。

十、那部爱情片王大海已经看了十多次了，可是主要内容他还是不人理解。

B. CONVERSATIONS 对话

Read out loud the following conversations, including the name or role of the person speaking. If possible, find a partner or partners and each of you play a role. Then switch roles, so you get practice reading all of the lines.

一、

小牛：太好了！我还从来没看过这类的电影儿呢。在什么地方？几点开始？

小李：北京图书馆，三点半。三点我来找你，怎么样？

小牛：好啊。

小李：好，再见。

小牛：再见。…… 几排的？

小李：位子不错，楼下十五排，十六、十八号儿。我们进去吧。……你觉得
　　这部片子怎么样？

小牛：太好了！很感人。

小李：他们说的话，你都能听懂吗？

小牛：大部分都懂，有的地方说得太快，听不太明白。不过电影的主要内
　　容我都能理解。

D. SUPPLEMENT: 台灣的地理

台北在台灣的北部
台南在台灣的南部
台東在台灣的東部
那麼，請問，台中在台灣的哪裏？

(芙蓉 **fúróng** means "lotus")

Notes 注解

A1.   ◉老一代 **lǎo yídài** "the older generation"

A8.   相当一部分 (相當一部分) "quite a number of," "a considerable portion of"

B2.   ◉包间 (包間) **bāojiān** "private room," "separate room" (in a restaurant) [PW]

C3a.   ◆搬家 **bānjiā** "move" (one's home) [VO]

C3b.   ◆休息 **xiūxi** "rest" [V]

C3c.   他走到我身边 (他走到我身邊) lit. "He walked to my body" or in idiomatic English, "He walked over to where I was."

C3d.   ◉只 (隻) **zhī** (measure for watches) [M]. Note that the simplified character 只 is here pronounced **zhī**, not **zhǐ** as when it means "only." The phrase 一只手表 (一隻手錶) means "a watch."

D.   The answer to the question, of course, is 中部.

(This sign was posted erroneously at Taipei Railway Station.)

Leisure Time Activities (II)

COMMUNICATIVE OBJECTIVES

Once you've mastered this unit, you'll be able to use Chinese to read and write about:

1. Sports and leisure activities.

2. Competitive games that are in progress: Who is playing whom? What is the score? Who is likely to win and lose? etc.

3. Watching television.

4. The Great Wall of China.

5. A Chinese joke.

6. A passage comparing home education in China and the US.

7. A passage on Taiwanese society.

8. A famous story from ancient China about adding legs to a snake.

9. A passage about the geography of mainland China, Hainan, and Taiwan.

10. A story called "The Three-Character Donkey."

New Words in ISC 21-1 Written with Characters You Already Know

比方说 (比方說)	**bǐfāng shuō**	for example [PH]
比如	**bǐrú**	for example [MA]
比如说 (比如說)	**bǐrú shuō**	for example [PH]
打	**dǎ**	play (a sport) [V]
个子 (個子)	**gèzi**	stature, build [N]
公园 (公園)	**gōngyuán**	a park [PW]
和	**hàn**	and [CJ] (**Hàn** is the pronunciation of the word in Taiwan; in Beijing it is pronounced **hé**.)
毛	**máo**	feather, fur, hair (on body) [N]
哪些	**nǎxiē**	which ones? which?
太极 (太極)	**tàijí**	t'ai chi (short for 太极拳 [太極拳] **tàijíquán** t'ai chi, "shadow boxing" [N])
有没有+VERB (有沒有+VERB)	**yǒu méiyou + VERB**	(to indicate Yes/No questions) [PT] (e.g., 你有没 [沒] 有去？"Did you go?")

Reading Exercises (Simplified Characters) 简体字

Now practice reading the new characters and words for this lesson in context in sentences, conversations, and narratives. Be sure to refer to the Notes at the end of this lesson, and make use of the accompanying audio disc to hear and practice correct pronunciation, phrasing, and intonation.

A. SENTENCES 句子

Read out loud each of the following sentences, which include all the new characters of this lesson. The first time you read a sentence, focus special attention on the characters and words that are new to you, reminding yourself of their pronunciation and meaning. The second time, aim to comprehend the overall meaning of the sentence.

一、各位同学，现在请你们把今天的功课交给老师！

二、我的运气常常不太好；我室友的运气倒是不错。

三、我的室友参加校队以后，都没有时间和我去看电影了。

四、你早上可以去人民公园学中国功夫、打太极或者做其他的运动。

五、"容力为先生，容力为先生，请您尽快到办公室来接电话！"

六、我虽然没有参加什么球队，但是我还是很喜欢跟朋友随便打打球。

七、各地吃饭的习惯都不一样，比方说中国人吧，北方人喜欢吃面，南方人爱吃米饭。

八、中国人觉得好的开始很要紧，比如说，有一句老话说："好的开始是成功的一半儿。"

九、我们中文课的教室在楼上，可是老师的办公室在地下室，这样跑来跑去对大家都不太方便。

十、王大海不怎么用功，他妹妹倒是很用功，也上了很多很难的课，比方说，化学、物理、心理学什么的。

B. CONVERSATIONS 对话

Read out loud the following conversations, including the name or role of the person speaking. If possible, find a partner or partners and each of you play a role. Then switch roles, so you get practice reading all of the lines.

一、

台湾同学：你喜欢做哪些运动？

美国同学：我喜欢打排球。其实，我以前高中的时候在排球校队，不过现在已经很久没打了。

台湾同学：不简单！那你来台湾这么久了，有没有做一些不一样的运动，比如说，中国功夫、太极什么的？

美国同学：我自己没有，不过我的室友倒是每个星期天早上都会到对面的公园去学中国功夫。

二、

马川：明天去哪里打球？

王可：要不要去加油站后面的那个小公园？

马川：我觉得我们应该换一个地方，比方说领事馆后面那一大块空地或者食品店前面的那个公园都行。

王可：随便你，去哪里都行。

三、

妈妈：你手里拿着什么呢？

儿子：是个球，我等一下要到公园去跟同学打球。对了，妈，我的运动鞋放在哪里了？我找不着了！

妈妈：今天不能打球，会下雨的！

儿子：这么干的天气，下什么雨？

妈妈：我刚才听天气预报说会下雨的。再说，你的功课还没做完呢！

儿子：好吧，好吧，不去就不去！

四、

美国华人：妹妹，你不是从小就不喜欢学中文吗？怎么现在倒学起中文来了？

女儿　　：我小的时候你跟爸爸天天要我学，所以我就不学。现在我长大了，知道学中文有用，所以倒想学中文了。你跟爸爸高兴吧？

美国华人：孩子，你现在这么用功地学习中文，我跟你爸爸好高兴啊！

"Huàzhuāngshì"

C. NARRATIVES 短文

Read the following narratives, paying special attention to punctuation and overall structure. The first time you read a narrative, read it out loud. The second time, read silently and try to gradually increase your reading speed. Always think of the meaning of what you're reading.

一、

我這個人個子長得比較高，跑步跑得也不慢。以前在成功大學學習的時候，我很喜歡運動。比如說跟室友們一起打球或是到公園去打太極、學中國功夫什麼的。可是現在我已經參加工作了，每天從早到晚得在辦公室裡頭上班，實在太忙了，根本沒有空到外頭去運動。

二、

金金小妹妹今年六歲了，今天是她上小學一年級的第一天。她的老師王老師開始教班上的小朋友寫中國字了。老師告訴他們，開始總是最難，只要用功學習，寫第二張就容易得多了。「那麼，老師，」金金說，「我一開始就寫第二張吧！」

Notes 注解

A1. ⊙ 交给 (交給) **jiāogěi** "hand over to," "give to" [V+PV]

A4. ⊙ 人民公园 (人民公園) **Rénmín Gōngyuán** "People's Park" [PW]. There are public parks with this name in many mainland Chinese cities, the most famous of which are in Shanghai, Tianjin, Guangzhou, and Chengdu.

B2. ⊙ 空地 **kòngdì** "empty land," "vacant land" [N]

B3a. ⊙ 再说 (再說) **zài shuō** "furthermore," "besides," or "moreover" [PH]

B3b. 好吧，好吧，不去就不去！ "O.K., O.K., then I just won't go!"

B4a. The mother addresses her daughter as 妹妹 not to indicate that the daughter is her own younger sister, but rather to describe her position among the children in the family. 哥哥，姐姐, and 弟弟 are used similarly as terms of address by parents and grandparents in many Chinese families.

B4b. 学起中文来了 (學起中文來了) "have started learning Chinese." This structure consists of the compound verb 学起来 (學起來) with the object 中文, resulting in a so-called split resultative compound verb construction. When 起来 (起來) is added to verbs, it often adds the sense "begin."

B4c. 我小的时候你跟爸爸天天说要我学，所以我就不学 (我小的時候你跟爸爸天天說要我學，所以我就不學) lit. "When I was little, you and Dad said every day you wanted me to learn, so I on the contrary refused to learn." When used with negatives, 就 may emphasize something that is in contradiction to a previous statement.

C1. 参加工作 (參加工作) "participate in work," "work"

New Characters and Words

Study the six characters below and the common words written with them, paying careful attention to each character's pronunciation, meaning, and structure, as well as similar-looking characters. After you've studied a character, turn to the *Practice Essentials* volume and practice writing it on the practice sheet, making sure to follow the correct stroke order and direction as you pronounce it out loud and think of its meaning.

535 假   **jià**   vacation, leave

                       jiǎ   false; if

Radical is 人 **rén** "person" (30), which is written 亻 when occurring at the left side of a character. The colloquial name for this radical is 人字旁 **rénzìpáng** "side made up of the character 人." Phonetic is 叚 **jià**.

假	**jià**	vacation, leave [N]
假日	**jiàrì**	holiday, day off [N]
放假	**fàngjià**	take a vacation [VO]
请假 (請假)	**qǐngjià**	request leave [VO]
假如	**jiǎrú**	if [MA]
假如…的话 (假如…的話)	**jiǎrú...-de huà**	if... [PT]

536 春   **chūn**   spring

Radical is 日 **rì** "sun," which is a pictograph of a squared-off sun with a sunspot in it (132).

春假	**chūnjià**	spring vacation [N]

六、

河南人：我們看足球吧！今天是甚麼隊對甚麼隊啊？

湖北人：今天是南非對比利時。

河南人：現在幾比幾？

湖北人：三平。

七、

上海人：足球，足球，我要看足球！快把電視機打開！

廣州人：好。已經打開了。

上海人：甚麼隊對甚麼隊？

廣州人：馬里對多哥。對不起，我說錯了，是也門對黑山。

上海人：也門對黑山啊？現在幾比幾？

廣州人：現在四比〇。

C. NARRATIVES 短文

Read the following narratives, paying special attention to punctuation and overall structure. The first time you read a narrative, read it out loud. The second time, read silently and try to gradually increase your reading speed. Always think of the meaning of what you're reading.

一、

大部分的美國小孩，每天都看好幾個鐘頭的電視節目，而且想看甚麼就看甚麼，沒人管。雖然我也是美國人，但是我們家不是那樣。我們家只有一台小小的電視機，放在爸爸媽媽的房間裡。爸爸從來不讓我跟哥哥看電視，每次我們想看的時候，他就叫我們去做作業。有時候父母不在家，我們就會到他們的房間打開電視機，站在那兒看幾分鐘。一聽見爸爸媽媽開車回來的聲音，就馬上把電視機關上，跑回自己的房間去學習。我剛上大學的時候，覺得很自由，沒人管，要做什麼都可以，當然也可以隨時看電視。不過後來才知道，根本沒有甚麼好看的節目，還不如不看。這樣不但可以節省時間，還能省電！

二、

畫蛇添足

從前有幾個人得到一壺酒。這壺酒只夠一個人喝。應該給誰喝呢？有一個人提議說：「我們每個人都在地上畫一條蛇吧。誰先畫完，這壺酒就給誰喝。」大家都同意這個辦法，就開始在地上畫。有一個人很快就把蛇畫完了。他看別人都還沒畫完，就很得意地說：「你們實在畫得太慢了！你們看，我的蛇已經畫完了，我現在再給它添上幾隻腳吧！」當他正在給蛇畫腳的時候，另一個人已經把他的蛇畫完了，就把酒壺拿過去，說：「蛇是沒有腳的，你現在給它添上了腳，就不是蛇了。所以第一個畫完蛇的人應該算是我而不是你！」說完這句話，他就把酒喝完了。這個故事叫「畫蛇添足」，一直到現在，如果有人做了什麼完全不需要做的事情，中國人可能會說：「你這真是畫蛇添足！」

Notes 注解

A1. 强是强（強是強）"as for being strong, it's strong all right" or, in idiomatic English, "is pretty strong"

A8. 在场（在場）**zài chǎng** "be present, be on the scene" [PH]

A10. The film 黄土地（黃土地）, known in English as *Yellow Earth*, appeared in 1984. The director was Chen Kaige and the cinematographer was Zhang Yimou. The film 人到中年 is known in English as *At Middle Age*, and appeared in 1982. It was directed by Qiming Wang.

B1a. ◆文艺（文藝）"literature and art"

B1b. ◆文艺晚会（文藝晚會）"variety show" [PH]. This literally means "literature and art evening party."

B1c. ◆赢（贏）**yíng** "win" [V]

B2. 我的意思是说（我的意思是說）"What I mean is"

B3. The Chinese names 张三（張三）and 李四 are used much like English "John Doe" and "Jane Roe" as placeholder names to stand for Chinese people who are unnamed.

B4. 北京台（北京臺）"the Beijing (television broadcasting) station"

B5. ◉海地 **Hǎidì** "Haiti" [PW]

B6. ◉比利时（比利時）**Bǐlìshí** "Belgium" [PW]

B7a. ◉马里（馬里）**Mǎlǐ** "Mali" [PW]

B7b. ◉多哥 **Duōgē** "Togo" [PW]

B7c. ◉也门（也門）**Yěmén** "Yemen" [PW]

B7d. ◉黑山 **Hēi Shān** "Montenegro" [PW]

C1. ◉省电（省電）**shěngdiàn** "conserve electrical power" [VO]

C2a. ◆蛇 **shé** "snake" [N]. The measure used with 蛇 is 条（條）, so to say "this snake," one would say 这条蛇（這條蛇）.

C2b. ◆添 **tiān** "add" [V]

C2c. The character 足, as you learned in this lesson, means "foot." The well-known four-character expression 画蛇添足（畫蛇添足）, which is the title of the story you are about to read, literally means "draw a snake and add feet." It refers to ruining an effect by adding something superfluous.

C2d. ◉得到 **dédào** "obtain," "get" [RC]

C2e. ◆壶（壺）**hú** "flask," "jar," pot" [M]

C2f. ◆提议（提議）**tíyì** "propose," "suggest" [V]

C2g. ◉得意 **déyì** "be pleased with oneself," "complacent," or "self-satisfied" [SV]

C2h. ◉只（隻）**zhī** (measure for feet) [M]. The phrase 给它添上几只脚（給它添上幾隻腳）means "add several feet for it."

C2i. ◆脚（腳）**jiǎo** "foot" [N]

C2j. ◉当···的时候（當···的時候）**dāng...-de shíhou** "when" or "while" [PT]

An Excursion to the Great Wall

长城是什么时候建的？
（長城是什麼時候建的？）

大约是在两千多年前，
战国时代就开始建了。（大约
是在两千多年前，戰國時代
就開始建了。）

New Characters and Words

Study the six characters below and the common words written with them, paying careful attention to each character's pronunciation, meaning, and structure, as well as similar-looking characters. After you've studied a character, turn to the *Practice Essentials* volume and practice writing it on the practice sheet, making sure to follow the correct stroke order and direction as you pronounce it out loud and think of its meaning.

547 底   **dǐ**   bottom, base; ground

Radical is 广 **yǎn** "eaves." This radical is referred to colloquially as 广字头 (廣字頭) **guǎngzìtóu** "top made up of the character 广." Phonetic is 氐 **dī**. Distinguish 底 from 低 **dī** (268) and 纸 (紙) **zhǐ** (324).

到底	**dàodǐ(r)**	after all, really [MA]
底下	**dǐxia**	underneath [PW]
桌子底下	**zhuōzi dǐxia**	underneath the table
◉年底	**niándǐ**	end of the year [TW]
◉月底	**yuèdǐ**	end of the month [TW]

548 建   **jiàn**   establish, build

Radical is 廴 **yǐn** "go," which should be distinguished from the completely different radical 辶 **chuò**, which also happens to mean "go." The whole character 建 serves as a phonetic in other characters, e.g., in the character 健, which is used in the word 健康 **jiànkāng** "be healthy."

建	**jiàn**	build [V]
◉建成	**jiànchéng**	build so that something is completed, build, construct [RC]

549 修　　**xiū**　　build, repair; study, take (a course)

Radical is 人 **rén** "person" (30), which is written 亻 when occurring at the left side of a character. The colloquial name for this radical is 人字旁 **rénzìpáng** "side made up of the character 人." Phonetic is 攸 **yōu** "distant." Distinguish 修 from traditional 條 **tiáo** (240).

修	**xiū**	build, repair; study, take (courses) [V]
修起来 (修起來)	**xiūqilai**	in the building of something
主修	**zhǔxiū**	major in [V]; major [N]
◉ 修建	**xiūjiàn**	build, construct [V]

550 靠　　**kào**　　depend on, lean on

Radical is 非 **fēi** "not" (385). Phonetic is 告 **gào** "tell" (441). Distinguish 靠 from 告, 非, and 排 **pái** (524).

靠	**kào**	depend on [V]
◉ 可靠	**kěkào**	be reliable, dependable [SV]

551 战（戰）　　**zhàn**　　battle, war

Radical is 戈 **gē** "spear." Phonetic of the simplified character is 占 **zhàn** "occupy" (439) while the phonetic of the traditional character is 單 **dān** "single" (388). Distinguish simplified 战 from simplified 占, and traditional 戰 from traditional 單.

战国时代 (戰國時代)	**Zhànguó Shídài**	Warring States Period [TW]
◉ 第一次世界大战 (第一次世界大戰)	**Dì'yīcì Shìjiè Dàzhàn**	World War I [TW]
◉ 第二次世界大战 (第二次世界大戰)	**Dì'èrcì Shìjiè Dàzhàn**	World War II [TW]

552 争（爭）　　**zhēng**　　compete; fight

Radical of the simplified form is 刀 **dāo** "knife," which appears in slightly altered fashion on top of the character. Radical of the traditional form is 爪 **zhuǎ** "claw," which also appears in altered fashion on top of the character. The character 争 (爭) can itself serve as a phonetic in other characters, e.g., in the character 静 (靜), which is used in the word 安静 (安靜) **ānjìng** "be quiet."

战争 (戰爭)	**zhànzhēng**	war [N]
战争片 (戰爭片)	**zhànzhēngpiàn**	war film [N]

New Words in ISC 21-4 Written with Characters You Already Know

公里	**gōnglǐ**	kilometer [M]
够···的 (夠···的)	**gòu...-de**	quite... , rather... [PT]
可真够不容易的 (可真夠不容易的)	**kě zhēn gòu bù róngyide**	really quite hard
可不是	**kě bú shì**	"that's for sure" [IE]

人工	**réngōng**	human labor [N]
时代 (時代)	**shídài**	period [N]
算上	**suànshang**	include; count [RC]
算得上	**suàndeshang**	can be regarded as [RC]

 ## Reading Exercises (Simplified Characters) 简体字

Now practice reading the new characters and words for this lesson in context in sentences, conversations, and narratives. Be sure to refer to the Notes at the end of this lesson, and make use of the accompanying audio disc to hear and practice correct pronunciation, phrasing, and intonation.

A. SENTENCES 句子

Read out loud each of the following sentences, which include all the new characters of this lesson. The first time you read a sentence, focus special attention on the characters and words that are new to you, reminding yourself of their pronunciation and meaning. The second time, aim to comprehend the overall meaning of the sentence.

一、中国的万里长城是战国时代修建的。

二、中国人常说："在家靠父母，出门靠朋友。"

三、今天天气很热，牛和马都在树底下吃草。

四、桌子底下到底是什么东西啊？好像是什么小动物的样子！

五、我们生活在这个时代，特别需要世界和平，战争对谁都不好。

六、希望我今年年底之前能修完人类学专业的四十五个学分。

七、听说最近在中国，越来越多的女人觉得爱情不可靠，房子比男人更可靠。

八、那部电影是战争片，是关于第二次世界大战的时候美国和日本之间的战争。

九、现在中国哪儿都在建新房子，可是因为人口太多，可能十年以内房子还是不够住。

十、那天王大海问我："什么样的朋友才算得上是一生的朋友呢？"

B. CONVERSATIONS 对话

Read out loud the following conversations, including the name or role of the person speaking. If possible, find a partner or partners and each of you play a role. Then switch roles, so you get practice reading all of the lines.

一、

美国人：长城到底有多长？

中国人：好像有六千多公里长。

美国人：长城是什么时候建的？

中国人：大概是在两千多年前，战国时代就开始建了。不过这里的这一部分是明朝的时候修的。

美国人：那个时候修起来可真够不容易的。

中国人：可不是！全得靠人工，死了不知道有多少人。

二、

张建树：小王，我刚看了一部新电影，战争片，是关于第二次世界大战的。
　　　　战争实在太可怕了！

王建中：对啊。我最近看了一本书，是关于第一次世界大战的，也是够可
　　　　怕的。

张建树：世界各国人民都要和平，谁都不要战争。

王建中：可不是。

张建树：所以大家都应该学习外国的语言和文化！

王建中：一点儿也不错。

C. NARRATIVES 短文

Read the following narratives, paying special attention to punctuation and overall structure. The first time you read a narrative, read it out loud. The second time, read silently and try to gradually increase your reading speed. Always think of the meaning of what you're reading.

一、从前的楼和房子都是靠人工修建的。虽然建起来很慢，但是建成了
　　以后都是很可靠的好房子，很多年都不会坏。现在随便要在哪儿建房
　　子，只要几个月就建好了。现在的新房子好看是好看，可是不一定比
　　老房子好。因为房子应该要慢慢儿地建，几个月建好的房子常常这里
　　坏，那里坏，你可能还得花很多钱去修。虽然很多人喜欢买新房子，可
　　是以后我买房子还是比较愿意买老一点儿的房子。所以很多人说："
　　鞋子是新的好，房子跟朋友是老的好！"

二、中国大陆东西有差不多五千两百公里长，南北有差不多五千五百公里
　　长。中国的海岸线有一万八千多公里。海南东西有一百八十九公里长，
　　南北有一百五十五公里长。海南的海岸线有一千五百多公里。台湾东
　　西有一百四十四公里长，南北有三百九十四公里长。台湾的海岸线也
　　有一千五百多公里。

三、三字驴

　　三国时代有一个大将名叫孙权。他手下有一个人叫诸葛子瑜。诸葛子
　　瑜是一个非常能干的人，可是长得不大好看，因为他的脸太长，看起
　　来像一只驴子。

　　　　有一天孙权请了很多朋友来喝酒。诸葛子瑜也去了，还带了他年
　　纪不到十岁的儿子。大家都知道那个孩子特别聪明，也很会说话。孙
　　权看见诸葛子瑜的儿子也来了，就想跟他开个玩笑。

　　　　孙权叫他的用人找来一只驴子，他在驴子的头上贴了一条白纸，
　　纸上写了四个字。孙权跟他的朋友喝酒喝到最高兴的时候，就让那只
　　驴子出来，让它走来走去。喝酒的人看见纸上写的是"诸葛子瑜"四
　　个字，都笑了起来。

　　　　可是只有那个孩子不笑。他想了一想，就站起来，走到那只驴子
　　前面，在那四个字下面又加了三个字。然后他笑着回到原来的座位坐
　　下。大家一看，都觉得这个孩子实在太聪明了。孙权一句话也没说，就
　　把驴子送给了诸葛子瑜。原来那个孩子在他父亲的名字底下加了"的
　　驴子"三个字！

Notes 注解

A4. 好像是什么小动物的样子 (好像是什么小動物的樣子) lit. "It seems like it's some kind of little animal."

A5. 生活在这个时代 (生活在這個時代) "live in this period." Note that 在 here functions as a postverb.

A10. ⊙ 一生 **yìshēng** "whole life long," "life-long" [AT]

B1. ◆ 明朝 **Míngcháo** "Ming Dynasty" (1368–1644 CE) [TW]

C2a. ◆ 大陆 (大陸) **dàlù** "continent" or "mainland" [PW]. The very common collocation 中国大陆 (中國大陸) means "mainland China."

C2b. 东西 (東西) **dōng xī** "east and west" or "from east to west." Be careful to distinguish this from the noun 东西 (東西) **dōngxi** "thing."

C2c. ⊙ 海岸线 (海岸線) **hǎi'ànxiàn** "coastline" [N]

C3a. ◆ 三字驴 (三字驢) **Sān Zì Lǘ** "The Three-Character Donkey." This is the title of a well-known story from 三国志 (三國志) **Sān Guó Zhì** *Records of the Three Kingdoms*, a famous Chinese historical text from the third century C.E.

C3b. ⊙ 三国时代 (三國時代) **Sān Guó Shídài** "Three Kingdoms Period" (220–280 CE) [TW]

C3c. ⊙ 大将 (大將) **dàjiàng** "high-ranking general" [N]. Note that the character 将 (將) is here pronounced as **jiàng**, not as **jiāng**.

C3d. ◆ 孙权 (孫權) **Sūn Quán** (person's name). The surname 孙 (孫) is rather common in Chinese and well worth learning.

C3e. ⊙ 手下 **shǒuxià** "under someone's command," "under someone's leadership" [N+L]

C3f. ◆ 诸葛子瑜 (諸葛子瑜) **Zhūgě Zǐyú** (person's name). The surname 诸葛 (諸葛) is one of the few two-syllable surnames in Chinese. Another fairly common two-syllable surname written with characters you have already learned is 司马 (司馬).

C3g. ⊙ 能干 (能幹) **nénggàn** "be capable," "able," or "competent" [SV]. Note that simplified 干 is here pronounced **gàn**, not **gān**.

C3h. ◆ 脸 (臉) **liǎn** "face" [N]

C3i. ⊙ 只 (隻) **zhī** (measure for many animals, including donkeys) [M]

C3j. ◆ 驴子 (驢子) **lǘzi** "donkey" [N]. To say "one donkey," you say 一只驴子 (一隻驢子).

C3k. ◆ 聪明 (聰明) **cōngming** "be smart," "clever" [SV]

C3l. ◆ 跟…开个玩笑 (跟…開個玩笑) **gēn...kāi ge wánxiào** "play a joke on" [PT]

C3m. ⊙ 用人 **yòngren** "servant" [N]

C3n. ◆ 贴 (貼) **tiē** "paste" or "stick" [V]

C3o. 一条白纸 (一條白紙) "a strip of white paper"

C3p. ◆ 座位 **zuòwèi** "seat" [N]

Street Sign in Taipei

Emergencies

COMMUNICATIVE OBJECTIVES

Once you've mastered this unit, you'll be able to use Chinese to read and write about:

1. Becoming ill, going to see the doctor, staying in the hospital, etc.

2. Explaining to a passerby or the police that your purse or wallet has been stolen.

3. Going to the police, security guard station, or lost or found to retrieve a missing item.

4. Dealing with a vehicular accident: Anyone hurt? Whose fault? Should you call the police or try to negotiate a settlement privately on the spot? etc.

5. Various passages on the brain drain, the history of Chinese immigration to the U.S., and famous stories from Chinese culture.

6. Several Chinese jokes.

C. NARRATIVES 短文

Read the following narratives, paying special attention to punctuation and overall structure. The first time you read a narrative, read it out loud. The second time, read silently and try to gradually increase your reading speed. Always think of the meaning of what you're reading.

一、

許志明同志從英國回來了。他瘦多了，變得我們都認不出來了。當《人民早報》記者問到他這次英國之行的時候，他說：「還好，該辦的事情都辦完了，不過這次運氣不太好，在英國的幾個月也過得不如意。原來許同志剛去英國的第二個星期就病了，住了兩個多星期的醫院。他覺得雖然英國的醫生還不錯，但是醫院裡的飯太難吃了。他也說雖然學了很多年的英文，可是英國英文的口音特別難懂，有時候他根本聽不懂大家在說甚麼。他還說英國的天氣不大好，常常下雨。最後他告訴記者：「現在回家了，我非常高興！」

二、

有一個小學老師想考考他的學生，看看他們的英語能力到底怎麼樣。他把「How are you?」三個字寫在黑板上，問學生誰能說說這句英文的意思？沒有人敢說話，所以他就隨便點了一個學生。那個學生想，這幾個單字他都認識，只是連在一起是甚麼意思，他真的不太清楚，只好猜猜看。他說，「這句話的意思是不是「怎麼是你？」」老師聽後，笑了一下說：「不對，再來一個試試」。那個學生說：「「How old are you?」的」問另一個學生。他就寫了「How old are you?」，問意思應該是「怎麼老是你？」，對不對，老師？」

Notes 注解

A3.   修 here means "build."

B3a.   ◆ 午 **wǔ** "noon" [BF]. The phrase 许 (許) 是言午许 (許) means "许 (許) is the 许 (許) that is made up of 言 and 午." This is the pattern for describing a character according to its component parts (BSC 4-2: 2). Chinese people often feel the need to clarify which of several similar-sounding characters they mean, especially in the case of personal names. In this case, there is another common surname 徐 **Xú** with which 许 (許) **Xǔ** is sometimes confused. Note also that the character 午 is used to write the following spoken words that you have learned previously: 上午 "morning," 中午 "noon," and 下午 "afternoon."

B3b.   ◆ 木 **mù** "tree," "wood" [BF]. The pictograph 木 is a common radical.

B3c.   ⊙ 立志 **lìzhì** "resolve to do something" (lit. "establish one's will") [VO]. The phrase 立志的志 means "志 as in the expression 立志." In this pattern, a character is described in terms of a common expression in which it occurs (BSC 4-2: 2).

B4.   ◆ 猴子 **hóuzi** "monkey" [N]

C1a. ◆瘦 **shòu** "be thin" [SV]

C1b. 变得我们都认不出来了 (變得我們都認不出來了) "He had changed to the extent that we were not able to recognize him." The compound 认出来 (認出來) means "recognize." It is often used in its negative potential form 认不出来 (認不出來) "can't recognize."

C1c. The word 当 (當) at the beginning of the third sentence means 当…的时候 (當…的時候) "When…." In this usage, 当 (當) can be pronounced either **dāng** or **dàng**.

C1d. ⊙…之行 …**zhī xíng** "trip to" (someplace) [PT]. With this phrase, the name of the place is placed before 之行. In the text here, 英国之行 (英國之行) means "trip to England."

C1e. ⊙口音 **kǒuyīn** "accent" (in speaking a language or dialect) [N]

C2a. ◆黑板 **hēibǎn** "blackboard" [N]

C2b. ⊙点 (點) **diǎn** "select," "choose," or "call on" [V]. This meaning is related to that of 点菜 (點菜) "order food," which you learned in ISC 14-1.

C2c. ⊙单字 (單字) **dānzì** "individual vocabulary word" [N]

C2d. ⊙连 (連) **lián** "join," "link" [V]. In this sentence, 连在   起 (連在   起) means "joined together" or "linked together."

C2e. ◆猜 **cāi** "guess" [V]. 猜猜看 means "try and guess" (BSC 3-2: 2B).

C2f. ⊙老是 **lǎoshi** "always" [A]

C2g. There are numerous versions of this story, some involving high-level Chinese political leaders testing each other's English. In that case, the incorrect Chinese translations of the English expressions "How come it's you?" 怎么是你 (怎麼是你) and "How come it's always you?" 怎么老是你 (怎麼老是你) carry a subtext of veiled criticism of the other person, i.e., "How come it's always you (who causes me political problems)?" Many Chinese speakers delight in this type of double entendre.

"**Shìmín** Dentist"

(牙医 [牙醫] **yáyī** means "dentist"; the symbols to the right of the rare character 旻 are from Taiwan's Chinese Phonetic Alphabet and indicate the pronunciation of the character)

PART 2

The Pickpocket

New Characters and Words

Study the six characters below and the common words written with them, paying careful attention to each character's pronunciation, meaning, and structure, as well as similar-looking characters. After you've studied a character, turn to the *Practice Essentials* volume and practice writing it on the practice sheet, making sure to follow the correct stroke order and direction as you pronounce it out loud and think of its meaning.

559 偷   **tōu**   steal; stealthily, secretly

Radical is 人 **rén** "person" (30), which is written 亻 when occurring at the left side of a character so as not to get in the way of the component at the right. The colloquial name for this radical is 人字旁 **rénzìpáng** "side made up of the character 人." The other component is 俞 **Yú** (surname).

偷	**tōu**	steal [V]
小偷	**xiǎotōu**	thief [N]
◉偷看	**tōukàn**	secretly look at, steal a glance at, peek at [V]

560 赶 (趕)   **gǎn**   rush, hurry, make a dash for

Radical is 走 **zǒu** "walk" (70). The colloquial name for this radical is 走字旁 **zǒuzìpáng** "side made up of the character 走." When 走 serves as the radical in another character, its last stroke is lengthened, with the component on the right side placed above the last stroke of 走. Phonetic of the simplified form is 干 **gān** "shield," while the phonetic of the traditional form is 旱 **hàn** "drought." Distinguish 赶 (趕) from 走, 起 **qǐ** (177), 越 **yuè** (265), and 趣 **qù** (438).

赶 (趕)	**gǎn**	rush, hurry, catch up [V]
赶到 (趕到)	**gǎndào**	rush to a place [RC]

尽快赶到 (盡快趕到)	**jìnkuài gǎndào**	rush as quickly as possible to a place
赶快 (趕快)	**gǎnkuài**	quickly [A]

---

561 读(讀)   **dú**   read, read aloud; study

Radical is 人 **rén** "person" (30), which is written 亻 when occurring at the left side of a character so as not to get in the way of the component at the right. The colloquial name for this radical is 人字旁 **rénzìpáng** "side made up of the character 人." The other component is 卖 (賣) **mài** (254). Distinguish 读 (讀) from 卖 (賣).

读 (讀)	**dú**	read, read aloud; study [V]
读书 (讀書)	**dúshū**	study [VO]
◉ 读者 (讀者)	**dúzhě**	reader [N]
◉ 读研究生 (讀研究生)	**dú yánjiūshēng**	study as a graduate student [PH]

---

562 护(護)   **hù**   protect, guard

Radical of the simplified form is 手 **shǒu** "hand" (305), which at the left side of a character is written as 扌 and is referred to colloquially as 提手 **tíshǒu** "raised hand." Radical of the traditional form is 言 **yán** "speech" (336), the colloquial name for which is 言字旁 **yánzìpáng** "side made up of the character 言." Phonetic of the simplified character is 户 **hù** "door."

护照 (護照)	**hùzhào**	passport [N]
保护 (保護)	**bǎohù**	protect [V]

---

563 皮   **pí**   skin; leather

This character is itself both a radical and a phonetic. It serves as a phonetic in numerous other characters, e.g., in 被 **bèi** (passive marker) (564) and 破 **pò** "break" (572), both of which are taught in this unit.

皮包	**píbāo**	purse [N]
皮带 (皮帶)	**pídài**	belt [N]
皮鞋	**píxié**	leather shoes [N]
皮鞋厂 (皮鞋廠)	**píxié chǎng**	leather shoe factory [PH]

---

564 被   **bèi**   quilt; by (indicates passive)

Radical is 衣 **yī** "clothing" (357), which at the left side of a character is written as 衤. Phonetic is 皮 **pí** "skin" (563). "Quilts" 被 are "clothing" 衤 for sleeping, and in ancient times were made of fur or animal "skins" 皮. This character was later borrowed to write the spoken word **bèi**, which indicates the passive voice. Distinguish 被 from 皮.

被	**bèi**	(indicates passive) [CV]
被打了	**bèi dǎle**	was hit
被偷了	**bèi tōule**	was stolen
被她拿走了	**bèi tā názǒule**	was taken away by her
◉ 被子	**bèizi**	quilt [N]

New Words in ISC 22-2 Written with Characters You Already Know

非…不可	**fēi...bù kě**	must [PT]
国语中心 (國語中心)	**Guóyǔ Zhōngxīn**	Mandarin Training Center [PW]
回来 (回來)	**-huílai**	come back [RE]
找回来 (找回來)	**zhǎohuílai**	find and get back [RC]
回去	**-huíqu**	go back [RE]
跑回去	**pǎohuíqu**	run back [RC]
急	**jí**	be worried, anxious [SV]
那些	**nèixiē**	those [SP + M]
跑到	**pǎodào**	run to [V+PV]
钱包 (錢包)	**qiánbāo**	wallet [N]
师大 (師大)	**Shīdà**	National Taiwan Normal University [PW]
怎么回事？(怎麼回事？)	**Zěnme huí shì(r)?**	"What's the matter?" [IE]
证件 (證件)	**zhèngjiàn**	identification papers, ID [N]

Reading Exercises (Simplified Characters) 简体字

Now practice reading the new characters and words for this lesson in context in sentences, conversations, and narratives. Be sure to refer to the Notes at the end of this lesson, and make use of the accompanying audio disc to hear and practice correct pronunciation, phrasing, and intonation.

A. SENTENCES 句子

Read out loud each of the following sentences, which include all the new characters of this lesson. The first time you read a sentence, focus special attention on the characters and words that are new to you, reminding yourself of their pronunciation and meaning. The second time, aim to comprehend the overall meaning of the sentence.

一、我将来要读医，我男朋友决定读人类学。

二、我的行李被别人拿走了，我非赶快找回来不可。

三、考试的时候，那个同学偷看手机，被老师看见了。

四、他新买的皮鞋和皮带都是意大利进口的，好看极了。

五、小谢在校时，不用功读书，现在只好在一家皮鞋厂工作。

六、我刚才放在桌子上的土司不见了，是不是被你吃了？说实话！

七、虽然有人说过"偷来的水果最香"，不过最好还是不要偷水果！

八、十二点的那班公车快要开了，我们得快一点儿赶到车站，要不然就来不及了。

九、清代的时候很多孩子一开始读书，都从《三字经》、《千字文》和《百家姓》读起。

十、王大海的护照被偷了，他非找回来不可，要不然怎么回国呢？

B. CONVERSATIONS 对话

Read out loud the following conversations, including the name or role of the person speaking. If possible, find a partner or partners and each of you play a role. Then switch roles, so you get practice reading all of the lines.

一、（在台北）

美国留学生：有小偷！有人偷了我的皮包！

行人　　　　：什么？怎么回事？

美国留学生：我是美国人，在师大国语中心读书。我的皮包、护照、各种
　　　　　　证件都被偷了。现在怎么办？那些东西我非找回来不可！

行人　　　　：别急，别急！我一定尽力帮你找。我们先到警察局去报告
　　　　　　警察。

美国留学生：好吧。

二、

男生：我的钱包不见了！好像被偷了！

女生：真的吗？是什么时候被偷的？你看见小偷了吗？

男生：我没看见，可是我非找回来不可。里头除了五千多块钱以外，还有
　　　我的护照和别的证件。怎么办？

女生：你先别急，让我帮你想个办法……

三、

小许：你下班以后怎么不赶快回家？在这儿等什么呢？

老张：我非得在这里等一会儿不可。你不知道，我和我爱人说好了，下班
　　　后谁先到家谁做饭。

小许：怪不得你爱人也在前面等着呢！

老张：什么？！

C. NARRATIVES 短文

Read the following narratives, paying special attention to punctuation and overall structure. The first time you read a narrative, read it out loud. The second time, read silently and try to gradually increase your reading speed. Always think of the meaning of what you're reading.

一、我爱说英文

我有个男同学，他的女朋友叫李文英。他有一次送了她一本英文书，前面写了他的名字和日期，还加了一句"我爱说英文"。请注意，"我爱说英文"这句话从左往右读也通，从右往左读也通。你们想这位男同学大概希望他的女朋友怎么读这个句子？为什么？

二、笨孩子

在北京城外头住着一个白老头儿。他的太太早死了。他有一个儿子，叫白二。这时候白二也有二十多岁了。白二的朋友给他介绍了一位张小

A Lost Bag

New Characters and Words

Study the six characters below and the common words written with them, paying careful attention to each character's pronunciation, meaning, and structure, as well as similar-looking characters. After you've studied a character, turn to the *Practice Essentials* volume and practice writing it on the practice sheet, making sure to follow the correct stroke order and direction as you pronounce it out loud and think of its meaning.

565 掉 **diào** fall, drop; lose

Radical is 手 **shǒu** "hand" (305), which at the left side of a character is written as 扌 and is referred to colloquially as 提手 **tíshǒu** "raised hand." Phonetic is 卓 **zhuó** "eminent." Distinguish 掉 from 桌 **zhuō** (373).

掉	**diào**	fall, drop; lose, misplace [V]
掉	**-diào**	away [RE]
跑掉	**pǎodiào**	run off, run away [RC]
死掉	**sǐdiào**	die [RC]
忘掉	**wàngdiào**	forget [RC]
卖掉 (賣掉)	**màidiào**	sell off [RC]

566 火 **huǒ** fire

This character, which is a pictograph representing fire, is itself a radical. As a radical at the left-hand side of a character, as in 炒 **chǎo** "stir-fry," it is referred to colloquially as 火字旁 **huǒzìpáng** "side made up of the character 火," and its last stroke is shortened so that it doesn't collide with the component to its right. When 火 occurs as a radical at the bottom of a character, it is written 灬 and is referred to colloquially as 四点火

(四點火) **sìdiǎn huǒ** "four dots of fire," e.g., 煮 **zhǔ** "boil." The character 火 can also serve as a phonetic in some characters, e.g., in the simplified character 伙, which is used in the word 伙伴 **huǒbàn** "companion." Distinguish 火 from 人 **rén** (30), 大 **dà** (13), and 太 **tài** (64).

火	**huǒ**	fire [N]
火车 (火車)	**huǒchē**	train [N]
⊙火山	**huǒshān**	volcano [N]
⊙火山口	**huǒshānkǒu**	crater of a volcano [N]

---

567 检(檢)   **jiǎn**   examine

Radical is the pictograph 木 **mù** "tree." This radical is referred to colloquially as 木字旁 **mùzìpáng** "side made up of the character 木." Note that when 木 is written at the left of a character as a radical, its last stroke is shortened so that it doesn't collide with the component to its right. Phonetic is 金 (僉) **qiān**.

⊙体检 (體檢)	**tǐjiǎn**	physical examination [N]

---

568 查   **chá**   examine, check
　　　　Zhā   Zha (a surname)

Radical is the pictograph 木 **mù** "tree," which is at the top of the character. The rest of the character is composed of 日 **rì** (132) and 一 **yī** (1). Distinguish 查 from 香 **xiāng** (39).

⊙查	**Zhā**	Zha [SN]
⊙查	**chá**	examine, check [V]
⊙查字	**cházì**	look up characters [VO]
检查 (檢查)	**jiǎnchá**	inspect, examine [V]; inspection [N]
查号台 (查號台)	**cháhàotái**	information, directory assistance [N]

---

569 危   **wēi/wéi**   danger

Radical is 卩 **jié**. Distinguish 危 from 色 **sè** (352) and 包 **bāo** (332).

危	**Wēi/Wéi**	Wei [SN]

---

570 险(險)   **xiǎn**   danger

Radical is 阜 **fù** "mound," which is written 阝 when occurring at the left-hand side of a character. This radical is referred to colloquially as 左耳旁 **zuǒ'ěrpáng** "side made up of a left ear." Phonetic is 金 (僉) **qiān**. Distinguish 险 (險) from 检 (檢) **jiǎn** (567) earlier in this lesson.

⊙危险 (危險)	**wēixiǎn/wéixiǎn**	be dangerous [SV]; danger [N]

New Words in ISC 22-3 Written with Characters You Already Know

错 (錯)	**cuò**	error, mistake [N]
没错 (沒錯)	**méi cuò**	"that's right" [IE]
国家 (國家)	**guójiā**	country [N]
还 (還)	**huán**	give back [V] (Note that the character is in this sense pronounced **huán**, not **hái**.)
还给 (還給)	**huángěi**	give back to [V+PV]
没什么 (沒什麼)	**méi shénme**	"You're welcome" [IE]
学生证 (學生證)	**xuéshēngzhèng**	student ID [N]
应该的 (應該的)	**yīnggāide**	"something one ought to do," "of course" [IE]

 ### Reading Exercises (Simplified Characters) 简体字

Now practice reading the new characters and words for this lesson in context in sentences, conversations, and narratives. Be sure to refer to the Notes at the end of this lesson, and make use of the accompanying audio disc to hear and practice correct pronunciation, phrasing, and intonation.

A. SENTENCES 句子

Read out loud each of the following sentences, which include all the new characters of this lesson. The first time you read a sentence, focus special attention on the characters and words that are new to you, reminding yourself of their pronunciation and meaning. The second time, aim to comprehend the overall meaning of the sentence.

一、从上海到南京，你看最好是坐飞机，火车，还是汽车？
二、火虽然有用，但也很危险，大人、小孩儿都应该特别小心。
三、这个火山很有名，每年有成千上万的人从世界各地来看它。
四、他越是想早一点儿把他的房子卖掉，
　　就越是卖不掉，真着急！
五、今天天气不好，开车太危险了，还是
　　坐火车吧，又省事又安全。
六、那个地方很危险，小偷特别多，你要
　　随时注意自己的皮包或钱包。
七、这个字我不认识，我查过可是查不
　　到，你能不能告诉我是什么意思？
八、你运气不错，钱包找回来了！快检查
　　一下，看里面的东西是不是都还在。
九、美国人常说中国是共产主义国家，但
　　是中国人自己说中国是社会主义国
　　家。
十、王大海小时候学的法语，现在全忘掉
　　了！

Danger Do Not Open
Bahaya Jangan Buka
危险　请勿打开
ஆபத்து　திறக்கக்கூடாது

Sign in Singapore

B. CONVERSATIONS 对话

Read out loud the following conversations, including the name or role of the person speaking. If possible, find a partner or partners and each of you play a role. Then switch roles, so you get practice reading all of the lines.

一、

马南喜：先生，我今天早上掉了一个皮包。不知道有没有人看到？

警卫　：你的皮包有多大？什么颜色？

马南喜：白色跟黑色，大概比我这个皮包大一点。上面写着WILLIAMS。里面除了一千多块钱以外，还有我的学生证跟护照。

警卫　：你是哪个国家的？叫什么名字？

马南喜：我是美国人，叫Nancy Miles。中文名字叫马南喜。

警卫　：你看，这是不是你的皮包？

马南喜：没错，没错，正是我的！

警卫　：请你检查一下看东西是不是都在？

马南喜：我看看。钱、学生证跟护照都在。真谢谢你！

警卫　：没什么，应该的。以后小心一点！

二、

许先生：你比较喜欢坐飞机，火车，还是汽车？

何小姐：坐火车或是汽车都可以，可是我不喜欢坐飞机。

许先生：为什么？

何小姐：安全检查越来越麻烦。什么都得检查，而且很多东西不准带。

许先生：没错！

何小姐：还有，我总怕飞机会掉下来。每一、两年都有飞机掉下来，每次都有好多人死掉。

许先生：其实，你不用怕这个。现在的飞机都很安全。我在哪儿读过，坐飞机比坐汽车还安全！当然坐火车也很安全。

C. NARRATIVES 短文

Read the following narratives, paying special attention to punctuation and overall structure. The first time you read a narrative, read it out loud. The second time, read silently and try to gradually increase your reading speed. Always think of the meaning of what you're reading.

一、我是加拿大的华人，在广州出生，十一岁的时候跟着父母来到加拿大。记得我刚开始学英文的时候，觉得很难。差不多每个字都看不懂，所以刚查完一个字马上又得查另外一个字。经过了十几年，虽然现在有时候还有生字得查，但现在，我英文读得、说得就跟加拿大人差不多一样，而且我很高兴我也没忘掉我的母语中文。我在大学的时候还学了一点日文，不过因为一直没有机会用，所以我的日文早就"还给"老师了！

C. NARRATIVES 短文

Read the following narratives, paying special attention to punctuation and overall structure. The first time you read a narrative, read it out loud. The second time, read silently and try to gradually increase your reading speed. Always think of the meaning of what you're reading.

一、

我是加拿大的華人，在廣州出生，十一歲的時候跟著父母來到加拿大。記得我剛開始學英文的時候，覺得很難。差不多每個字都看不懂，所以剛查完一個字馬上又得查另外一個字。經過了十幾年，雖然現在有時候還有生字得查，但現在，我英文讀得、說得就跟加拿大人差不多一樣，而且我很高興我也沒忘掉我的母語中文。我在大學的時候還學了一點日文，不過因為一直沒有機會用，所以我的日文早就「還給」老師了！

二、人才外流

不少外國留學生在美國讀完研究生，拿到學位以後，都不想回國。他們想盡了辦法要留在美國工作，因為美國的生活好，而且也比較自由，比方說言論自由－就不是每個國家都有的。所以很多國家都有人才外流的問題，也可以說是人才外「留」。當然，不住在自己的國家，也不應該完全忘掉自己的「根」。所以，如果我們能夠把我們的母語傳給下一代，是非常好的事情。

Notes 注解

A3a. ⊙成千上万 (成千上萬) **chéng-qiān-shàng-wàn** "tens of thousands (of)" [EX]

A3b. 世界各地 "all over the world" (lit. "all places in the whole world")

A4. 卖不掉 (賣不掉) "can't sell," "can't get rid of something by trying to sell it"

A5. ⊙安全 (安全) **ānquán** "be safe," "secure" [SV]

B1. ◆颜色 (顏色) **yánsè** "color" [N]

B2a. ⊙安全检查 (安全檢查) **ānquán jiǎnchá** "safety inspection," "security check" [PH]. This is nowadays often abbreviated to 安检 (安檢).

B2b. ◆麻烦 (麻煩) "be troublesome," "bothersome" [CV]

B2c. ⊙准 **zhǔn** "allow," "permit" [V]. This verb is commonly used in the negative.

C1a. ⊙跟 **gēn** "follow" [V]. 跟着 (跟著) means "following."

C1b. ⊙经过 (經過) **jīngguò** "pass through," "go through" [RC]. The phrase 经过了十几年 (經過了十幾年) lit. means "having gone through more than ten years" or, in idiomatic English, "after more than a dozen years."

C1c. ◉母语 (母語) **mǔyǔ** "mother tongue," "native language" [N]

C2a. ◉人才 **réncái** "capable person," "person of talent" [N]

C2b. ◉外流 **wàiliú** "flow outward" [V]; "outflow" [N]

C2c. ◉人才外流 **réncái wàiliú** "brain drain" [PH]

C2d. ◉学位 (學位) **xuéwèi** "degree" [N]

C2e. ◉想尽办法 (想盡辦法) **xiǎngjìn bànfǎ** "try every possible way or means" [PH]

C2f. ◉言论自由 (言論自由) **yánlùn zìyóu** "freedom of speech" [PH]

C2g. 人才外 "留" "people of talent 'stay' abroad". This is a Chinese pun, since 人才外流 "brain drain" sounds exactly the same as 人才外 "留"

C2h. ◉根 **gēn** "root" [N]

C2i. ◉能够 (能夠) **nénggòu** "can" [AV]

C2j. ◉代 **dài** "generation" [M]. The common phrase 下一代 means "the next generation."

C2k. 把我们的母语传给下一代 (把我們的母語傳給下一代) "transmit our mother tongue to the next generation"

危險
有電
未經授權不得內進

DANGER
ELECTRICITY

"Danger, (there is) electricity, without authorization (you) may not enter" (sign in Hong Kong)

The Accident

怎么样？怎么样？
您受伤了没有？
（怎麼樣？怎麼樣？
您受傷了沒有？）

我倒没什么大事。不过，
您看，我的自行车成了什么样儿了？
（我倒沒什麼大事。不過，您看，我
的自行車成了什麼樣兒了？）

New Characters and Words

Study the six characters below and the common words written with them, paying careful attention to each character's pronunciation, meaning, and structure, as well as similar-looking characters. After you've studied a character, turn to the *Practice Essentials* volume and practice writing it on the practice sheet, making sure to follow the correct stroke order and direction as you pronounce it out loud and think of its meaning.

571 伤（傷） **shāng** wound, injury; injure, hurt

Radical is 人 **rén** "person" (30), which is written 亻 when occurring at the left side of a character so as not to get in the way of the component at the right. The colloquial name for this radical is 人字旁 **rénzìpáng** "side made up of the character 人." Distinguish traditional 傷 from traditional 場 **chǎng** (227) and traditional 陽 **yáng** (285).

| 受伤（受傷） | **shòushāng** | suffer injury, be hurt [VO] |

572 破 **pò** break, tear, split

Radical is 石 **shí** "stone" (420). Phonetic is 皮 **pí** "skin" (563). If a person is hit by a "stone" 石, it might "break" 破 the "skin" 皮. Distinguish 破 from 皮 **pí** (563) and 被 **bèi** (564).

破	**pò**	break, tear [V]
◉打破	**dǎpò**	break, smash [RC]
◉破坏（破壞）	**pòhuài**	destroy, damage [RC]

573 结（結）   **jié**   tie; knot

Radical is 丝（絲）**sī** "silk." When at the left side of a character, this radical is referred to colloquially as 绞丝旁（絞絲旁）**jiǎosīpáng** "side made up of twisted silk" and is written as 纟（糹）. Phonetic is 吉 **jí** "auspicious." Distinguish 结（結）from 给（給）**gěi** (192).

结果（結果）	**jiéguǒ**	as a result, in the end [CJ]; result [N]
◉结（結）	**jié**	knot [N]
◉打结（打結）	**dǎjié**	tie a knot [VO]
◉打中国结（打中國結）	**dǎ Zhōngguo jié**	tie Chinese-style knots [PH]

574 发（發）   **fā**   put forth, issue, distribute

Radical of the simplified form is 又 **yòu** "again" (210), and of the traditional form it is ⼔ **bō** "legs." Distinguish simplified 发 from 友 **yǒu** (172).

发生（發生）	**fāshēng**	happen [V]
发票（發票）	**fāpiào**	receipt, itemized bill [N]
发音（發音）	**fāyīn**	pronunciation [N]
◉发明（發明）	**fāmíng**	invent [V]; invention [N]
◉发现（發現）	**fāxiàn**	discover [V]; discovery [N]

575 费（費）   **fèi**   spend; expense

Radical is 贝（貝）**bèi** "cowrie shell," which gives an idea of the meaning, since cowrie shells were used as a form of money in ancient China. Phonetic is 弗 **fú** "not." One way to remember this character is by the similarity of the character 弗 to a "reverse dollar sign." Distinguish 费（費）from 贵（貴）**guì** (85).

费（費）	**Fèi**	Fei [SN]
修车费（修車費）	**xiūchēfèi**	cost of repairing a vehicle [N]
水费（水費）	**shuǐfèi**	water fee [N]
电费（電費）	**diànfèi**	electricity fee [N]
水电费（水電費）	**shuǐdiànfèi**	water and electricity fee [N]
破费（破費）	**pòfèi**	go to great expense [VO]
◉费用（費用）	**fèiyòng**	expenses, cost, fee [N]
◉小费（小費）	**xiǎofèi**	tip, gratuity [N]
◉费城（費城）	**Fèichéng**	Philadelphia [PW]

576 合   **hé**   be in accord with

Radical is 口 **kǒu** "mouth" (140). When at the bottom of a character, as here, this radical is referred to colloquially as 口字底 **kǒuzìdǐ** "bottom made up of the character 口." The whole character is itself a phonetic in other characters, e.g., in 哈 **hā** (the sound of laughter) or in 给（給）**gěi** (192). Distinguish 合 from 拿 **ná** (314) and 给（給）**gěi** (192).

合算	**hésuàn**	be worthwhile; reasonable (in price) [SV]
◉合身	**héshēn**	be well-fitting (of clothes) [SV]
◉合作	**hézuò**	cooperate; cooperation [V/N]

	区	區	qū	area, district, region
472				
474	帮	幫	bāng	help; gang, clique
477	尽	盡	jìn	to the very limit; to exhaust
480	流	流	liú	flow
482	试	試	shì	try; test
485	飞	飛	fēi	fly
486	船	船	chuán	boat, ship
488	体	體	tǐ	body
489	绩	績	jī	achievement, merit
491	于	於	yú	be located at, in, on, to
492	论	論	lùn/lún	discuss, debate/The Analects
495	连	連	lián	even
497	产	產	chǎn	produce
498	义	義	yì	righteousness
499	责	責	zé	duty, responsibility
508	观	觀	guān	look at
509	画	畫	huà	paint; painting
515	华	華	huá/Huà	China/(surname)
516	亲	親	qīn	parent, relative; to kiss
520	将	將	jiāng/jiàng	will; take/general
521	计	計	jì	calculate; plan
522	划	劃	huà	plan
523	类	類	lèi	kind, type
	楼	樓	lóu	building; floor
30	队	隊	duì	team, group

	运	運	yùn	move, transport
531				
538	育	育	yù	education
540	团	團	tuán	group; organization
544	视	視	shì	look at, regard, inspect
545	强	強	qiáng	strong, powerful
551	战	戰	zhàn	battle, war
552	争	爭	zhēng	compete; fight
553	医	醫	yī	medical doctor; heal
555	变	變	biàn	change, transform
666	许	許	xǔ	permit
560	赶	趕	gǎn	rush, hurry
561	读	讀	dú	read; study
562	护	護	hù	protect, guard
567	检	檢	Jlǎn	examine
570	险	險	xiǎn	danger
571	伤	傷	shāng	wound; injure
573	结	結	jié	tie; knot
574	发	發	fā	issue, distribute
575	费	費	fèi	spend; expense
578	导	導	dǎo	guide, lead
579	组	組	zǔ	organize; group; set
580	并	並	bìng	moreover, and
581	济	濟	jì	cross a river; help
583	银	銀	yín	silver
585	统	統	tǒng	lead; unify; all together

594	周	週	**zhōu**	week
596	历	歷	**lì**	experience, undergo
599	达	達	**dá**	reach, attain
601	据	據	**jù**	according to; based on
602	创	創	**chuàng**	create, start
603	约	約	**yāo/yuē**	weigh out/approximate
606	响	響	**xiǎng**	echo; sound, noise
608	环	環	**huán**	ring, link; surround
610	断	斷	**duàn**	break off; cut off
611	绝	絕	**jué**	break off; cut off
613	独	獨	**dú**	single; independent; unique
620	脑	腦	**nǎo**	brain
621	无	無	**wú**	not have, not exist
622	网	網	**wǎng**	net; network; web
623	装	裝	**zhuāng**	install; pretend; clothing

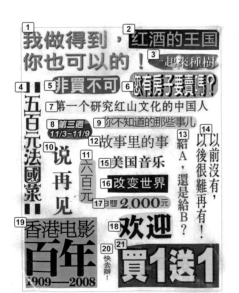

English Translations, p. 14

1. I can do it, you can, too!
2. Kingdom of red wine
3. Let's plant trees together
4. 500 dollar French dish
5. Must buy
6. Do you have a house you want to sell?
7. The first Chinese to study Hongshan culture
8. Week 3, 11/3–11/9
9. Those things you didn't know
10. Say goodbye

11. Six hundred dollars
12. The things in the story
13. Give it to A, or give it to B?
14. In the past there weren't any, and in the future it would be difficult to have any again!
15. American music
16. Change the world
17. 3 pairs for 2000 dollars
18. Welcome
19. One hundred years of Hong Kong films, 1909–2008
20. Do it soon!
21. Buy 1, get 1 free